Grade 4

# The Complete Year in Reading and Writing

## Daily Lessons ● Monthly Units ● Yearlong Calendar

### Laurie Pastore and Pam Allyn

■SCHOLASTIC

NEW YORK • TORONTO • LONDON • AUCKLAND • SYDNEY
MEXICO CITY • NEW DELHI • HONG KONG • BUENOS AIRES

To all fourth-grade teachers, who care so much, and:

To my mother, for showing me what it means to be a teacher;
to my father, for teaching me to love books; and my sister,
for reminding me what is truly important in life.
~ *Laurie Pastore*

To Lois Bridges and Danny Miller.
~ *Pam Allyn*

Scholastic Inc. grants teachers permission to photocopy the activity and stationery pages from this book for classroom use only. No other part of this publication may be reproduced in whole or in part, or stored in a retrieval system, or transmitted in any form or by any means, electronic, mechanical, photocopying, recording, or otherwise, without written permission of the publisher. For information regarding permission, write to Scholastic Inc., 557 Broadway, New York, NY 10012.

Cover design by Jay Namerow

Interior design by Maria Lilja

Photos by LitLife Archives (interior and cover), Maria Lilja (inside cover and pages 75, 93, 110, 150)

Acquiring Editor: Lois Bridges

Development and Production Editor: Danny Miller

Copy Editor: Chris Borris

ISBN 13: 978-0-545-04638-1

ISBN 10: 0-545-04638-6

Copyright © 2008 by LitLife Publishing LLC

# Contents

As a bonus, use our Spotlight Units to journey through day-by-day lessons in all the Complete 4 components.

# Acknowledgments

We would like to thank the teachers, the children, and our colleagues in the LitLife network of schools who believe in the power of words.

There was a team of people who gave of themselves in the deepest and most generous of ways to this project. We are full of gratitude for the wise and thoughtful Delia Coppola, Janet Knight, Debbie Lera, and Michelle Yang. Their insights, feedback, and creations glow brightly throughout this series.

We are grateful for the support of our extraordinary LitLife team: the remarkable and talented Jenny Koons, who understands life and people and kids and curriculum and enriched the books with her careful eye; and the marvelous Rebekah Coleman, whose spirit kept us going and whose wise attention completed us. With thanks to our dedicated interns Jen Estrada and Alyssa McClorey, and to Deb Jurkowitz, LitLife grammarian and in-house linguist. We deeply appreciate our agent, Lisa DiMona, for shining the light that guides our way. And we thank Fiona and Muriel, two magical girls who helped us to know what third and fourth graders like to read and write about.

Danny Miller may very well be one of the funniest people on earth. He is also a brilliant editor. His dedicated efforts to this series are appreciated beyond compare by us all. Lois Bridges—inspiration, mentor, friend, champion of children and humanistic education, connector of all dots, editor extraordinaire—we thank you. All our appreciation to the team at Scholastic: the creative Maria Lilja, and Terry Cooper for her vision and dedication to the work of supporting teachers. In addition we thank Eileen Hillebrand for her genius way of getting the word out there, and Susan Kolwicz for her genius in getting the message heard.

This experience of writing six books together has been by turns precious, wild, funny, exhausting, scary, joyous, and deeply satisfying. We collectively gave birth to three babies during this process, visited hundreds of schools, took our own kids to school, and tried to have dinner with our husbands once in a while. From the beginning we committed to one another that when the work felt hard, we would always remember that relationships come first. We are most proud of this and hope our readers can feel the power of our bonds in every page of every book in this series. We thank one another, always.

Pam Allyn sends boundless gratitude to Jim, Katie, and Charlotte Allyn for their love and for their countless inspirations. She would especially like to thank her coauthor Laurie Pastore for her fearlessness in the face of the open roads and the empty page, and for the wisdom and care she brings to them.

Laurie Pastore would like to thank several key learning partners over the years: Anne Powers, Betsy Henley, and Monica Ware. These fellow teachers and friends taught her the value of collegial planning and reflection, which ultimately led her toward her current work as a literacy consultant. She would like to thank the fourth-grade team at Ridge Street Elementary for piloting many of the units in this book, and Adrienne Laitman for welcoming us into her classroom. She would also like to express her deep gratitude toward Nick and Tom Pastore for their enduring patience and tender support when yet another take-out dinner was delivered or there were no clean socks in the house. Finally she would like to thank her coauthor Pam Allyn for inspiring her to try new, hard things every day—like writing books!

# Chapter 1

# All About the Complete Year

## Dear Fourth-Grade Teacher,

Your fourth graders are busy. They are busy with their imaginations, their lively experiences, their curiosity, their investigations, their friendships, their home relationships. Their lives are rich with the interconnectedness of all of these parts. Their minds are wide awake, humming, singing with possibility.

Do not be deceived by how old they look, and how they may dress like preteens. At home, they put together a Lego® set after school, a complex project of creation that takes several days to complete. They have a pretend game with a group of friends which goes on and on, where parts are added and discarded over weeks at a time. They generate creative ideas constantly: writing songs, making plays, doing art projects.

They are your greatest allies in any good idea waiting to be hatched, any class project waiting to be done, any fun adventure waiting to be launched. They are coming into their own. You can see the stirrings of true talent: the child whose singing voice suddenly stops your class in its tracks, the child who can zing through ten books in two weeks, the child who draws a face with a startling understanding of human emotion in it. Suddenly, what looks like play is also the early indication of all kinds of passions and interests that child may embrace as she grows to adulthood.

The process work this year, then, is about all of that. It is about helping our students integrate new aspects of their identities and synthesize all the different ways they are experiencing the world through literacy. In the ARCH units that begin this year of instruction, your students are looking across texts to explore common themes and interests and passions. Across the year, your students are learning how to talk with one another in meaningful and joyous ways about texts, their own and others'.

Your fourth graders can absorb all the newness of their expanding worlds. They are soaking it all in. Let this year be a feast in genre. Mysteries and plays are two genres to explore, discover, and admire; the emphasis on nonfiction connects them to their content areas and to the demands of the state and national assessments while offering them ample opportunity to roam with pleasure through all kinds of text resources and explore their own topics of interest.

Our students are making connections everywhere. Their minds are working at a fast and furious rate, and so units in strategies are opportune and eagerly received. They study theme, character, and more ethereal elements of literature such as mood and tone, all to capture those essential connections across books, across ideas, and across genres.

Fourth graders see links everywhere. What better areas to study this year than punctuation that links and connects, grammar that is used to enhance a steady sentence, modifiers, and a deepened knowledge of parts of speech? They are builders, constructors, fort-makers, play-makers, plan-makers, and goal-setters. They are fully into the conventional world and the world of conventions. They are part of the adult world, yet they also like to be just who they are, deeply themselves, quirky, intriguing, eccentric. Let us create a year that embraces all of that: the wanting to belong with the wanting to be themselves, the desire for mastery alongside the deeply creative potential that is in them. This duality is the miraculous world of the fourth grader.

Warmly,

*Laurie Pastore   Pam Allyn*

# At-a-Glance Overview of the Complete Year

Organized around the Complete 4 components (Process, Genre, Strategy, and Conventions) and four unit stages (Immersion, Identification, Guided Practice, and Commitment), each book in the Complete Year series features a year's worth of integrated reading and writing curriculum. Because we honor your professional decision-making, you will find that the Complete Year provides a flexible framework, easily adapted to your state standards and to the needs and goals of your community, your students, and your teaching style.

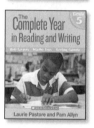

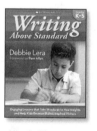

Pam Allyn's *The Complete 4 for Literacy* and Debbie Lera's *Writing Above Standard* are foundational texts for the Complete Year. LitLife and RealeBooks provide innovative professional and technological support for the Complete Year.

## What Will You Find Inside the Complete Year Series?

### Yearlong Curricular Calendar

### Units of Study

- More than 25 detailed unit outlines spanning every season of the school year.
- 8 Spotlight Units including more than 100 day-by-day lessons
- 2 ARCH units to start your year right
- 2 reflective units to end your year on a powerful note

### Assessment

- Individualized assessments for every unit
- Complete 4 Assessment (C4A)

### Lists of Anchor Texts for Each Unit

### Parent Letters

### Resource Sheets and Homework Assignments

### Professional Reading Lists

### Glossary of Terms

**DVD** that features Pam Allyn sharing the benefits of the Complete 4 for the Complete Year as well as ALL downloadable assessment forms and resources. You will also find helpful links to professional development support from LitLife and easy-to-use technological support from RealeBooks to help you publish your students' work.

## The Complete Year Supports...

**Individual teachers** wanting a clear road map and detailed lessons for reading and writing and for reading/writing connections.

**School or district teams** wanting to plan a continuum together with specific lessons and units that address the needs of all students—ELL, gifted, and special needs.

**Administrative leaders and literacy coaches** wanting to guide their school to a consistent, standards-rich plan for reading and writing instruction.

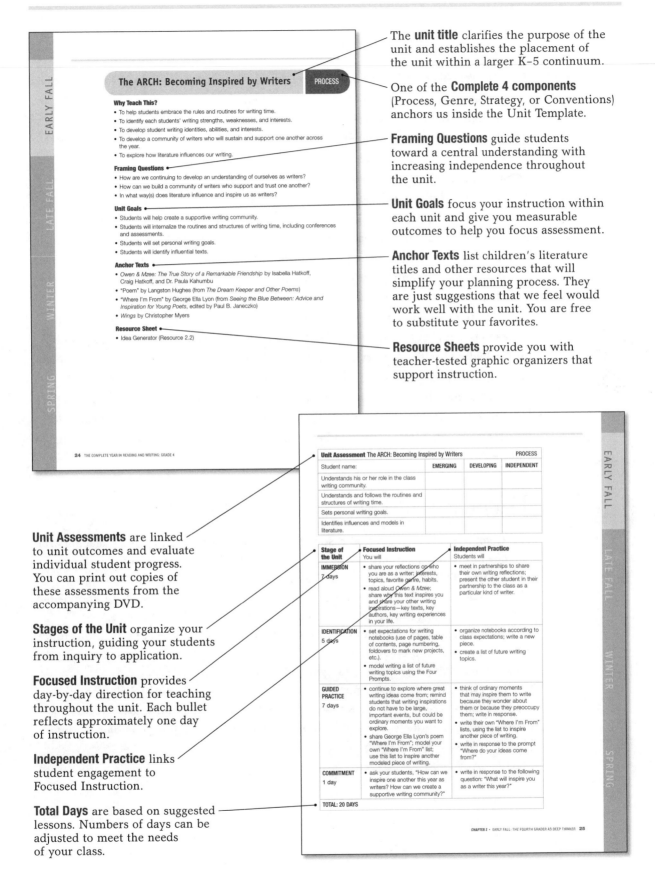

The **unit title** clarifies the purpose of the unit and establishes the placement of the unit within a larger K–5 continuum.

One of the **Complete 4 components** (Process, Genre, Strategy, or Conventions) anchors us inside the Unit Template.

**Framing Questions** guide students toward a central understanding with increasing independence throughout the unit.

**Unit Goals** focus your instruction within each unit and give you measurable outcomes to help you focus assessment.

**Anchor Texts** list children's literature titles and other resources that will simplify your planning process. They are just suggestions that we feel would work well with the unit. You are free to substitute your favorites.

**Resource Sheets** provide you with teacher-tested graphic organizers that support instruction.

**Unit Assessments** are linked to unit outcomes and evaluate individual student progress. You can print out copies of these assessments from the accompanying DVD.

**Stages of the Unit** organize your instruction, guiding your students from inquiry to application.

**Focused Instruction** provides day-by-day direction for teaching throughout the unit. Each bullet reflects approximately one day of instruction.

**Independent Practice** links student engagement to Focused Instruction.

**Total Days** are based on suggested lessons. Numbers of days can be adjusted to meet the needs of your class.

---

### The ARCH: Becoming Inspired by Writers — PROCESS

**Why Teach This?**
- To help students embrace the rules and routines for writing time.
- To identify each students' writing strengths, weaknesses, and interests.
- To develop student writing identities, abilities, and interests.
- To develop a community of writers who will sustain and support one another across the year.
- To explore how literature influences our writing.

**Framing Questions**
- How are we continuing to develop an understanding of ourselves as writers?
- How can we build a community of writers who support and trust one another?
- In what way(s) does literature influence and inspire us as writers?

**Unit Goals**
- Students will help create a supportive writing community.
- Students will internalize the routines and structures of writing time, including conferences and assessments.
- Students will set personal writing goals.
- Students will identify influential texts.

**Anchor Texts**
- *Owen & Mzee: The True Story of a Remarkable Friendship* by Isabella Hatkoff, Craig Hatkoff, and Dr. Paula Kahumbu
- "Poem" by Langston Hughes (from *The Dream Keeper and Other Poems*)
- "Where I'm From" by George Ella Lyon (from *Seeing the Blue Between: Advice and Inspiration for Young Poets*, edited by Paul B. Janeczko)
- *Wings* by Christopher Myers

**Resource Sheet**
- Idea Generator (Resource 2.2)

---

### Unit Assessment — The ARCH: Becoming Inspired by Writers — PROCESS

| Student name: | EMERGING | DEVELOPING | INDEPENDENT |
|---|---|---|---|
| Understands his or her role in the class writing community. | | | |
| Understands and follows the routines and structures of writing time. | | | |
| Sets personal writing goals. | | | |
| Identifies influences and models in literature. | | | |

| Stage of the Unit | Focused Instruction — You will | Independent Practice — Students will |
|---|---|---|
| IMMERSION 7 days | • share your reflections on who you are as a writer: interests, topics, favorite genre, habits.<br>• read aloud *Owen & Mzee*; share why this text inspires you and share your other writing inspirations—key texts, key authors, key writing experiences in your life. | • meet in partnerships to share their own writing reflections; present the other student in their partnership to the class as a particular kind of writer. |
| IDENTIFICATION 5 days | • set expectations for writing notebooks (use of pages, table of contents, page numbering, foldovers to mark new projects, etc.).<br>• model writing a list of future writing topics using the Four Prompts. | • organize notebooks according to class expectations; write a new piece.<br>• create a list of future writing topics. |
| GUIDED PRACTICE 7 days | • continue to explore where great writing ideas come from; remind students that writing inspirations do not have to be large, important events, but could be ordinary moments you want to explore.<br>• share George Ella Lyon's poem "Where I'm From"; model your own "Where I'm From" list; use this list to inspire another modeled piece of writing. | • think of ordinary moments that may inspire them to write because they wonder about them or because they preoccupy them; write in response.<br>• write their own "Where I'm From" lists, using the list to inspire another piece of writing.<br>• write in response to the prompt "Where do your ideas come from?" |
| COMMITMENT 1 day | • ask your students, "How can we inspire one another this year as writers? How can we create a supportive writing community?" | • write in response to the following question: "What will inspire you as a writer this year?" |

**TOTAL: 20 DAYS**

# How This Book Will Support You

*The Complete Year in Reading and Writing: Grade 4* is written by two authors, Laurie Pastore, a team leader at LitLife and experienced classroom teacher, and Pam Allyn, the executive director of LitLife. Together, we have spent thousands of hours in fourth-grade classrooms, pondering the unique experiences that comprise this year.

LitLife is a global organization dedicated to teacher training in the area of literacy education. Every lesson in this book has been field tested in a wide variety of classrooms. LitLife team leaders coach teachers and work alongside students to create a practical, meaningful curriculum that is well suited to each grade level because it exists inside a broader continuum. See this book as a compass you can use to chart a course in reading and writing instruction that feels true to your beliefs about the developmental needs and interests of fourth graders.

Many programs do not differentiate sufficiently by grade level. Fourth-grade teachers are often combined into a grade 3–5 grouping in professional literature and workshops. And yet the span between these grades is psychologically, socially, and intellectually gigantic. A curriculum for fourth grade needs to match the development of the learner and the uniqueness of this age of student.

In creating this book for you, we also keep in mind the entirety of the child's learning experience throughout the elementary grades. While specifically written for fourth graders, the units presented here were created with the big picture in mind: children's entire K–5 experience.

# The Complete 4

The Complete 4 was devised in response to the need expressed to us by teachers for balance in literacy instruction. We believe students should be well-rounded readers and writers. This means they should learn about reading and writing strategies. They should also develop a strong understanding of genre and a working knowledge of the conventions of the English language and begin to take on the passions, habits, and behaviors of lifelong readers and writers. The Complete 4 includes four key components of literacy instruction that will help us teach into these varied expectations: Process, Genre, Strategy, and Conventions.

The Complete 4 components help us to plan the school year by balancing the types of units across the year. Knowing whether a unit falls under the category of Process, Genre, Strategy, or Conventions helps us to focus the unit so that all our lessons lead up to several key understandings.

Here is what we mean by the Complete 4:

| Process | Your students will practice the processes shared by all successful readers and writers, at an appropriate developmental level. These include fluency, stamina, and independence. |
|---|---|
| Genre | Your students will learn to identify and use various literary containers, including narrative, nonfiction, poetry, and standardized tests. |
| Strategy | Your students will learn to be strategic readers and writers, practicing how writers make plans on a page, and how readers approach text differently depending on their needs. |
| Conventions | Your students will learn grammar and punctuation in contexts that are real, practical, and relevant to their reading and writing experiences. |

In planning a complete year of literacy instruction for fourth grade, we have created reading and writing units that reflect a deep balance. All four Complete 4 components are represented. Take a look at the color calendar on the inside front cover to see how the units in the fourth-grade year focus on the key components of literacy instruction—Process, Genre, Strategy, and Conventions. We have selected these units for you as a way to create balance and provide a solid foundation upon which a productive year of learning can occur.

## Will this book help me connect other aspects of the curriculum to the Complete 4?

Absolutely! One of the best features of the Complete 4 system is its flexible capacity to help you integrate all the areas of your curriculum. For example, in fourth grade your students are studying history and science topics of all kinds. They are expanding their research skills. Units on nonfiction reading and writing support cross-content work. You can teach the skills and strategies for reading and writing in the content areas inside one or more of these units.

Alignment to standards is critical, and these units are constructed in such a way as to reflect the standards and to allow for adjustment to your state standards.

## Can this book help me if I have other demands in my day and cannot teach all the units?

Yes, it can. Here are three suggestions for how you could adapt this calendar to your particular situation:

- You can choose one reading and one writing unit from each Complete 4 component to teach during the year.
- You can focus on the units of study that pair well with your existing themes.
- You can teach only the reading or writing strand.

## Will the Complete 4 help me forge reading and writing connections with my students?

This is another great aspect of the Complete 4 program: we link reading and writing units as "companions." Although the instruction may not always be identical, the units should be "talking" to one another. You will see how we take special care to make sure reading and writing units echo and parallel each other, or to stagger them so students see, feel, and understand those essential connections. Indeed, reading and writing are interrelated processes that are mutually supportive when taught together. You may have noticed that your strongest writers are typically your most passionate readers.

## Can I use this book to support just my writing instruction since I already use another reading program?

Yes. You can use this book to guide you in either writing or reading. Take a look at the writing calendar only: with your grade-level team, you can look into your reading program and see where you can link your instruction. For example, if your reading program has a set of stories on friendship, you could link that set to our Uncovering Theme unit in the spring. This calendar is designed so that you can use it flexibly. Use the reading calendar alone, or the writing calendar alone. They work that way, but they have been written to match for those of you who want the "complete" package. The Complete 4 is also a way to reintroduce quality children's literature into your classroom even if you use a core reading program.

## Can I still benefit from this yearlong approach if my school has commitments that must be addressed at different times of the year?

One of the most exciting aspects of the Complete 4 is that the reading and writing units are interconnected and follow a logical sequence. However, we have also constructed the calendars to allow for flexibility. If, for example, your standardized testing comes earlier in the year, you can easily move units around to suit your test preparation schedule. Or if your entire school studies poetry together in the fall rather than the spring, you can move the units to accommodate that. The calendar is designed to be used either as a whole unit, as a step by step program, or as building blocks to construct your own unique program.

## Will the Complete 4 help me meet the needs of all learners in my classroom?

The range of ability levels and learning modalities in each of our classrooms reminds us to balance our own teaching. The Complete 4 can help us accomplish this. For example, we tend to work with our English language learners mostly on conventions of print, while we work with writers whose first language is English more on strategies or genre. The Complete 4 reminds us that our English language learners flourish with exposure to the habits and passions of readers and writers, the study of different genres, and practice with complex strategies. Similarly, your students who have a comparatively strong sense of conventions are often not given intensive instruction in that area, but they too would enjoy and benefit greatly from inspiring lessons on the construction of a sentence or the artful use of a punctuation mark. The Complete 4 guides us to teach with an eye to creating a Complete Year for all students.

## Will this book help me with the flow of my day?

Yes! We are very aware of your time constraints and the benefits of predictable routines. We have created a very simple, easy-to-follow outline for each day's work during reading and writing time that follows a whole/small/whole pattern. These are the three parts of every lesson:

- Focused Instruction: the whole-class lessons
- Independent Practice: individualized or small-group work
- Wrap-Up: more whole-class teaching with planning for the next day's lesson

| Focused Instruction | Students gather for a period of Focused Instruction for 5 to 15 minutes. <br> • Warm up your students with a reference to prior teaching and learning. <br> • Teach one clear point. <br> • Ask students to quickly try your point. <br> • Clarify your teaching point. <br> • Set the stage for Independent Practice. |
|---|---|
| Independent Practice | Students practice independently while you confer with students and/or conduct small instructional groups. <br> • Encourage students to read or write independently (at their level). <br> • Have students practice your teaching point as they read and write. <br> • Meet with individual students, partnerships, and/or groups regularly for informal assessment and instruction. <br> • Look for future teaching points or an example to use in the Wrap-Up. |
| Wrap-Up | Students return for a focused, brief discussion that reflects on the day's learning. <br> • Restate your teaching point. <br> • Share examples of students' work or learning. <br> • Set plans for the next day and make connections to homework. |

## What are my students actually doing during Independent Practice?

As you will see from the scripted lessons in our Spotlight Units, during Independent Practice students practice a skill you have demonstrated. In addition, they are doing something that seems fairly simple on the surface but in fact is the heart of our work and the driving energy for all the lessons in this book: **they are reading and writing independently**, every day. We suggest that 50 percent of all reading and writing time be Independent Practice. Of this time, approximately 20 percent should be spent practicing a specific skill associated with their reading, and 80 percent of the time should be spent actually reading and writing! Students should be given time every day to read and write in a comfortable manner, at their reading and writing levels, and in books and topics that are of great personal interest to them. Here are the approximate amounts of time your students can and should be reading and writing for each day (you may have to work toward these minutes as the year unfolds):

| Grade Level | Actual Reading Time | Actual Writing Time |
| --- | --- | --- |
| KINDERGARTEN | 10–15 minutes | 10–20 (writing/drawing) |
| FIRST GRADE | 10–20 | 10–20 |
| SECOND GRADE | 20–30 | 20–25 |
| THIRD GRADE | 30–40 | 25–30 |
| FOURTH GRADE | 35–45 | 25–30 |
| FIFTH GRADE | 40–45 | 30–40 |

## Are there essential materials I must use in order to make the Complete 4 program a success?

You can use any of your support materials, including a core reading program or a phonics program, alongside the Complete 4 approach. The heart of our approach is that every child has time to practice skills, strategies, and processes through reading and writing that is at his level and is as authentic as possible. A seminal National Endowment for the Arts study (2007) found, not surprisingly, that "students who read for fun nearly every day performed better on reading tests than those who reported reading never or hardly at all." The study points to the "failure of schools and colleges to develop a culture of daily reading habits." In addition, an analysis of federal Department of Education statistics found that those students who scored lower on all standardized tests lived in homes with fewer than ten books (Rich, 2007). This study then points to two pivotal factors in ensuring lifelong literacy: children must have time to read a lot, and children must have easy, continual access to books.

Our work throughout this book and this series is designed to focus on daily Independent Practice: Students are reading authentic literature and reading a lot, every day, at their own level. Students are writing about topics of authentic interest and writing a lot, every day, at their own level. Students are navigating texts and have easy access to understandable texts throughout the day, especially during literacy time. These, then, are the two keys to our work: giving students time to practice reading and writing, and giving them access to texts that inspire them both as readers and as writers.

The access is critical and is best accomplished by establishing a well-stocked classroom library. Your library should have a variety of genres: nonfiction, fiction, and poetry. Approximately 20 to 30 percent of your library should be leveled through a clearly organized system in which children can find books that are truly comfortable for them to read at their independent reading levels.

Your students should have a way to bring their books between home and school, and to store the stack of books they have been reading most recently, either in baggies or baskets. Organization is one of two keys to life (the other being passion!). Don't let disorder get in the way of helping your children do a lot of reading in your classroom. They can help you organize your library, too.

It is also crucial for students to have a way to record thinking about reading, either in a reading notebook, a folder, or even a binder. The important thing to remember is that this should be a system that works for you and your students. It does not matter so much what you select or what you call it, as long as you know your children can easily access it, and they feel comfortable writing in it and, if they are our youngest readers and writers, drawing in it.

During writing time, your students need order as well. Keep a separate writing area neat and stocked, equipped with all the helpful tools a writer loves: sticky notes, staplers, tape, and date stamps. And as with reading time, your students should have a clearly identified, easy-to-use container to capture their writing. In this series we use writing notebooks with our students from second grade to fifth grade, and writing folders with students in kindergarten and first grade. Using folders allows us to provide our students with a variety of paper choices if they need them. The key to keeping containers for students' writing work is that it is easy for them to revisit, reread, and reflect upon, and it is easy for you to look at before conferences and to assess on an ongoing basis. Again, it does not matter what you call these containers, or which ones you choose, as long as they are truly useful for both you and your students.

## I don't have access to all the anchor texts you recommend in this book, or there are other texts I prefer to use instead. Will my units be as effective if my anchor text selections are somewhat different from yours?

We want to give you as many specific suggestions as we can, and so we have recommended many anchor texts for each unit. You can find them both in the unit templates and also in the back of the book in a seasonally organized bibliography so you can order all of them for your classroom library if you wish. However, if you can't find them all, or you have others you wish to use instead, you are more than welcome and the units will absolutely be as successful. Take a close look at why we chose the texts we did so you can replace them with selections that will still match the outcomes for the units and will feel comfortable for you.

## I use the elements of balanced literacy: shared reading, guided reading, read-aloud, and more. Where do they fit in to the Complete 4 system?

See your elements of balanced literacy as the "how" of your teaching and the Complete 4 as the "what." Teachers who use balanced literacy elements are still asking: But WHAT do I teach tomorrow? The Complete 4 answers that age-old question. Your balanced literacy structures, then, can truly become the engines that drive your content home. For example, shared reading and the read-aloud are structures you can use present your content, both in the Focused Instruction and in the Wrap-Up. Guided reading is a structure you can use to practice content with smaller groups of children. This can be done during Independent Practice, so while some of your children are reading independently others are meeting with you in small groups.

## What if I've never taught in units like this before?

In a Complete Year unit of study, students learn about one aspect of reading or writing (process, genre, strategy, or conventions) in a one- to six-week cycle of learning. Inside this book you will find all the units for a Complete Year of reading and writing instruction. In each unit, we have set a specific focus for instruction and created framing questions to guide you and your students. We have set a time frame and established goals for each unit and put together a list of anchor texts that you can use to teach the lessons. Most important, we have provided helpful templates to take you through *all* the units.

To help you implement and pace your instruction, we have divided the instruction in each unit into four key lesson stages: Immersion, Identification, Guided Practice, and Commitment. The premise behind this concept was inspired by the work of Pearson and Gallagher (1983). They delineated a gradual release of responsibility from teacher to student as the ideal conditions for learning. These stages help us make the necessary turns in our teaching so that we move in an efficient and effective way through any unit of study and our students have the best chance for success.

| **Immersion** | We immerse our students in a topic of study. |
| --- | --- |
| **Identification** | We name or define what students must know about the topic by the end of the unit. |
| **Guided Practice** | We model reading and writing for our students and give them time for practice, so that we can guide them toward the goals of the unit. |
| **Commitment** | We ask students to reflect on their learning and commit to the use of this knowledge in their future reading and writing. |

## You use specific language to identify the parts of a unit and the parts of a lesson. How can I be sure I can follow along easily?

The language in this book is extremely user-friendly. We try to steer clear of jargon as much as we can. To best help teachers plan units and teach lessons, we have identified terms that help us all move forward easily. We have included a helpful Glossary of Terms for you on page 233.

## What is the role of the Spotlight Units in the Complete Year books?

Each Complete Year book features eight bonus Spotlight Units, designed to help you understand what each unit of study can look and feel like in your classroom—both in terms of the concrete day-to-day details as well as the "learning energy" that you create through your instructional language and strategies. During the Spotlight Units, we invite you into our classrooms to sit by our sides and listen as we interact with our students. While we know you'll use your own language that reflects your unique teaching personality, we provide examples of language we use in our classrooms as a model for you to adapt. Learning how to craft our teaching language in artful ways that encourage active student participation takes practice; for example, knowing how to design open-ended questions rather than questions that just elicit a yes–no response is an art, typically learned through classroom-tested trial and error. Sometimes, it's helpful to listen in on another teacher and notice how she uses language to frame each teaching moment.

Inside the Spotlight Units, you'll find one reading unit and one writing unit in each of the Complete 4 components (Process, Genre, Strategy, and Conventions). Our Spotlight Units also include unit templates, so you can see how we translate the templates into day-by-day lesson plans. You'll notice that not all bullets are translated directly into lessons and that the flow of the unit is fluid and flexible so you can adapt it in ways that fit your students' unique needs and interests.

## How do I use the unit templates?

We envision teachers taking the templates we provide for each unit and adapting them to their students. Perhaps you have favorite books you love to read in your nonfiction unit. Or perhaps your students need more than one day on a bulleted lesson. Although the templates offer guidelines for the overall structure of a unit and suggestions for how the unit might be paced, we see them as a road atlas, a guide that leads you toward your goal but also gives you the opportunity to add your own special touches along the way. Many teachers like to keep these unit templates on their desks as a reminder of where they are going, to help them plan each day's lesson.

## How will I assess my students through the Complete Year?

The structure of the Complete 4 classroom gives you a rich opportunity to assess your students during their Independent Practice. Units of study give you regular, frequent opportunities to take stock of your students' progress. At the end of each unit is an assessment form for you to use.

Chapter 6 is dedicated to the C4 Assessment (C4A): a comprehensive tool designed for your grade level. You can use the C4A three times a year for both reading and writing. Quick and easy, the C4A will provide valuable information on your students' progress in all areas of reading and writing instruction.

# The Complete Year in Grade 4

These books are organized around the seasons of the year. Our learning time with our students, bound by the parameters of the school year, is also organized by seasons, and so we thought it would be helpful to organize our books that way, too.

As the year begins, fourth graders have great confidence about their place in school. They are the "big" kids and can go places independently; they may have new privileges at lunch and recess. Winter brings new growth. They are changing in many ways and are quite aware of the world outside their classrooms. They have a vibrant interest in the conversations of adults around them. They are building stamina. They are interested in how to read and write in the sciences and history. The spring brings with it more blooming possibilities. Students are reading in new genres and discovering the joys of reading a lot: quantity feels as good as quality. They have forged friendships that truly matter to them, and talk about things of great importance to them. At this spring season, they suddenly seem to grow another ten inches. They may be doing new after-school activities and sports that are important to them in ways that are becoming more than activities—they are passions. They are reading and writing poetry; together with friends, they are creating plays and performing them. Their world is changing, expanding, unfolding. They are gloriously young, seriously growing. This is a year like no other.

Get ready now for the Complete Year experience. Timely and timeless (and won't cost YOU time). Flexible and friendly (and fun). Easy to use and easy to navigate (and easy to explain to parents). Standards based and field tested (in hundreds of classrooms). Made for you (to simplify your teaching life and to reconnect you with the joy of teaching). Made for your fourth graders (especially).

Have a great year!

# Chapter 2

## EARLY FALL

# The Fourth Grader as Deep Thinker

*"Ma spits on her finger. She wipes at a smudge on my chin. I lift my head and let her wash me all she wants. That finger of hers reminds me of the ginger cat who washes her kittens down in the Land of the Car Bones, where Pa and I take our walks sometimes."*

—from *Just Juice* by Karen Hesse

Our fourth graders are seized by ideas, becoming passionate about their own and intrigued by others'. This season is one of expanding for students: thinking across books, across ideas, making connections to all of the world, finding writers they love, collaborating with one another in productive and joyous ways as readers and writers. They are still so young, too, as you well know, and so the reading and writing times still represent tender moments of belonging, identity-shaping, and community-building. They are thinking deeply about themselves and about their relationships to others. Join us in this first season with our fourth graders for eight units of study in the teaching of reading and writing.

SPOTLIGHT UNITS

# Beginning the Year With the ARCH

Our first units, known as the ARCH, are designed to bring our students together into a reading and writing community. This acronym stands for Assessment, Routines, Choice, and Healthy Community. The units balance the need to assess students as readers and writers with lessons on the routines of reading and writing time, the community-building aspects of reading and writing time, and how to make choices both in terms of topics and texts.

We must actively construct this community by establishing the daily routines for reading and writing time, discovering personal and shared interests, and introducing our students to our libraries and writing tools. Fountas and Pinnell (2001) remind us that during the first month of school you have two important goals: to help your students think of themselves as readers and to establish roles and routines. They remind us to repeat key lessons, chart the routines and roles of the reader and writer, and refer our students back to these reference points regularly.

As teachers, we are always a bit uncertain about how to begin the year in terms of content. We want to get to know our students, and we know we need to establish these routines, but we wonder what the content and outcomes are for this work. The ARCH is designed to blend both process and products: the beautiful work we do in coming together for the first time, as well as the important work we do in generating products that represent our students and move them forward at the very beginning of this school year's journey.

Each Complete 4 year begins with an ARCH unit at every grade level, but each year should feel different because of your students' changing developmental needs. (See page 112 of *The Complete 4 for Literacy* to see all the ARCH articulations for each grade level.) In fourth grade, our ARCH focus is Thinking Across Books and Becoming Inspired by Writers. In the reading and writing units that follow, we continue to build upon that theme with units that help our students discover the value of thinking and working across text.

The ARCH units set the foundation for the entire year. The ARCH incorporates teaching of all of those routines and habits you long for and need when you are in the midst of your work with your students. If you set the stage now, you are guaranteed a happy, truly productive year in the teaching of reading and writing.

## The ARCH: Thinking Across Books

**PROCESS**

### Why Teach This?

- To embrace the rules and routines of reading time.
- To develop student reading identities, abilities, and interests.
- To develop a community of readers who will sustain and support one another across the year.
- To develop the importance of thinking critically across text.

### Framing Questions

- How are we continuing to develop an understanding of ourselves as readers?
- How can we build a community of readers who support and trust one another?
- How can we think across multiple texts?

### Unit Goals

- Students will internalize the routines and structures of reading time.
- Students will set personal reading goals.
- Students will practice thinking critically across text, making important discoveries and connections.

### Anchor Texts

- "Anti-Bullying Buddies," a nonfiction article by Elizabeth Carney, *Scholastic News* (10/9/06)
- "The Bully" in *Baseball, Snakes, and Summer Squash: Poems About Growing Up* by Donald Graves
- *Riding the Tiger* by Eve Bunting
- *Whoever You Are* by Mem Fox
- *Zen Ties* by Jon J. Muth

### Resource Sheet

- Reading Goals Planner (Resource 2.1)

| Unit Assessment The ARCH: Thinking Across Books | | | PROCESS |
|---|---|---|---|
| Student name: | EMERGING | DEVELOPING | INDEPENDENT |
| Understands and follows the routines and structures of reading time. | | | |
| Has an accurate sense of oneself as a reader, including challenges faced. | | | |
| Sets personal reading goals. | | | |
| Uses classmates for book/genre/author suggestions. | | | |
| Demonstrates a developing ability to talk across text. | | | |

| Stage of the Unit | Focused Instruction<br>You will | Independent Practice<br>Students will |
|---|---|---|
| IMMERSION<br>4 days | • introduce the class to your classroom library, the routines for borrowing books, the way the library is organized.<br>• review prior knowledge and experience in key fictional genres.<br>• read aloud from *Whoever You Are* by Mem Fox; explore similarities, as people and as readers, despite differences in classroom community.<br>• read aloud *Zen Ties* by Jon J. Muth; explore what it means to be a friend, a classmate, and a member of a reading community. | • explore the library, listing books of interest and their location.<br>• list favorite genres and favorite titles within genres; share these with a partner; explore these genre baskets in the library.<br>• find classmates with similar interests; interview them, explore their reading preferences, explore genre baskets together.<br>• set personal goals as readers and as members of a reading community; get acclimated to the flow of the reading period. |
| IDENTIFICATION<br>4 days | • model goal-oriented book selection and plans for future reading.<br>• define the job specifications of being in a reading community.<br>• create list of students and each one's preferred genre.<br>• explain the role of the teacher and the student in a reading conference. | • identify the next three books they plan to read.<br>• practice flow of the reading time and reading independently.<br>• meet in genre interest groups to add books to reading plans.<br>• read with the plan of preparing for a conference. |

| | | |
|---|---|---|
| **GUIDED PRACTICE**<br>6 days | • read aloud a theme-based picture book like *Riding the Tiger* by Eve Bunting; model a reading conference with a student based on this shared text.<br><br>• read aloud a theme-based poem like "The Bully" by Donald Graves; model thinking aloud as you read and connect this poem to yesterday's picture book.<br><br>• ask what kind of a community we will have this year and how we will we treat each other; read aloud a passage from a theme-based article like "Anti-Bullying Buddies" by Elizabeth Carney; model making additional connections across text; ask the class why authors often write about this topic.<br><br>• establish expectations for thinking inside of text this year: good readers make connections across text, looking for larger ideas, issues, and themes.<br><br>• establish expectations for reading across a wide range of genres this year, challenging students to try on new genres and new authors; use the Reading Goals Planner (Resource 2.1).<br><br>• establish expectations for reading behaviors this year—including building stamina and reading a certain number of books across the year; use the Reading Goals Planner. | • read independently; practice daily routines; participate in teacher conferences.<br><br>• read independently, think about how connections can be made across texts.<br><br>• work at table groupings to write a classroom community charter.<br><br>• read independently, noticing when they stop and think as they read; share their reading behavior with a partner.<br><br>• set up three-month reading goals for genre and number of books using the Reading Goals Planner and tape into reading notebook; read independently.<br><br>• add to the Reading Goals Planner by considering reading behaviors, capacities, routines, and collaborations. |
| **COMMITMENT**<br>1 day | • review total reading expectations for the class reading goals across the Complete 4—process, genre, strategy, and conventions (this serves as a general introduction to the units in the year). | • share draft reading goals with a partner; discuss and revise reading goals based on discussion. |
| **TOTAL: 15 DAYS** | | |

## The ARCH: Becoming Inspired by Writers

PROCESS

### Why Teach This?

- To help students embrace the rules and routines for writing time.
- To identify each student's writing strengths, weaknesses, and interests.
- To develop student writing identities, abilities, and interests.
- To develop a community of writers who will sustain and support one another across the year.
- To explore how literature influences our writing.

### Framing Questions

- How are we continuing to develop an understanding of ourselves as writers?
- How can we build a community of writers who support and trust one another?
- In what way(s) does literature influence and inspire us as writers?

### Unit Goals

- Students will help create a supportive writing community.
- Students will internalize the routines and structures of writing time, including conferences and assessments.
- Students will set personal writing goals.
- Students will identify influential texts.

### Anchor Texts

- Lois Lowry's Newbery acceptance speech (found at www.loislowry.com/pdf/Newbery_Award.pdf)
- *Owen & Mzee: The True Story of a Remarkable Friendship* by Isabella Hatkoff, Craig Hatkoff, and Dr. Paula Kahumbu
- "Poem" by Langston Hughes (from *The Dream Keeper and Other Poems*)
- *Stone Soup* magazine (downloadable from www.stonesoup.com)
- "Where I'm From" by George Ella Lyon (from *Seeing the Blue Between: Advice and Inspiration for Young Poets*, edited by Paul B. Janeczko)
- *Wings* by Christopher Myers

### Resource Sheet

- Idea Generator (Resource 2.2)

| Unit Assessment The ARCH: Becoming Inspired by Writers | | | PROCESS |
| --- | --- | --- | --- |
| Student name: | EMERGING | DEVELOPING | INDEPENDENT |
| Understands his or her role in the class writing community. | | | |
| Understands and follows the routines and structures of writing time. | | | |
| Sets personal writing goals. | | | |
| Identifies influences and models in literature. | | | |

| Stage of the Unit | Focused Instruction<br>You will | Independent Practice<br>Students will |
| --- | --- | --- |
| IMMERSION<br>7 days | • share your reflections on who you are as a writer: interests, topics, favorite genre, habits.<br><br>• read aloud *Owen & Mzee*; share why this text inspires you and share your other writing inspirations—key texts, key authors, key writing experiences in your life.<br><br>• read aloud *Wings*; introduce your class to the writing routines and tools in your classroom by beginning a writing piece in your own notebook that is inspired by this book and its message.<br><br>• read aloud "Poem" by Langston Hughes; remind writers of the variety of choice they have in topic and form.<br><br>• introduce the Four Prompts to your class (I wonder, I remember, I observe, I imagine); write in response to one of these prompts.<br><br>• ask students to generate a baseline piece of writing of their choice to be used for assessment; write in front of your class as a model of this exercise, making sure to keep it short and fun! | • meet in partnerships to share their own writing reflections; present the other student in their partnership to the class as a particular kind of writer.<br><br>• meet in partnerships to look through last year's writing portfolios; explore their writing inspirations (mentor texts, authors, etc.).<br><br>• practice working within routines by beginning a writing piece in their writing notebooks.<br><br>• meet in partnerships to look through last year's writing notebooks; explore the range of writing topics and forms.<br><br>• use one of the Four Prompts to write another piece in their writing notebooks.<br><br>• create a baseline piece of writing for assessment; choose their own topic and their own form.<br><br>• write an explanatory author's note to explain what the writing sample demonstrates about the writer. |

| IDENTIFICATION<br>5 days | • set expectations for writing notebooks (use of pages, table of contents, page numbering, foldovers to mark new projects, etc.).<br>• model writing a list of future writing topics using the Four Prompts.<br>• model thinking about the literature that you would like to write in response to this year; demonstrate this kind of free writing for your class (for example, write in response to a different Langston Hughes poem: What does this poem inspire you to say in your own words in response?).<br>• ask a student to share her writing with the class; use the Idea Generator (Resource 2.2) to help this writer go deeper or in other possible directions with her topic.<br>• model a writing conference with a student volunteer; establish responsibilities and expectations for writing conferences during Independent Practice. | • organize notebooks according to class expectations; write a new piece.<br>• create a list of future writing topics.<br>• browse through picture books and poetry collections; find at least one text that inspires new writing and free-write in response to this text.<br>• use the Idea Generator to explore other approaches and development ideas for their topic.<br>• plan in writing for a possible conference based on yesterday's writing; share with partners. |
|---|---|---|

| | | |
|---|---|---|
| **GUIDED PRACTICE**<br><br>7 days | • continue to explore where great writing ideas come from; remind students that writing inspirations do not have to be large, important events, but could be ordinary moments you want to explore.<br><br>• share George Ella Lyon's poem "Where I'm From"; model your own "Where I'm From" list; use this list to inspire another modeled piece of writing.<br><br>• read aloud a snippet from Lois Lowry's Newbery acceptance speech (1994), in which she shares where her own writing ideas come from.<br><br>• walk students through an issue of *Stone Soup*, a literary magazine by and for children; comment on the range of writing children are inspired to undertake for publication (poems, personal narratives, fiction, book reviews).<br><br>• share your own personal writing goals with your students; document them and put them in a public place.<br><br>• share a volunteer student's baseline writing piece; ask the class to name the strengths of the writer and suggest areas for development, considering these as additional fodder for writing goals.<br><br>• discuss with the class how you will work on your writing goals over the next several months. | • think of ordinary moments that may inspire them to write because they wonder about them or because they preoccupy them; write in response.<br><br>• write their own "Where I'm From" lists, using the list to inspire another piece of writing.<br><br>• write in response to the prompt "Where do your ideas come from?"<br><br>• read a story or poem from *Stone Soup*; they will use their emotional responses to these texts as inspiration for their own notebook writing.<br><br>• meet with a partner and discuss possible writing goals for the next several months; list these in their writing notebooks.<br><br>• revisit the baseline writing piece; consider personal strengths and areas for development and add these thoughts to individual writing goals.<br><br>• copy personal writing goals onto index cards and place in library pockets with student names (these will be used for writing conferences). |
| **COMMITMENT**<br><br>1 day | • ask your students, "How can we inspire one another this year as writers? How can we create a supportive writing community?" | • write in response to the following question: "What will inspire you as a writer this year?" |
| **TOTAL: 20 DAYS** | | |

# SPOTLIGHT on Conventions

- Getting to Know the Job of Words: Parts of Speech
- Adding Description to Writing: Using Modifiers

As fourth-grade teachers, we often either dread teaching conventions because they feel so detached from the liveliness of our students' literacy experiences or we cram in lots of instruction in concentrated periods of time, worried that we are not covering it all before they move on to the next grade. The Complete 4 approach advocates finding a middle ground. We are not going to teach conventions in isolation (although we do advocate regular word work time for practice with patterns and strategies), nor are we going to ignore them. Instead, we are going to carefully place conventions instruction where it belongs—alongside students' authentic work. We celebrate language, punctuation, and grammar in ways that respect and give dignity to the way fourth graders are coming to print. The writer Eudora Welty recalled her first glimpse of the alphabet inside her storybooks as a child and how magical the swirls and curves of each letter seemed. Let us capture that magic in units on conventions. See pages 62 to 72 in *The Complete 4 for Literacy* for more guidelines for this component.

*Pam Allyn*

## Functional Language Users

Most fourth graders love to read if given the chance to read the books they love. As they read from a wide variety of texts, they encounter new words every day. Some of these words make the books they are reading more vivid and descriptive. Some of these words are modifiers. But many students don't ultimately understand these words or the nuances the writer is trying to describe. To help your students appreciate the text they read, to encourage them to write in similarly beautiful ways, you must teach them the fundamentals of the parts of speech. The best way to do so is by calling their attention to the wonder of language in the texts they are reading independently, at their levels. Michael Smith and Jeffrey Wilhelm (2007) remind us that we should "teach terms that students need in order to do important work in their writing and reading by creating occasions in which students can see the necessity of the terms they're learning." Together, we explore the basic parts of speech, keeping in mind that language is functional as well as beautiful. Knowing the functions of language helps our students see the beauty of it, too.

> Nouns
> - person, place, thing
> - subject of a sentence Who or What
> - can be proper nouns or common nouns
> - proper nouns are capitalized because they name something
> - common nouns are not capitalized
> - can be singular or plural
> - without a noun the sentence would fall apart
> - more than one subject can be in a sentence

## Getting to Know the Job of Words: Parts of Speech

CONVENTIONS

### Why Teach This?

- To review prior knowledge of nouns and verbs.
- To introduce the concept of modifying nouns and verbs.
- To practice applying our knowledge of parts of speech to our real-world reading.

### Framing Questions

- What is the job of certain words in a sentence?
- How can this understanding help us identify parts of speech?

### Unit Goals

- Students will identify nouns, proper nouns, and pronouns.
- Students will identify verbs.
- Students will identify modifiers—adverbs and adjectives—with assistance.
- Students will name and explain the primary parts of speech.

### Anchor Text

- *From the Mixed-up Files of Mrs. Basil E. Frankweiler* by E. L. Konigsburg

| Unit Assessment Getting to Know the Job of Words: Parts of Speech | | | CONVENTIONS |
|---|---|---|---|
| Student name: | EMERGING | DEVELOPING | INDEPENDENT |
| Identifies common nouns, pronouns, and proper nouns. | | | |
| Identifies action verbs. | | | |
| Identifies helping verbs. | | | |
| Identifies state-of-being verbs. | | | |
| Identifies and explains adjectives. | | | |
| Identifies and explains adverbs. | | | |

| Stage of the Unit | Focused Instruction<br>You will | Independent Practice<br>Students will |
|---|---|---|
| **IMMERSION**<br>1 day | • ask students to wonder about the job of certain highlighted words in a shared passage. | • notice highlighted words in shared text; collaborate toward a collective working description of these words. |
| **IDENTIFICATION**<br>4 days | • review the job of the noun in a sentence.<br>• review the job of the verb in a sentence.<br>• define the job of an adjective in a sentence.<br>• introduce and define the adverb in a sentence. | • find other noun examples in shared text.<br>• find other verb examples in independent reading.<br>• find other adjective examples in independent reading.<br>• find other adverb examples in independent reading. |
| **GUIDED PRACTICE**<br>9 days | • model how you use context clues in the sentence and the location of a masked word to guess the part of speech.<br>• use the masked word activity to review different types of nouns—proper versus common (mask all but the first letter).<br>• use the masked word activity to match for singular/plural agreement. | • find one interesting sentence in independent reading; label any known parts of speech.<br>• search for proper and common nouns in independent reading.<br>• search for examples of singular and plural noun-verb pairs in independent reading. |

| GUIDED PRACTICE *(continued)* | • use the masked word activity to review action versus helping and state-of-being verbs.<br><br>• use the masked word activity to review subject-verb agreement.<br><br>• use the masked word activity to show different possible locations of the adjective in a sentence (e.g., the dog is excited, the excited dog).<br><br>• use the masked word activity to introduce possessive pronouns (my, his, her, its, our, their, your).<br><br>• use the masked word activity to review the introduction to the adverb; limit discussion to adverbs that modify verbs.<br><br>• model creating your own masked word activity. | • notice and compare different kinds of verbs in independent reading.<br><br>• search for examples of subject-verb agreement in independent reading.<br><br>• copy an adjective sentence onto a strip; turn into covered word activity.<br><br>• search for examples of possessive pronouns in independent reading.<br><br>• search for examples of adverbs in independent reading.<br><br>• create their own masked word exercises as a culminating project. |
|---|---|---|
| COMMITMENT 1 day | • model the basic naming of sentence parts as a final assessment. | • select a favorite sentence strip and highlight and name parts as final assessment; respond to framing questions. |
| **TOTAL: 15 DAYS** | | |

# Getting Started

Let's face it: we are all a bit intimidated by the prospect of studying grammar with our students. We know the basics of grammar, and we can probably fill out a grammar worksheet better than the next person, but certain words in the complex sentences we read and write each day are far more mysterious, and it is harder to identify their purpose in a sentence. Language is much more complex in use than in definition. Sure, you can and should dust off your copy of *The Elements of Grammar* by Margaret Shertzer, or buy a new, more amusing review of grammar like *Woe is I* by Patricia T. O'Connor. But the best way to study grammar is by perusing your own reading. When you read a sentence you love, stop and examine it. Your favorite sentences are your very best teachers.

# Teaching Materials

Every day your students are reading their own independent reading books and can find many wonderful examples of beautiful conventions inside those books.

## Choosing Teaching Texts

We have selected an anchor read-aloud text, *From the Mixed-up Files of Mrs. Basil E. Frankweiler* by E. L. Konigsburg. All the shared reading passages used to teach parts of speech will come from this book. Read the book aloud to your students and then revisit a short passage from that day's reading to study more closely. You can use typed excerpts, a SMART Board, or a document camera to share a passage of text with a large group of students.

## Choosing Student Texts

As this conventions unit does not require reading a particular genre, your students should be free to make choices based on their own interests and abilities and have plenty of time to read these texts! Don't "spoil" the books by having them only look at conventions. Let the conventions work be a part of the bigger picture of their independent reading.

### Setting Up Your Classroom Library

Access is the key component for success in reading. A classroom library that is inviting helps to motivate children to read and become readers. Books in the library should represent a variety of genres, including nonfiction, fiction, and poetry. Books should be placed in baskets in a way that encourages browsing, with the covers facing out. The baskets of books can be sorted by topics, genres, and authors.

### Independent Book Bags or Baskets

Ideally your students will be borrowing books from your classroom library, reading in school and at home, and returning each day with the same books. Books placed in large plastic bags transport well and protect paperback covers. A book bag can be used another way to help fourth graders set aside books for future reading: they can each have their current read and then two or three other titles set aside in a basket or bag for future reading.

## Differentiation

If we ask all of our students to read the same text all of the time, we are ignoring the reality that for some this text will be too easy, and for others too hard. A child who is flying high as a reader needs an appropriate challenge. A vulnerable reader needs an appropriate scaffold, so that she, too, can be successful. One way to accomplish this differentiation is to offer leveled books in your classroom library that will assist students in making appropriate book choices.

### Leveled Books

Devote a section of your library to baskets of leveled books. In the lower grades, in order to level a book, we look at the amount of print on a page, the number of words, the placement of the words and pictures, and the vocabulary in the book. In the upper grades, we add to these criteria by identifying the number of characters, episodic versus arching plot, sentence structure, and other features that make reading more difficult for middle-grade readers. For more information about leveling, Irene Fountas and Gay Su Pinnell have many books on this topic. They have created an A to Z system to level books. Many of our fourth-grade students come to us at a level M and the goal is to get them to a level P by the end of the year.

Leveled books should comprise approximately 20 to 30 percent of your library. Children can choose from the nonleveled books once they have learned how to make wise book choices. If you choose to use the A to Z leveling system, you may want to assign the letters a color sticker to minimize the issue of children feeling competitive about levels. If you are positive and excited about their choices, they will be less competitive with one another.

# Stages of the Unit

## Immersion

Read aloud, and then highlight parts of speech. Here is an example of such a passage from the first chapter of *From the Mixed-up Files of Mrs. Basil E. Frankweiler*:

> When Claudia decided to run away, she planned very carefully. She would be gone just long enough to teach her parents a lesson in Claudia appreciation. And she would go in comfort—she would live at the Metropolitan Museum of Art. She saved her money, and she invited her brother Jamie to go, mostly because he was a miser and would have money.

In this stage of the unit, you are introducing your students to the concept of naming parts of speech in ways that are relevant to reading they really like to do.

## Identification

Each day during this stage you review and define the parts of speech that a fourth grader should already know, the noun and the verb, and introduce and define the adjective and adverb. At the end of each day's read-aloud, feature a small passage of text for your class to reread. Here is a passage used from *Mixed-up Files* to focus on and review the noun:

> Jamie found his list of instructions under his pillow pinned to his pajamas.

Model identifying and naming the parts of speech of key highlighted words. The nouns will be the subjects and objects of all the attention in the sentence. The verbs will be, as Georgia Heard (2002) describes them, "the engines of sentences." All adjectives and adverbs will "modify" or change their nouns and verbs to be more specific. Here is an example of a class chart you might create with students after the lesson reviewing and defining the noun.

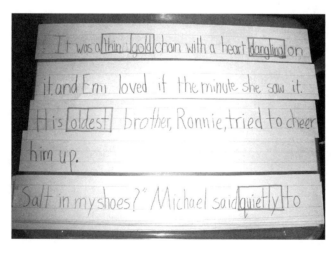

Here students copy mentor sentences from their independent reading and box out key parts of speech.

> **What We've Learned About the NOUN:**
> - A noun is a person, place, or thing. It is the subject and/or object of the verb.
> - Nouns are considered proper or common.
> - Proper nouns include specific names of people, places, or things.
> - Proper nouns are always capitalized.
> - All other nouns are common and are not capitalized.

It is important to remember that students are gathering examples from their reading, but they are still reading and enjoying their books. The "task" of connecting to conventions is just a part of what they do during Independent Practice each day.

## Guided Practice

Now the fun begins! Remember the old-fashioned cloze exercise? Well, it's back—but in a new and fresh way. Read aloud from your novel, and pull a short passage from the text to share with your class, but rather than highlighting the words, you mask them with a small sticky note. Now your students have to work harder to "uncover" the word. The first step in this process is to use the remaining unmasked words to recreate the job of the word that is covered. Here is an example from Chapter 5 of *From the Mixed-up Files of Mrs. Basil E. Frankweiler*:

> They had been gone from home for ▓▓▓ days now. Claudia insisted on a fresh change of underwear every day. That was the way she had been brought up. She insisted for Jamie, too. No question about it: their ▓▓▓ was becoming a problem. They had to get to a laundromat. That night they removed all their ▓▓▓ clothes from their instrument cases and stuffed those that would fit into various pockets. Those that didn't fit, they wore. A double layer of clothes never ▓▓▓ anyone in winter, as long as the clean ones are worn closest to the skin.

Use the masked word activity each day after your read-aloud. In independent reading, students find interesting sentences full of tricky parts of speech and copy them onto sentence strips, creating their own masked word strips to share with their

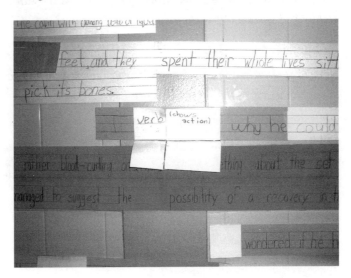

**This bulletin board features student-generated masked word strips. Sticky notes cover key words; flipping the blank note reveals the part of speech.**

classmates. In addition, students find ongoing practice for this new skill by playing online games for homework.

## Commitment

Students are asked to select a favorite sentence strip from their independent reading work and "diagram" the sentence by naming the parts of speech.

# How to Use the Lessons in the Spotlight Units

In every Spotlight Unit, we have scripted each lesson: Focused Instruction, Independent Practice, and Wrap-Up. Where you see italics, we have provided model language; you are free to use it as is, or you may prefer to adapt the language to suit your needs. For example, if we mention a book we might read aloud to our class, and you have one you like better, feel free to use that one instead. Or if we use a personal anecdote as a demonstration, you should replace it with one of your own. Where there are no italics, the lesson plan includes guidelines for what you and the students could be doing at that point in the lesson. You will notice that there is always a balance of teacher talk and suggested actions.

## Day-by-Day Lessons

### DAY 1 Immersion

#### Focused Instruction

- Read aloud from the novel. Highlight certain nouns and verbs in a key passage.

*Let's look at a paragraph from our read-aloud. Notice the words I've highlighted. What is the job of the word* decided? *How about* planned? *Turn and talk to a partner. Are there any other words in this paragraph that have the same job? What about the other highlighted words? What do they have in common?*

#### Independent Practice

*Here is another paragraph from our read-aloud. Work with a partner to see if you can describe the job of the words that are highlighted.*

- Students collaborate over passage.

#### Wrap-Up

- Categorize highlighted words. Write working job descriptions for these "types" of words.

## DAY 2 Identification

### Focused Instruction

- Read aloud from the novel, then highlight nouns in a key passage.

*Some of the words highlighted yesterday are nouns. The job of a noun is to be the subject or the object of a sentence. Let's look at this sentence from our read-aloud.*

- Highlight nouns.
- Explore differences and definitions of nouns.
- Show an example of when a word sounds like a noun and isn't a noun (e.g., "Let's paddle down the river").

### Independent Practice

- Partnerships work with another excerpt from read-aloud, searching for other examples of nouns.

### Wrap-Up

*Some of you noticed that nouns are often capitalized. These are proper nouns: they are the names of people, events, or places. Common nouns are still nouns, but because they aren't a specific name, they are not capitalized. Some of you thought* he, she, *and* they *are nouns because they act as subjects or objects in sentences. What do you think now?*

## DAY 3 Identification

### Focused Instruction

- Read aloud from the novel, then select a passage to read. Highlight key verbs in the passage.

*The words highlighted today are not nouns, they are verbs. The verb is the "engine" of every sentence. Most verbs drive the sentence forward. They are called action verbs.*

- Show examples from the passage.

*Some verbs are quieter. They are harder to identify. Some of these are called state-of-being, or linking verbs.*

- Show examples from the passage.

### Independent Practice

- Students read their independent books and find one interesting verb. They write the verb on a sticky note.

### Wrap-Up

- Share and list found verbs.
- Categorize verbs found.

## DAY 4 Identification

### Focused Instruction

- Read aloud from the novel. Revisit a passage that you have highlighted for adjectives.

*Every complete sentence has at least a subject and a verb. Writers add detail to their sentences using adjectives. Adjectives make writing more interesting, but they aren't needed to make a sentence complete. Let's write a class definition of the adjective and see if it fits our highlighted words.*

### Independent Practice

*As you read your books today, find examples of interesting adjectives. Write one or two on a sticky note to share.*

### Wrap-Up

- Students place sticky notes on a board.
- Discuss what all adjectives have in common with one another.

## DAY 5 Identification

### Focused Instruction

- Read aloud from the novel. Revisit a passage of text where you have highlighted adverbs that modify verbs.

*Adjectives help us paint a mental picture as we read. We know to adjust our image to add color or texture, shape, taste, smell, size, or emotion. All adjectives modify, or change, nouns. Adverbs modify other parts of speech. Let's look at this sentence from our read-aloud. I've highlighted the adverb. What word does this modify?*

- Students turn and talk.

### Independent Practice

*One job of an adverb is to provide more description to verbs. We can be reminded of this by seeing the word* verb *inside of* adverb. *Adverbs tell us more about time and place, manner, or degree. Look for examples of adverbs in your independent reading today.*

### Wrap-Up

*Did you notice that there are not many adverbs? They are harder to find than adjectives. Where should you look for an adverb in a sentence? What part of speech is it likely to be close to?*

## DAY 6 Guided Practice

### Focused Instruction

*Today I'm going to teach you a game that will help you practice naming the parts of speech in a sentence. I'm going to show you an excerpt of text, but I am going to mask several words with sticky notes. Let's see if we can guess the job of these covered words.*

- Play the game several times with students. Present a passage, then ask them to guess the job of a masked word and make educated guesses as to the meaning of the word. Validate students who identify the proper part of speech and use context clues to make thoughtful educated guesses about the actual word.

### Independent Practice

- Students find and copy one sentence from their reading onto a sentence strip and label the parts of speech in the sentence that can be identified.

### Wrap-Up

*What parts of speech are easy to find in our sentences? What parts are hard to find?*

## DAY 7 Guided Practice

### Focused Instruction

- Read aloud.

*We are going to play the masked word game again. This time I am going to cover all but the first letter of the masked words. Use what you know about parts of speech to make educated guesses about the type of word that is covered, and what that word might be.*

- Identify words with capital letters as proper nouns.

### Independent Practice

*As you read today, I want you to find two common nouns and two proper nouns. List them on sticky notes.*

### Wrap-Up

*Who found a proper noun by looking for capitalization?*

### DAY 8 Guided Practice

**Focused Instruction**

- Read aloud.

*Today we are going to play the masked word game again. But this time, I have covered only nouns. I want you to look at the pronouns in the sentence and see if you can tell me whether the noun is a plural noun or a singular noun. Remember, a plural noun means more than one of something, a singular noun means only one of something.* Tree *is* singular, trees *is plural.*

- Model and explain noun-pronoun agreement.

**Independent Practice**

*Find examples of plural and singular agreement in your reading today. Copy one singular noun, singular verb sentence and one plural noun, plural verb sentence onto sentence strips. Be prepared to share them.*

**Wrap-Up**

- Gather sentence strips into singular and plural columns. Note that nouns and pronouns in sentences are often teammates and need to agree in number.

### DAY 9 Guided Practice

**Focused Instruction**

- Read aloud.

*Can we use the masked word game to find different kinds of verbs? How would we recognize an action verb rather than a state-of-being verb? Let's try and see what you figure out.*

- Present a passage where the state-of-being verb is masked. Present a passage with an action verb masked.

**Independent Practice**

*As you read today, notice when your author uses action verbs, and when he or she uses state-of-being verbs.*

**Wrap-Up**

*Often a writer uses state-of-being verbs to fill you in on how the characters in the story are feeling, and action verbs to describe what they are doing. You can make the same choices when you write stories.*

## DAY 10 Guided Practice

### Focused Instruction

- Read aloud. Notice one or two examples of subject-verb agreement as you read.

- Play the masked word game. Cover nouns and ask students to use the verb to determine whether the noun is singular or plural.

### Independent Practice

*As you read today, find one example of subject-verb agreement you would like to share with the class. Copy the sentence onto a sentence strip. Underline the verb and circle the noun.*

### Wrap-Up

*Did anyone find an example of a plural noun that ended in s with a plural verb that didn't? Here are two examples to consider:* The cat chases the mouse. The cats chase the mouse. *Did you expect this? It almost feels backward, doesn't it? But s does not always signal plural in a noun.*

## DAY 11 Guided Practice

### Focused Instruction

*Sometimes, just to make things challenging, the adjective we are looking for is not always right next to the noun. Sometimes the adjective still describes the noun, but it is a distance away. Look at these two examples:* The dog is excited. It was an excited dog.

*You would all say that* excited *is an adjective in the second example. It is also an adjective in the first example. And separating the noun from the adjective is a linking verb!*

### Independent Practice

*Today as you read independently, find a sentence that you could use to create a masked word activity. Copy the sentence onto a sentence strip and then cover the word you want us to figure out with a sticky note. Just cover one word in one sentence today.*

### Wrap-Up

*Who would like to share their masked word sentence? We'll try to guess the part of speech and then the word itself.*

## DAY 12 Guided Practice

### Focused Instruction

*Today we are going to study a new kind of describing word. These don't tell us what color something is, or how big it is, or what it smells like. These words tell us to whom something belongs. They are called possessive pronouns because their root words are pronouns, but they act like modifiers. Let's list all the ways we can say something belongs to someone.*

- List: my, your, his, her, its, our, their.

*Most of you use these kinds of words all the time and don't know what they are. Also, some of you tend to misuse a couple of these. Let's be clear, for example, when we use* its *as a possessive pronoun, it is not the contraction* it's, *which means something completely different. Don't include the apostrophe unless you want the word to be a contraction. Also, some students confuse* your *and* you're. *Only use the apostrophe for a contraction, meaning "you are."*

- Use masked word activity to practice identifying possessive pronouns.

### Independent Practice

*Search for examples of possessive pronouns in your independent reading. Copy the sentence correctly onto a sentence strip.*

### Wrap-Up

*Let's share several of our sentence strips.*

## DAY 13 Guided Practice

### Focused Instruction

- Read aloud.

*Today we are going to play our masked word game again. Do you remember what we said an adverb is? What job does it have in a sentence?*

- Cover adverbs, using the game to reinforce adverbs that clearly modify verbs.

### Independent Practice

*Find another sentence in your independent reading featuring an adverb. Use this sentence to create a masked word sentence strip. Cover the word you want us to guess with a sticky note.*

### Wrap-Up

*Let's try to guess another student's masked word.*

## DAY 14 Guided Practice

### Focused Instruction

*Today I am going to show you how to create your own masked word game. I am going to take a paragraph from our read-aloud and choose a range of parts of speech to cover. I am going to make sure not to cover too many words, or to cover more than one word in a sentence, because that will make it too hard to guess.*

### Independent Practice

- Partners create their own masked word game using a paragraph of text found in the classroom library.
- Partners trade paragraphs and try to guess masked words.

### Wrap-Up

*What did you notice about playing this game on your own with your partner? Were you able to figure out the parts of speech that were covered? Did this help you figure out what the word might be?*

## DAY 15 Commitment

### Focused Instruction

*I went back and found my favorite sentence in our read-aloud novel. I copied it here on the board. Now I am going to show you how I identify the nouns, the verbs, and the adjectives. I am going to write the part of speech below the word, after I have highlighted it. Choose your favorite sentence from your independent reading book and label its parts of speech during Independent Practice.*

### Independent Practice

- Students select their favorite sentence strip and highlight and name all the nouns, verbs, and adjectives that they can find. Bonuses will be awarded to students who find sentences with adverbs.

### Wrap-Up

*So what have you learned about jobs of words in a sentence? What could you teach a new fourth grader? Turn and tell a classmate.*

# Painting Pictures With Our Words

This conventions unit serves a dual purpose: it gives your students additional practice and application with the concept of descriptive modifiers, and it helps students recognize that this understanding of conventions will help them write with greater voice and craft.

## Adding Description to Writing: Using Modifiers

**CONVENTIONS**

### Why Teach This?

- To teach the concept of modifiers in writing.
- To encourage students to use vivid language and build effective descriptive vocabulary.
- To build richer, more elaborate simple sentences.
- To continue to develop personal voice when writing.

### Framing Questions

- How can we create richer, more descriptive sentences?
- How can we transfer our growing knowledge of parts of speech to our own writing?

### Unit Goals

- Students will demonstrate an understanding of modifying a noun with a descriptive adjective or string of adjectives.
- Students will demonstrate a growing understanding of modifying a verb with an adverb.

### Anchor Text

- *Fox* by Margaret Wild

| **Unit Assessment** Adding Description to Writing: Using Modifiers | | | CONVENTIONS |
|---|---|---|---|
| Student name: | EMERGING | DEVELOPING | INDEPENDENT |
| Explains the concept and purpose of modifiers. | | | |
| Makes effective use of descriptive adjectives. | | | |
| Demonstrates an understanding of the rules of punctuating an adjective string. | | | |
| Attempts to use adverbs thoughtfully to indicate time, place, manner, or degree. | | | |

| Stage of the Unit | Focused Instruction<br>You will | Independent Practice<br>Students will |
|---|---|---|
| **IMMERSION**<br>2 days | • read aloud *Fox*; discuss the author's use of adjectives.<br><br>• revisit *Fox*; discuss the author's use of adverbs. | • read as writers, exploring the beautiful descriptive language of picture books with a partner; focus on adjectives and copy favorite sentences onto sentence strips.<br><br>• read again as writers, from the same beautiful picture books, looking for examples of adverbs; copy sentences onto sentence strips. |
| **IDENTIFICATION**<br>3 days | • name the adjectives and adverbs found in the class sentence strips from the Immersion stage.<br><br>• explain that *modify* means "to change," and that modifiers in our language allow us to become more specific with our thoughts, feelings, and descriptions.<br><br>• model how to select the most appropriate modifier for a sentence of your own creation; use visualization as a strategy to prompt your word choice of descriptive adjectives and adverbs that modify verbs. | • copy one favorite sentence from the Immersion stage at the top of a page in their writing notebooks; explore the impact the modifier had on the meaning of the sentence.<br><br>• find a sentence in their writing notebooks that they want to modify or change to become more specific; practice changing that sentence several times on the adjacent page, naming how the specific modifier changes the meaning every time.<br><br>• find a piece of their own writing in need of description, and practice visualizing this scene; use prewriting techniques such as describing the moment to a partner, sketching to remind oneself of that moment, and list sensory details, then rewrite a sentence or two using appropriate modifiers. |

| GUIDED PRACTICE 4 days | • list examples of descriptive adjective families (collections of adjectives of similar but different meaning), then build word banks for all students to use on class charts (consider arranging them in order of magnitude or degree).<br>• list examples of adverb families; build word banks for all students to use on class charts.<br>• explore the confusion between descriptive adjectives and adverbs modifying verbs (e.g., *bad* vs. *badly*, *good* vs. *well*, *real* vs. *really*).<br>• read a passage in your writing notebook; rework it using the strategy of visualizing and the technique of adding modifiers. | • use a thesaurus to gather and rank additional words to fit descriptive adjective families (e.g., *solid*, *strong*, *muscular*, *powerful*, *robust*, *burly*, *beefy*, *sturdy*); add to cumulative class charts.<br>• use a thesaurus to gather additional words to fit descriptive adverb families (e.g., *slowly*, *gradually*, *steadily*, *unhurriedly*); add to cumulative class charts.<br>• select their own passage from writing notebooks and rework to feature their newfound understanding of modifiers.<br>• use visualizing as a strategy to revise a piece of writing. |
| COMMITMENT 1 day | • share revised writing; model writing a caption to explain use of modifiers. | • celebrate the unit by reading before and after passages to a partner; write a caption to accompany celebrated writing. |
| **TOTAL: 10 DAYS** | | |

# Getting Started

Writing is basically about building. We are building sentences all the time. As adults, this has become unconscious, but every now and then, we stop and think: Was that right? By trusting our instincts and sensing and hearing what sounds right, we generally construct sentences that are fluid and sensible. In writing, it is easier to judge oneself, to look back upon it and say: That's not good enough! But knowledge is power, and by knowing the names of the building blocks and where they belong, we can construct beautiful and purposeful sentences.

# Teaching Materials

## Choosing Your Teaching Texts

Ideally, choose from books your students know, books you won't have to read again, but can just reintroduce and then lift a line worth admiring and name its parts. Every line of every text is a potential teaching tool for you. Make your choices, and prepare this featured text to share with the class. Copy key sentences on sentence strips to hang on your bulletin board. Have a short passage of text ready to share. Leave sticky notes on key pages of a basket of books, reminding you of the lines you want to study.

## Choosing Student Texts

In this unit, your students return to their own independent reading lives to find examples of modifiers they want to try out themselves. This means every student will be reading a text at his or her level that meets his or her interests. One student is reading *Look Who's Playing First Base* by Matt Christopher; she notices the very first sentence of this chapter book: "The boy was tall, dark-haired, and left-handed."

Or another student is finishing *Holes* by Louis Sachar: "A woman sitting in the chair behind Hector was absent mindedly fluffing his hair with her fingers. She wasn't very old, but her skin had a weathered look to it, almost like leather."

They don't all have to be reading fiction, either. They may read poetry or nonfiction texts, as long as they are looking for examples of wonderfully descriptive text.

## Differentiation

For those vulnerable students who are still grasping the world of print, noticing simple adjectives and trying them in their own writing will be challenge enough. For those strong readers and writers who are ready to soar, we can use our time in writing conferences to help them take the concept of the modifier to the next level— to craft descriptive phrases that are set off with commas. In both cases our students will be learning something new about being a writer—and this message will and should match their ability level.

## Setting Up Student Writing Notebooks

You will find it useful to have your students keep a simple notebook in which they can explore being a writer. This might be a composition notebook or a tabbed section of a binder, but it should be a place your students can return to throughout the year, to read and reread their writing, to collect writing ideas and look for new ones, to reflect on their growing abilities as writers. Set aside the back of the notebook for lists of writing topics, and as students come up with new writing ideas they can add these to their lists, moving farther into the notebook as they go. Set up the first several pages for a table of contents so students can keep track of the units and the work generated in each unit. Ask students to paginate their notebooks so that the table of contents can help the student find material quickly. Set up writing "rules" for their notebooks, such as only writing on the right-hand pages, leaving the left for notes and try-its done with the teacher during conferences. Or ask students to skip lines so they can go back later and add missing words or phrases for clarity.

## Stages of the Unit

### Immersion

Where you come upon an adjective or a descriptive phrase in your shared reading, wonder what the author's intention was in using these exact words. Admire sentence construction together.

### Identification

Your students find examples of modifiers in mentor texts and their own writing notebooks. Have writers revisit scenes, sketch them, or describe them to a classmate, then list the descriptors and work these into a revised passage of writing featuring adjectives. Focus on intention and specificity with your students.

### Guided Practice

This stage allows us the opportunity, if we choose to do so, to introduce the thesaurus as a reference tool. As with any reference book, we must teach our students how to use the thesaurus, and one way to do so is within a unit on modifiers. Here is an example of one adjective family constructed by students during this stage. They were looking for other ways to describe *small*.

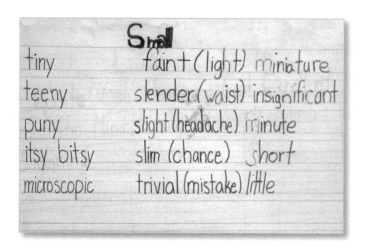

Toward the end of this stage, students will select and correct a passage in their writing notebooks, adding modifiers to describe the scene or person more accurately.

### Commitment

Ask your students to reflect on their learning. What do they understand about being a writer now that they didn't know before? How will it help them as they continue to write?

# Day-by-Day Lessons

## DAY 1 Immersion

### Focused Instruction

- Read aloud *Fox* by Margaret Wild.

*Let's look at the first sentence of* Fox:

> "Through the charred forest, over hot ash, runs Dog, with a bird clamped in his big, gentle mouth."

*Let's find the adjectives in this sentence:* charred, hot, big, gentle. *Think about these words. If we took them away, the sentence would read:*

> "Through the forest, over ash, runs Dog, with a bird clamped in his mouth."

*Why do you think the author added these adjectives? And why these specific modifiers? Why does she make the ash hot, and the forest charred? Why does she make the dog's mouth big, but gentle?*

### Independent Practice

*Today let's read from our picture book collection with a partner. Explore the language that the authors use. Find a favorite sentence. Copy it onto a sentence strip.*

### Wrap-Up

*Do any of your sentences feature amazing adjectives? Why do you think your author chose those words to modify or change his sentence? What did this word add to the meaning and the intention of that sentence?*

## DAY 2 Immersion

### Focused Instruction

*Let's look again at* Fox *by Margaret Wild. Here is the scene where the bird, who can no longer fly, clings to the dog's back as he runs through the woods. The author describes the moment in this way:*

> "He runs so swiftly, it is almost as if he were flying."

*Can you spot the adverb? Remember, most adverbs help describe the verb, and the verb in this sentence is* runs. *Why do you think the author wants you to know how fast the dog is running?*

### Independent Practice

*With your partner, read from our picture books again and see if you can find examples of adverbs. They are harder to find! Copy the sentences onto sentence strips.*

## Wrap-Up

*Near the end of* Fox, *Magpie, the bird, is lured away by the jealous fox. Do you remember what he says?*

*He says:*

> *"I can run faster than Dog. Faster than the wind. Leave Dog and come with me."*

*Margaret Wild does not use many adverbs in her book. Why would she use them to describe how fast Dog runs, and then use them again to show Fox luring Magpie away? What is the author's intention?*

### DAY 3 Identification

### Focused Instruction

*Today we are going to look at the sentence strips you gathered over the last two days. I have highlighted all the adjectives in yellow and any adverbs I found in green. Let's read the sentences with and without these modifiers. How does it change the meaning?*

### Independent Practice

*Take your sentence strip from earlier this week, or a new sentence from a picture book that you really like that is really descriptive and powerful, and copy this sentence on the top of a new page in your writing notebook. Then write to explore what makes this sentence so powerful. What does it make you think? What other descriptions could the author have included?*

### Wrap-Up

- Two students read their writing to the class.

### DAY 4 Identification

### Focused Instruction

*When we refer to an adjective or an adverb as a modifier, it is because the word* modify *means "to change". Modifiers help us as writers to be more specific with our thoughts, our feelings, and our descriptions. Let's look at another example from* Fox *by Margaret Wild:*

> *"After the rains, when saplings are springing up everywhere, a fox comes into the bush; Fox with his haunted eyes and rich red coat."*

*Why is it so important for the author to specify that the fox's eyes are haunted, and his coat is rich and red? What does this imply about the fox character? Why describe the fox in scary terms, in the same sentence where the author talks about the forest coming back to life after the fire? Why does she want us to compare the red of his coat with the image we get in our minds of green things growing all around? What does red suggest?*

## Independent Practice

*Take a sentence in your writing notebook today that you want to change to be more specific and more powerful. Put the original sentence at the top of a new page in your notebook, and then change it by adding adjectives. Notice how the meaning changes each time you vary the adjectives you choose. Pick your favorite.*

## Wrap-Up

- Students turn and read their before and after sentences to a classmate.

### DAY 5 Identification

## Focused Instruction

*Writers are very specific when they choose their words. They make sure the words they use paint the picture they intended in the mind of the reader. As writers, we have to be careful to choose the adjectives that will really show the reader what we mean. And the more specific, the better.*

*I am going to practice this in front of you. Listen to this sentence in my writing notebook.*

*Now I am going to change this sentence to paint a more complete picture. To help me do this, I am going to close my eyes and visualize the moment I am writing about. This will help me pick the adjectives and adverbs that match the pictures in my head.*

## Independent Practice

- Students find a sentence they want to revise for description.
- Students use visualizing as a strategy to help them choose modifiers to add to their writing. Before revising, they sketch the scene in their minds (or even on paper) to help them hold onto the image.

## Wrap-Up

- Two students share their before and after sentences.

### DAY 6 Guided Practice

## Focused Instruction

*On the board I have listed some of the adjectives that Margaret Wild uses to describe Dog and Fox.*

| Part of Speech | Dog | Fox |
|---|---|---|
| Adjective | big, gentle, silent, blind | haunted, rich, red, truly alone |

*Let's take one of these adjectives: big. She uses this word to describe Dog, especially in relation to the bird. What other words mean gentle? What else could we say to describe his nature?*

- List synonyms for gentle.
- Do the same activity for *haunted.*

*Sometimes it helps us as writers to think of all the adjectives that belong to the same "family" of descriptors. This allows us to choose the very best adjective, the one that does the best job of painting the picture we want. I am going to try this in my own writing. Here I have described my son as "wiggly." I could also say he was "jumpy" or "twitchy" or "squirmy" or "fidgety." In fact, "fidgety" would have been a better choice, because that is exactly what he was doing.*

### Independent Practice

- Students find an adjective of interest in their writing notebooks.
- Students work in partnerships to use a thesaurus to build lists of adjective families that match their word(s).
- Students record these word families on chart paper.

### Wrap-Up

- Hang charts in the front of the class. Admire the lists of related adjectives.

### DAY 7 Guided Practice

### Focused Instruction

*We can make lists of adverbs that are similar to one another just as we did with adjectives.*

 *Dog was fast, but Fox was faster in our picture book. What are other adverbs we could use to describe the speed of these animals? Which fit them better? Why?*

- List synonyms for *fast,* using a copied page from a thesaurus to reinforce its use.

### Independent Practice

*Choose an adverb from a favorite picture book. Work with a partner and your thesaurus to build a list of adverb families. Copy these words onto a chart.*

### Wrap-Up

- Hang the charts in the front of the class. Admire the wealth of synonyms.

## DAY 8 Guided Practice

### Focused Instruction

*Sometimes when students start to use adjectives and adverbs, they use certain words incorrectly. I am going to show you several sentences, and I want you to tell me which ones look correct, and which ones do not.*

- Feature sentences misusing *bad* and *badly, good* and *well*, and *real* and *really*.

*If we uncover the job of the word in the sentence, we will know whether we are using it properly. If I say, "I smell bad," that means don't get too close to me, I probably need a bath. But if I say, "I smell badly," then that probably means there is something wrong with my nose. This is because* badly *is an adverb and it is describing my ability to smell, whereas* bad *is an adjective and it is describing ME!*

### Independent Practice

*As we come to the end of this unit, I want you to select a passage in your reading notebook, or write a new passage. I want you to use wonderful descriptions in your writing—lots of adjectives that help paint a picture of the moment you are describing, and an adverb or two if it feels right. You will have today to draft this passage and tomorrow to polish it and reflect on what you have learned. Then I will ask you to hand these in.*

- Students work on personal writing samples.

### Wrap-Up

- Share your own writing sample with the class.

## DAY 9 Guided Practice

### Focused Instruction

*Let's look at one of my writing samples. Shut your eyes while I read it aloud. Use my words to paint a picture in your mind of the scene. What do you see?*

- Students share visualizations with one another.

*As you revisit and polish your writing sample today, I want you to use this same strategy of visualizing. You can shut your eyes and visualize your scene and then check your writing, or you can ask a partner to read your piece aloud while you close your eyes. Do the words convey the image you want to create? If not, revise your writing so that they do.*

### Independent Practice

- Students revise and edit their writing pieces.
- Confer with students who you know generally require editing help.

### DAY 10 Commitment

#### Focused Instruction

*Yesterday I read you my writing sample. Today I am going to read through it aloud to make sure it makes sense and that I have edited it for clarity and convention. Then I am going to write a short caption that will accompany my sample. Watch as I underline several of my favorite adjectives or adverbs, and then write why I think these additions improved the quality of my writing.*

#### Independent Practice

- Students polish their own writing samples and write accompanying captions.

#### Wrap-Up

- Students celebrate the end of the unit by reading their passages to a partner.

## Talk Informs Thinking

Fourth graders are fabulously social. They are developing a strong awareness of one another and are hugely influenced by the ideas of their peers. Let us take advantage of these inclinations by talking about what it means to collaborate honestly and gently.

Reading and writing partners nourish and support one another, and do not criticize or pass judgment on the habits of a fellow reader or the quality of his writing. As Douglas Kaufman (2000) says in *Conferences & Conversations: Listening to the Literate Classroom*, "When students talk honestly about their work, they hear themselves and are often able to solve their own problems. They learn, perhaps for the first time, what they know." This is true only if the conditions are right for partners to trust one another and feel comfortable sharing and listening. These units, then, are all about those processes. Fourth graders are enormously efficient and capable. They are your best coteachers, your best compeers in the reading and writing journey. Let them help you and help one another throughout the year by creating structures that really work.

## Deepening Collaboration: Reading Partners

PROCESS

### Why Teach This?

- To familiarize students with how to talk in thoughtful ways about reading.
- To generate greater understanding of text through interactive discussions.

### Framing Question

- How can reading and talking together deepen our reading comprehension?

### Unit Goals

- Students will identify important topics in their reading that will make for rich conversation.
- Students will listen well to their partners, incorporating a different perspective into their understanding of text.
- Students will stay on topic and talk long and strong—building stamina and substance into conversations.
- Students will talk across a variety of texts and genres.

## Anchor Texts

- *Bone Detective: The Story of Forensic Anthropologist Diane France* by Lorraine Jean Hopping
- *A Lucky Thing* by Alice Schertle
- *The Van Gogh Cafe* by Cynthia Rylant

| Unit Assessment Deepening Collaboration: Reading Partners | | | PROCESS |
|---|---|---|---|
| Student name: | EMERGING | DEVELOPING | INDEPENDENT |
| Understands the responsibilities of the ideal reading partner. | | | |
| Listens to partner and connects to partner's ideas. | | | |
| Collectively goes deeper into text through talk. | | | |
| Explains the differences in talk within different genres. | | | |

| Stage of the Unit | Focused Instruction<br>You will | Independent Practice<br>Students will |
|---|---|---|
| IMMERSION<br>4 days | • read aloud a passage from *The Van Gogh Cafe* by Cynthia Rylant; ask for a student volunteer and model a partnership discussion.<br><br>• read aloud a passage from *Bone Detective: The Story of Forensic Anthropologist Diane France* by Lorraine Jean Hopping; ask for another volunteer and model a partnership discussion for the class.<br><br>• read aloud a poem from Alice Schertle's book *A Lucky Thing*; model a partnership discussion with a volunteer.<br><br>• summarize with the help of your students what they've noticed about partnership talk: When does it go well? When does it feel hard? How does it change across genre? | • read a short shared fiction text, then talk in informal partnerships, noticing the content and process of their talk.<br><br>• read a short shared nonfiction text, then talk in informal partnerships, noticing the content and process of their talk.<br><br>• read another shared poem, then talk in informal partnerships, noticing the content and process of their talk.<br><br>• select partners and a shared text from a particular genre; read together, then talk in thoughtful ways. |

| IDENTIFICATION 4 days | • list great ways to talk about fiction, then continue reading aloud from *The Van Gogh Cafe*; ask two students to model talking about this text, using ideas from the list; have students name what conversational moves the speakers made.<br><br>• list great ways to talk about nonfiction, then continue reading aloud from *Bone Detective: The Story of Forensic Anthropologist Diane France*; ask two students to model talking about this text, using ideas from the list; have students name what conversational moves the speakers made.<br><br>• list great ways to talk about poetry, then read aloud another poem from *A Lucky Thing*; ask two students to model talking about this text, using ideas from the list; have students name what conversational moves the speakers made.<br><br>• list examples of when the discussion is not successful; brainstorm suggested solutions to keep talk going. | • select partners and a shared fiction text, reading side by side, planning for a thoughtful discussion of text, using the class list.<br><br>• select partners and a shared nonfiction text, reading side by side, planning for a thoughtful discussion of text, using the class list.<br><br>• select partners and a collection of poems by the same author, reading side by side, planning for a thoughtful discussion of the text, using class list.<br><br>• select partners and read a short text of their choice of genre, then talk together, using strategies outlined on the class list. |
|---|---|---|
| GUIDED PRACTICE 1 day | • discuss the value of a strong reading partner; identify the characteristics of this individual: someone who will push us to think deeper, someone who is focused and accountable, someone who does their share of the work; identify the characteristics of a weak partner: someone who wants to socialize, someone who didn't pay attention while reading, someone who dominates or doesn't share. | • work on being an ideal reading partner. |
| COMMITMENT 1 day | • reflect on what you've noticed your students are doing well as collaborators; name what you'd like to see them try that they are still not doing. | • write a reflection in their reading notebooks, including a self-assessment of their performance in partnerships and a reflection on what type of student makes the best partner. |
| **TOTAL: 10 DAYS** | | |

## Deepening Collaboration: Writing Partners

PROCESS

### Why Teach This?

- To teach students to support one another in the writing process.
- To explore the different roles of the writing partner.
- To help students become less dependent upon your support when they encounter difficulties.

### Framing Questions

- What is the job of a writing partner?
- When do we turn to writing partners for help?

### Unit Goals

- Students will write a piece with focus and development.
- Students will learn that a writing partner can help them generate writing topics.
- Students will learn that a writing partner can help them develop a chosen topic.
- Students will learn that a writing partner can be a supportive audience who asks clarifying questions.

### Anchor Text

- *A Chair for My Mother* by Vera B. Williams
- *Family Pictures/Cuadros de Familia* by Carmen Lomas Garza

### Resource Sheet

- Idea Generator (Resource 2.2)

| Unit Assessment Deepening Collaboration: Writing Partners | | | PROCESS |
|---|---|---|---|
| Student name: | EMERGING | DEVELOPING | INDEPENDENT |
| Uses a partnership to explore writing topics. | | | |
| Uses a partnership to develop a writing topic. | | | |
| Uses a partnership as an audience for clarifying questions. | | | |
| Completes a piece with focus and development. | | | |
| Celebrates writing with a partner. | | | |

| Stage of the Unit | Focused Instruction<br>You will | Independent Practice<br>Students will |
|---|---|---|
| **IMMERSION**<br>4 days | • name times when another person has helped you with your own writing process; chart these examples for future reference.<br>• read aloud *A Chair for My Mother*; model a writing partnership with a volunteer student; focus the meeting on helping each other get writing ideas for a narrative from this text.<br>• using the Idea Generator (Resource 2.2), model a writing partnership with a volunteer student; focus the meeting on prewriting strategies; help each other explore and develop a writing topic.<br>• model a writing partnership with a student, asking clarifying questions about her piece; record questions as they arise in text using sticky notes. | • brainstorm with a partner times when working with someone else helped their writing process; list these in writing notebooks; write side by side.<br>• work with a partner to develop a list of possible writing ideas for a narrative, using favorite picture books to stimulate discussion; write side by side, each writer using one topic from their list.<br>• work in partnerships, using the Idea Generator to help each other list the directions and detail they can use that will develop their topic; write side by side.<br>• work with a partner to listen to a piece written previously, asking clarifying questions; record these questions on sticky notes and leave them in the notebook, writing to clarify based on their partner's comments. |
| **IDENTIFICATION**<br>3 days | • name effective ways that writers can support each other in the writing process; list these possible interventions for future reference on a class chart.<br>• explain the difference between a writing partner and an editor, or between a writing partner and a teacher, explaining that it is not the job of the partner to revise or suggest specific changes, but instead to be a supportive audience for ideas.<br>• name and list the characteristics of an effective writing partner. | • meet with a partner, choosing one of the listed approaches to help each other.<br>• write independently, then meet with a partner, making sure to act as a partner and not as an editor.<br>• list three peers whom they think would be good writing partners for them; include explanations and examples, and submit this list to the teacher. |

| | | |
|---|---|---|
| **GUIDED PRACTICE**<br>6 days | • place students in formal writing partnerships; explain that they will help each other through the writing process this week at several points, and that each partner will be evaluated based on their constructive support.<br><br>• model writing to develop a narrative idea by reading aloud *Family Pictures/Cuadros de Familia* by Carmen Lomas Garza; show students how they can lift a line from existing writing to explore their topic in a new, fresh way.<br><br>• select one writing technique (adding dialogue, for example) and model writing in this way for your students.<br><br>• model rereading the passages written so far on your topic, then create a writing plan so you can begin to draft in front of your students.<br><br>• read aloud your draft in progress to a volunteer partner; ask the partner to ask clarifying questions, then revise or add onto writing to address these questions.<br><br>• finish your draft in front of your students; ask them to be a supportive audience, sharing one compliment with the class. | • meet in selected partnerships and discuss possible writing ideas; develop a list of possibilities and then select the idea of greatest interest for each writer; begin writing.<br><br>• write independently, trying the technique of lifting a line; after writing, meet in partnerships to share the outcome of this writing session.<br><br>• meet in selected partnerships, and fill out the Idea Generator, using this web to stimulate discussion around developing additional writing; write side by side, sharing their successes at the end of the period.<br><br>• reread entries and begin to draft a first pass at the topic; share writing with partner at the end of the period.<br><br>• meet in selected partnerships and share drafts in progress; ask each other clarifying questions and write side by side to add to or revise writing for clarity.<br><br>• finish their drafts; reread and polish for grammar and conventions. |
| **COMMITMENT**<br>1 day | • celebrate the effectiveness of partnerships; share anecdotes with the class that you observed during this unit to demonstrate how partners help each other through the writing process. | • meet in small groups formed by several partnerships; share how they helped their partner in their writing process; read their finished draft aloud to the collective group.<br><br>• write to reflect on how they were helped by the partnership and how they believe they were helpful to another student. |
| **TOTAL: 14 DAYS** | | |

# Meeting People Who Change Us

It has been said that there are only two plots in great literature: a stranger comes to town, or a character sets off on a journey. Either way, change in characters shifts the landscape in literature, and from those little earthquakes, we find an essence of the human condition that we can relate to. Fourth graders love the characters they meet in literature. They love them so much they wish for sequels and imagine prequels. They put themselves in Sal's shoes in *Walk Two Moons* by Sharon Creech, and they shiver with worry for Maniac in *Maniac Magee* by Jerry Spinelli. These units wrap around those passions with a study of how characters change, and how we as writers can convey the essence of great characters. Fourth graders are pondering the universe while making forts in their backyards. They are characters in their own stories, open to life's new experiences, ready to set off on their own journeys.

## Exploring Changes in Characters  STRATEGY

### Why Teach This?

- To extend a reader's insight into characters beyond appearance and action by including characters' thoughts, feelings, and motivations.
- To explore how character change is connected to the author's purpose or intention.

### Framing Questions

- What are the different ways we can learn about the characters in the books we read?
- How do main characters go through some sort of change or transformation?
- How does exploring this change help us become stronger readers?

### Unit Goals

- Students will identify and define point of view.
- Students will identify the ways in which a character changes over time.
- Students will gather text evidence to substantiate this change.
- Students will use this insight into character to begin to explore the author's purpose.

### Anchor Texts

Select a novel to read aloud that demonstrates a powerful change in character.
Suggestions include:

- *The Birchbark House* by Louise Erdrich
- *Bud, Not Buddy* by Christopher Paul Curtis
- *In the Shade of the Nispero Tree* by Carmen T. Bernier-Grand
- *Junebug* by Alice Mead
- *Just Juice* by Karen Hesse
- *Milkweed* by Jerry Spinelli
- *My Name Is Maria Isabel* by Alma Flor Ada
- *The Paint Brush Kid* by Clyde Robert Bulla

- *A Single Shard* by Linda Sue Park
- *The Storyteller's Beads* by Jane Kurtz
- *When Zachary Beaver Came to Town* by Kimberly Willis Holt

| **Unit Assessment** Exploring Changes in Characters | | | STRATEGY |
|---|---|---|---|
| Student name: | EMERGING | DEVELOPING | INDEPENDENT |
| Identifies point of view in independent reading. | | | |
| Demonstrates ability to build understanding of main character (appearance, thoughts, feelings, actions, motivations). | | | |
| Finds text examples of evidence of character change. | | | |
| Effectively explores the author's purpose in changing the main character. | | | |

| Stage of the Unit | Focused Instruction<br>You will | Independent Practice<br>Students will |
|---|---|---|
| **IMMERSION**<br>2 days | • introduce your new read-aloud (see Anchor Texts); notice the voice of the storyteller as you read.<br>• share how you are feeling about the main character and why you feel this way. | • explore the storyteller in their own chapter books.<br>• develop opinions about their main characters and explore why they feel this way. |
| **IDENTIFICATION**<br>4 days | • define and identify point of view.<br>• name the ways we learn about character (appearance, thoughts, the character's and other people's comments and actions).<br>• identify and explain inner monologue.<br>• identify the ways in which a character changes or develops through a story. | • identify the point of view of the main character in their independent reading books.<br>• look for other types of character discovery as they read independently.<br>• identify examples of inner monologues in independent reading.<br>• write in reading notebooks to explore the way(s) in which main characters change in their independent reading books. |

| GUIDED PRACTICE 7 days | • read aloud from a novel; model stopping, thinking, and using sticky notes to mark changes in character. <br><br> • revisit sticky notes from the previous day; model developing a theory about a character based on these observations. <br><br> • read aloud from the novel; gather evidence in support of your theory; record on a class chart. <br><br> • read aloud again; gather evidence; record findings. <br><br> • revisit findings on the class chart; model asking whether findings support or refute your theory. <br><br> • model writing to revise your theory about your character, using the latest evidence and your personal insight. <br><br> • finish reading aloud; think aloud to explore the author's intention in illuminating a character's change across the life of a book. | • use sticky notes to mark changes in characters within their independent novels. <br><br> • revisit sticky notes from from the previous day; write to develop a theory about their character in their reading notebooks; read in search of evidence for their theories. <br><br> • continue to read independently in search of evidence for their theories. <br><br> • share theories and evidence with a partner; allow their partner to suggest alternative theories; read. <br><br> • read independently, searching for additional evidence to support or refute theories. <br><br> • write to develop or revise character theories in reading notebooks. <br><br> • read; consider the author's intention in highlighting the main character and the change this character undergoes; jot thoughts in reading notebooks. |
|---|---|---|
| COMMITMENT 1 day | • reflect on how focusing on character helps our reading comprehension. | • reflect on two learning points relating to character. |
| **TOTAL: 14 DAYS** | | |

# Adding Thoughts and Feelings to Writing

**STRATEGY**

## Why Teach This?

- To encourage writers to include inner monologues in their narrative accounts.
- To provide insight into their main characters by adding thoughts and feelings to their writing.
- To develop a stronger sense of mood or tone based on the character's feelings in the story.

## Framing Question

- How can we include our thoughts and feelings in our narratives?

## Unit Goals

- Students will select mentor texts to provide them with models from which to include thoughts and feelings in their narratives.
- Students will experiment with short infusions of thought and longer, more developed inner monologues to allow greater insight into the character.
- Students will add to this exploration of character by exploring gesture and dialogue.

## Anchor Texts

Select a novel featuring strong characters to read aloud. This may be the same novel you used in the companion reading unit. Suggestions include:

- *The Birchbark House* by Louise Erdrich
- *Every Living Thing* by Cynthia Rylant
- *Just Juice* by Karen Hesse
- *Milkweed* by Jerry Spinelli
- *A Single Shard* by Linda Sue Park

| Unit Assessment Adding Thoughts and Feelings to Writing | | | STRATEGY |
|---|---|---|---|
| Student name: | EMERGING | DEVELOPING | INDEPENDENT |
| Demonstrates ability to add thoughts and feelings to narrative scenes. | | | |
| Explains what an inner monologue is, and writes one. | | | |
| Adds meaningful, appropriate dialogue to narrative scenes. | | | |
| Attempts to include gesture as a further indication of character feelings. | | | |

| Stage of the Unit | Focused Instruction<br>You will | Independent Practice<br>Students will |
|---|---|---|
| **IMMERSION**<br>3 days | • read aloud an inner monologue from an anchor novel; ask students to consider why an author would want the reader to hear the inner thoughts and feelings of the character.<br><br>• think aloud about how writers listen carefully for that inner voice as they write—the voice that tells them how the main character is feeling, or what he is thinking about in that moment; model transferring this inner voice to the page as you write in front of your students.<br><br>• create a web to represent the ways you have learned about the main character in your read-aloud. | • find an example of character thoughts and feelings in independent reading; share with a partner and have a discussion about the author's intention.<br><br>• reread several entries in their writing notebooks, selecting one where they can revisit that moment and listen for their inner voices (thoughts and feelings should be added on the left page, adjacent to the original selected entry).<br><br>• plan out how they will reveal a character's feelings to the audience in a real or imagined narrative. |
| **IDENTIFICATION**<br>2 days | • name and define the techniques writers use to develop characters: inner monologue, dialogue, action, gesture; provide specific examples of each and model one for students.<br><br>• model another example of developing a character's thoughts and feelings. | • draft a scene that provides insight into a character.<br><br>• use a different characterization technique to draft another scene that provides insight into the same or different character. |
| **GUIDED PRACTICE**<br>4 days | • select an existing piece from your writing notebook; rewrite two adjacent lines onto a new page, placing one at the top of the page and one at the bottom; slow down this moment by adding thoughts, feelings, observations, wonderings, and memories.<br><br>• present a mentor example of an extended inner monologue; use this text as inspiration to practice speaking directly to the audience with your own inner monologue. | • choose two adjacent lines from their writing notebooks and place them at the top and bottom of a new page; write to elaborate on this moment, adding thoughts and feelings.<br><br>• write an inner monologue.<br><br>• use a T-chart to make their own decisions—what will be public information (actions, dialogue), what will be private (thoughts, feelings, subtle gestures)—then write to incorporate both forms of communication in a real or imagined scene. |

| GUIDED PRACTICE (continued) | • model the decisions a writer makes between the public and private worlds of the main character, using a T-chart to share your decisions; write to model how the public and private will reveal themselves (gesture and inner monologue for private transmission; dialogue and action for public transmission).<br><br>• revisit scenes written in this unit; select a favorite and model polishing it for craft and convention. | • select their own favorite scene entries, polishing them for craft and convention; publish them by mounting on textured paper or with a colored tape border. |
|---|---|---|
| COMMITMENT 1 day | • model writing a reflection. | • write their own reflections. |
| TOTAL: 10 DAYS | | |

# From Early Fall to Late Fall

Your year is in full swing. Your students have learned their roles and the routines of your classroom. They have experienced reading and writing in a range of genres. You have asked them to practice working collaboratively as readers and writers, and to go deeper with their analysis in reading and their craft in writing. What an important start to an equally important year. But now it's time for the next phase of your students' growth. They will build independence as readers and writers. They will delve into research. They are ready for change and can do so much.

# Chapter 3

# LATE FALL

# The Fourth Grader as Decision-Maker

*"Midnight approaches. It's ⁻40 outside and I'm shivering in my tent. But being cold is nothing compared to how exhausted I feel from the lack of oxygen up here. I am panting as if I've just run a marathon. I am so tired that it takes me one hour just to tie my laces and put on my coat. Am I going to reach the top of the world in twelve hours? It's now or never. I am determined!"*
—from "Everest: On Top of the World" by Marie-Piel Elie, *Owl* magazine

Fourth graders are bold and confident in some ways, still worried and young in others. They are capable of so much as the year unfolds. This season brings with it the opportunity for them to build their reading and writing stamina, and to engage in deep study of themselves as readers and writers. They can make new decisions about how they go to the blank page, and how they make book choices. They are indeed on top of the world. Come with us as we explore this next set of units.

LATE FALL UNITS

- Developing Identity and Independence in Reading, *page 69*  SPOTLIGHT UNITS

- Developing Identity and Independence in Writing, *page 82*

- Reading the Test, *page 94*

- Writing to the Literary Prompt, *page 97*

- Building Stamina: Reading Longer and Stronger, *page 100*

- Building Stamina: Writing Longer and Stronger, *page 102*

- Planning and Organizing Research, *page 104*

- Developing Expertise: Informational Articles, *page 107*

# SPOTLIGHT on Process

- Developing Identity and Independence in Reading
- Developing Identity and Independence in Writing

In my book *The Complete 4 for Literacy*, I explain in detail how process units are designed to build identity, capacity, collaboration, and responsibility. Although these form the foundations upon which readers and writers grow, they often take a backseat in our instructional plans because they are so intangible. A student's understanding of herself and the actions that move her forward as a reader and writer are all such an important part of her growth as a fourth grader. Establishing a strong understanding of processes now will help us move forward smoothly, rather than having to grapple with management issues later on in the year. Our explicit instructions for working with a partner give our students a structure for growing ideas and supporting one another. Lessons on building community will create a spirit of joy and collaboration that is indispensable in sustaining the atmosphere of safety and trust in your room. In these units, students learn how to develop the essential process skills of reading and writing stamina. These capacities are critical to establishing lifelong independence as readers and writers, and so we have created lessons that take our students through the experience of choice in a supported, layered approach.

For more information on process units, please see pages 37 to 47 of my book *The Complete 4 for Literacy*.

*Pam Allyn*

# Self-Motivated Learners

Find a willing fourth grader and have her sit down and talk to you about school. She'll talk about her friends and something that happened on the playground. She might mention a favorite book she is reading, or whose birthday was celebrated that day. But she isn't likely to mention us—her teachers—or the content of our teaching. There is a disconnect with many children between their lives, hearts, and minds, and our time with them each day. Classic research like John Goodlad's (2004) study of American public schools and classrooms show this disconnect more completely. Often, students are not engaged in the work of the classroom, and there is an absence of enthusiasm and connection between the teacher and the student. Frequently, this occurs because students have little or no say in their own learning. We decide their reading and the questions they answer. But what would happen if we empowered our students, at key points in time during the year, to decide their own course of study?

If we ask students to be reflective and give them some control over their own learning experiences, we will generate a group of self-motivated, accountable learners. Karen Szymusiak and Franki Sibberson (2001) have realized this: "When we make self-reflection a part of our reading workshops, children learn how to recognize their own strengths and limitations as readers. Being reflective helps them make better book choices about their reading and notice when they are having difficulties." The next two Spotlight Units present models of this type of approach—enabling students to set their own reading and writing goals, and making plans to achieve these goals. Also, these units give our students the opportunity to explore their own passions. Fiona tells us she has always wanted to read more mythology. Peter tells us he loves science fiction. Sarah reminds us she has a passion for reading about movie stars. In writing, Fiona would like to make a movie with her two best friends. John would like to write about the trip he took with his grandfather. Susie wants to study and write about the effects of zoos on animals. The absolute beauty of these units is that they will bring you closer to the unique inner lives of your students. No prompts or ideas you ever develop could be half as interesting as these children naturally are.

## Developing Identity and Independence in Reading

PROCESS

### Why Teach This?

- To give students the opportunity to work with greater independence and less teacher direction.
- To give students longer-range projects that will help them build their organizational skills and individual sense of responsibility for their own outcomes.
- To give students more opportunity for personal-choice reading in an effort to build a lifelong love of reading.

## Framing Questions

- What are our dreams for ourselves as readers?
- How can we become more independent as readers?

## Unit Goals

- Students will select individual short-term reading goals—whether based on process, genre, strategy, or conventions.
- Students will make a reading plan to achieve these goals.
- Students will learn to be more autonomous readers.

## Resource Sheets

- Reading Goals Across the Complete 4 (Resource 3.1)
- Reading Conference Request (Resource 3.2)
- Project Planner (Resource 3.5)

| **Unit Assessment** Developing Identity and Independence in Reading | | | PROCESS |
|---|---|---|---|
| Student name: | EMERGING | DEVELOPING | INDEPENDENT |
| Selects appropriate individual reading goal. | | | |
| Works thoughtfully toward the achievement of this goal. | | | |
| Succeeds in achieving that goal. | | | |
| Works with greater independence during reading time. | | | |
| Asks for reading conferences when necessary. | | | |
| Sets ongoing personal reading goals. | | | |

| Stage of the Unit | Focused Instruction<br>You will | Independent Practice<br>Students will |
|---|---|---|
| **IMMERSION**<br>3 days | • share your own reading "dreams" with your class; let them know what you'd love to do as a reader if given the opportunity.<br><br>• share with your students something you would like to try as a reader that you have never done before.<br><br>• share with your students something that you would like to get better at as a reader. | • share their own reading wishes and dreams with a partner; list these in their reading notebooks.<br><br>• consider new reading try-its with a partner; list these in reading notebooks.<br><br>• share with a partner ways in which they'd like to get better as a reader; list these in reading notebooks. |
| **IDENTIFICATION**<br>4 days | • explain that readers can set personal goals (in areas of process, genre, strategy, or conventions) and work toward these goals; show Reading Goals Across the Complete 4 (Resource 3.1).<br><br>• share a reasonable short-term goal that you can achieve by the end of this unit.<br><br>• identify that some students have similar goals, and that one way to support one another in achieving our goals is to work together; share examples of group projects (united around genre, media, author, or interests).<br><br>• ask all students to share and commit to goals publicly; model planning for your own goal (gathering texts, planning using a calendar, etc.) using the Project Planner (Resource 3.5) if necessary. | • review reading wish lists and label as process, genre, strategy, or conventions goals; add to these columns with other possible goals and share with a partner.<br><br>• review lists of goals, select one that can be achieved by the end of this unit, and share it with a partner; write the goal on loose-leaf paper and hand in.<br><br>• conduct short sharing sessions to find other students who may share similar goals; determine whether the goal will be an individual or group goal.<br><br>• meet in groups or individually to plan for achieving that goal; use the Project Planner if necessary. |

| **GUIDED PRACTICE**<br>6 days | • ask your class what it means to be an independent reader; list their suggestions (making good book choices, being prepared, etc.).<br>• ask students to share progress toward their goal.<br>• teach students how to ask for help as readers; introduce the Reading Conference Request form (Resource 3.2).<br>• demonstrate using the Project Planner to stay on track as a reader.<br>• reflect on progress and insight into your reading goal.<br>• consider possible goals for ongoing reading work and share with students; introduce the class to reading goal pockets. | • work independently (or in small groups) toward achievement of that goal.<br>• work independently toward goal.<br>• request a conference if necessary.<br>• monitor goal progress on a calendar or in a book planner.<br>• share progress with another reader (or group); work toward completion of the goal.<br>• revisit list of reading goals; select a new goal and write it on an index card; place it in reading goal pockets. |
|---|---|---|
| **COMMITMENT**<br>1 day | • share your observations and pride in individual efforts and goals; explain that setting personal goals helps us build our reading identity and performance. | • share reflections on the experience of an independent project with the class; celebrate goals or plan to continue them. |
| **TOTAL: 14 DAYS** | | |

# Getting Started

Ask any reader to describe a positive memory of reading. Regardless of the circumstances, this memory almost always involves personal choice. Readers choose when, where, what, and how to read a book of their choice. This unit is all about choice and independence. Let your students guide you. They have many marvelous ideas, and this is a time in the year to let them shine. Ask your students to let you know, through conversation and through writing, what they think they might want to pursue in this unit. You will be surprised and delighted by what they come up with.

# Teaching Materials

You will need the books and texts that you like to read, and that you'd like to see your students try. Students with wider-ranging interests may need to turn to the school or public library, or even a safe and secure search of the Internet, but no other special materials are required for this process unit.

## Choosing Teaching Texts

Gather the pile of books that sits at your bedside. Bring the books to class so that you can share your reading life and personal goals with your students. If you have been too busy to read much, let your children know this. If your favorite thing to read is the sports section of the paper, let your students know this. If you want to make a plan to read more sports sections, let them know this. If you want to read mysteries by a new writer, let them know that. If you have always felt like a slow reader and want to get a bit faster this month, let them know that, too. Make your own reading goals as authentic as you can. Your students can help motivate you.

## Differentiation

Your students will do much of the differentiation work in this unit. With appropriate discussions, conferences, and modeling, a reader who struggles to finish a book will set an achievable goal for this three-week unit. A strong reader may stretch himself into a new genre, or undertake reading across several works by the same author. Students who prefer nonfiction may develop this passion by conducting further research, or they may read fiction instead. Know your students and their habits, and help steer those students who cannot identify or set appropriate reading goals toward an objective that makes sense and holds interest for them.

# Stages of the Unit

## Immersion

Take several days to talk to your students about who you are, and who they are, as readers. Explore the areas in which they feel proud and confident. Explore the areas to which they are reticent to go as readers. Create lists of wishes and dreams—books they would like to read, series they would like to complete, genres they would like to try, media (such as magazines and newspapers) they would like to learn more about. Create parallel lists of challenges that they need to work on to become stronger readers—finishing texts, keeping focus while reading, keeping track of multiple characters, holding onto important details. Create a menu of appetizing choices from which your students will choose their own short-term reading goals.

## Identification

The next four days are spent selecting reading goals and making plans to achieve these goals. It is useful to help explain to your students that they can set goals that are based in process, genre, strategy, or conventions. Most students think in terms of genre. They will say, "Let's try to read science fiction and see whether we like it." There are other kinds of goals, too. Use the Complete 4 categories (Resource 3.1) to organize the goals in this unit. Process goals help a reader who wants to improve her stamina or focus. Strategy goals can help a reader make connections across genres. Conventions goals may include learning to read with greater expression through an awareness of punctuation. Help students identify goals across the Complete 4 that would allow each reader to work on an independent project that matches their identity as a reader.

In many cases, students have very unique goals and will want to work independently to achieve them. Other students will discover they have common interests, challenges, or goals, and so they may decide to work together. There may be a group that wants to investigate reading newspapers. Or a group may want to read about baseball, even though the material they each want to read is different. This is fine, also. This is the reading community at work, with readers helping readers, working side by side.

## Guided Practice

During this stage, your students will work independently or in small groups. During daily Independent Practice, confer with your readers as they actively read from texts of their own choice and monitor their progress in achieving their goals. Show your students how to plan the incremental steps on a calendar so they can set reasonable "assignments" for themselves. If a group is trying to explore a nonfiction topic of interest, they need to set dates for gathering materials, researching and note taking, and sharing their findings. If a student is trying to finish an "uphill" book for the first time, and it is longer than he is used to, he needs to see how to divide the page count over the available dates to determine how many pages he needs to read in a sitting and whether it is a realistic goal. Your students can request a conference with you. Introduce the Reading Conference Request form (Resource 3.2) and model its use.

Finally, challenge your students to envision a new set of goals that will stretch beyond the boundaries of this unit. Have them commit to these new individual goals, write them on index cards, and place them in the library pockets that have been set aside with their names on them.

**Reading Conference Request**

_____ would like a reading conference. Date: _____
(Student Name)

I am reading: _____

I want to share with you:
☐ a problem I'm having  ☐ something I've figured out about my book
☐ something I'm proud of  ☐ something I am wondering about

Details: _____

RESOURCE 3.2

## Commitment

On this final day of the unit, share your observations with the class. Let them know how proud you are of their enthusiasm, independence, passion, and drive. Celebrate by sharing everyone's personal goals.

# Day-by-Day Lessons

## DAY 1 Immersion

### Focused Instruction

*This unit is going to be about making choices that allow you to follow your reading passions. If I could choose what I want to read right now, I would say that I want to read more poetry. I want to read silly poetry and serious poetry. I want to read poetry that is going to make me laugh and poetry that will make me think. I asked the teacher across the hallway what she would like to read and she knew right away—a series of historical fiction books about England. What would you want to read if you could choose? What is your reading dream?*

- List student ideas.

### Independent Practice

- Students browse library book baskets.
- Students share their own reading wishes and dreams with a partner and list ideas in reading notebooks.

### Wrap-Up

- Two students share their lists with the class.

## DAY 2 Immersion

### Focused Instruction

*Sometimes when I think about my reading dreams, I think about doing something I've never done before—like read a book in a genre I have never read before, or read a certain number of books in a certain amount of time. Some readers like to read books written by the same author so they can compare them. Other readers like to read on a subject, like baseball, and read lots of different things—magazine articles, biographical profiles, statistics books. Last year I decided to read historical fiction, and I found I really liked it! What is something you would like to try as a reader that you have never done before?*

- List student ideas.

### Independent Practice

- Students browse library baskets and discuss possible goals with partners.
- Students list reading ideas in their reading notebooks.

### Wrap-Up

- Two students share the things they want to try as readers.

## DAY 3 Immersion

### Focused Instruction

*Sometimes readers choose to read something that they love to read; sometimes they decide to try something as a reader that they have never done before. Readers also challenge themselves to improve, so if they know something is hard, they work at that hard part until they get better. For me, I try to work at not getting lazy as a reader when I get to the hard parts or the boring parts of a book. My tendency is to skip these parts, but sometimes I miss important information, so I challenge myself to read these parts carefully even if the writer isn't capturing my attention. What is hard for you as readers?*

- List student ideas.

### Independent Practice

- Students write in their reading notebooks in response to this prompt.
- Students share their writing with another reader.

### Wrap-Up

- Two students share specific improvements they would like to make in their reading.

## DAY 4 Identification

### Focused Instruction

*I have been asking you about your hopes and dreams and goals as readers because we have begun a unit that focuses on building your independence as readers. I am excited to see what you choose as your reading goals and the kinds of passions you follow this month during reading time.*

*If I think about my own goals, I can take what I've shared with you this week, and put these goals into certain categories:*

| Process | Genre | Strategy | Conventions |
|---------|-------|----------|-------------|
|  | Read more poetry. Try a new genre. | Pay attention to the slow parts. |  |

*So far, I've thought of two genre goals and one strategy goal for myself. Before I decide on my goal for this unit, I want to think of goals that would fit the other two categories. For example, I could work on noticing the punctuation in the books I read and use this to help me figure out how to read with expression. I might not read aloud, but I want the voice of the writer in my head to help me make meaning. If I pay close attention to the punctuation, I can recreate how she wanted me to read her words. This would be a conventions goal.*

*A process goal would be something that had to do with my habits and behaviors as a reader. I could try to read at another time of day rather than right before I go to sleep because this is when I am most tired. Or I could choose a new place to try out reading. We just moved our couch into the sunroom, so I could see if this is a better reading spot for me.*

### Independent Practice

*Together, we have made a list of possible reading goals any student might pursue. I want you to notice these goals, and think about the goals you have already written in your reading notebooks and add to these, if possible. Make sure you try to think of personal goals for each category: process, genre, strategy, and conventions. When you are done, share your goals with a partner.*

### Wrap-Up

- Ask for students to share goals that fit the four categories. Add these to your class list.

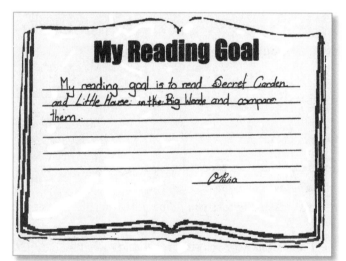

**My Reading Goal**

My reading goal is to read *Secret Garden* and *Little House in the Big Woods* and compare them.

*Olivia*

Olivia has set a reading strategy goal. She wants to read two books from two different genres and compare them. They both feature strong female characters. This should be an interesting project.

## DAY 5 Identification

### Focused Instruction

*Today we are going to choose our goals. The goal that each of us chooses should be something we can accomplish in the next two weeks. What goal will you choose?*

### Independent Practice

- Students review possible goals with a partner and select a preferred goal.
- Students write recommended goals on loose-leaf paper and hand it in to you.

### Wrap-Up

- Go around the room and have each student declare his or her goal.

## DAY 6 Identification

### Focused Instruction

*Some of you have similar goals. For example, three of you are interested in trying the genre of science fiction. This unit is all about building your independence, so all of you are welcome to read independently, but I want you to know it is a choice to work with others if they have similar goals. Sometimes we need one another to be successful. I have posted each of your goals on the chart so you can see if other students have a goal similar to your own.*

### Independent Practice

- Each student determines whether reaching their goal will be an individual pursuit or a small-group effort. Students can "interview" one another to discuss this possibility.

### Wrap-Up

*Did anyone decide to work together in a small group? What is your goal?*

### DAY 7 Identification

### Focused Instruction

*Each of us has set a personal goal that we hope to achieve in the next two weeks. I have posted these goals here on a chart so we can remember what we are working on. Our job now is to get ready to begin working on our goals. What do we need to do to begin?*

- List student suggestions.

*We will need to plan our reading, so we can use our Project Planner (Resource 3.5) to accomplish this. It will help us determine what and how we need to read each day to accomplish our goals. We also need our materials. Today use some of your independent reading time to gather the materials you need and make whatever plans you need to make.*

### Independent Practice

- Students gather materials, plan the steps to achieve their goals, and begin reading toward their personal goals.

### Wrap-Up

*Does anyone still need materials that they haven't been able to find? How can we help you?*

### DAY 8 Guided Practice

### Focused Instruction

*What does it mean to be an independent person? What about an independent reader?*

- List student suggestions.

### Independent Practice

- Students work independently toward their goals.

### Wrap-Up

- Students share how reading time went today.

### DAY 9 Guided Practice

#### Focused Instruction

*Today I want to hear how someone's project is progressing. Who would like to share their goal with us, and what you have done so far toward that goal?*

#### Independent Practice

- Students work independently toward their goals.

#### Wrap-Up

*Does anyone else want to share how his or her independent project is going?*

### DAY 10 Guided Practice

#### Focused Instruction

*Even though we are working independently, we still may need help from time to time. Usually I ask you to confer with me. Now I want you to take more responsibility and request conferences with me when you want to share your learning or something you have figured out about yourself as a reader. We have a new system for you to request a reading conference.*

- Model filling out the Reading Conference Request form (Resource 3.2).

#### Independent Practice

- Students work independently toward their goals.
- Students request conference if necessary.

#### Wrap-Up

- Report on a conference you had and what was accomplished together.

### DAY 11 Guided Practice

#### Focused Instruction

- Demonstrate revisiting the Project Planner to see whether you are on track for completing your goal in the time allotted.

#### Independent Practice

- Students work independently toward goal.
- Students check their progress on the Project Planner.

#### Wrap-Up

- Students share progress with a partner.

### DAY 12 Guided Practice

#### Focused Instruction

*What have you learned about yourself as an independent reader as you have worked toward your goal?*

- List student responses.

#### Independent Practice

- Students finish working on their independent reading projects.

#### Wrap-Up

*How does it feel to set a goal, work toward that goal, and then achieve that goal?*

### DAY 13 Guided Practice

#### Focused Instruction

*I am glad we took this time to focus on our own interests and independence. Making our own choices is one way to love reading. I want us to look back on the list of goals we made at the beginning of this unit and ask ourselves, "What's next? What will our next goals be?" We can list our goals on index cards and place them in library pockets with our names on them so that we can always have a place to keep track of our independent work.*

#### Independent Practice

- Students revisit reading notebooks, look at their lists, and set future goals. They write new goals on index cards and place them in library pockets.

#### Wrap-Up

*Who would like to share their new reading goal?*

### DAY 14 Commitment

#### Focused Instruction

*I am so proud of the work you did this week. Each of you chose a thoughtful goal, worked hard to be independent, and had fun! This kind of work will help all of us grow as readers. How should we celebrate our goals?*

#### Independent Practice

- Students discuss and select a way to celebrate their goals.
- Students write a reflection on their learning in this unit.

#### Wrap-Up

- Plan celebration.

## Developing Identity and Independence in Writing

### Why Teach This?

- To give students the opportunity to work with greater independence and less teacher direction.
- To give students a longer-range project that will help them build their organizational skills and individual responsibility and accountability.
- To give students more opportunity for personal-choice writing in an effort to build a lifelong love of writing.

### Framing Questions

- What are our hopes and dreams for ourselves as writers?
- How can we become more independent as writers?

### Unit Goals

- Students will select short-term writing goals—whether based on process, genre, strategy, or conventions.
- Students will make a writing plan to achieve these goals.
- Students will learn to be more autonomous and responsible in writing.

### Anchor Text

- Meet the Authors and Illustrators series by Deborah Kovacs and James Preller

### Resource Sheets

- Writing Conference Request (Resource 3.3)
- Writing Goals Across the Complete 4 (Resource 3. 4)
- Project Planner (Resource 3.5)
- Comments for the Author (Resource 3.6)
- Parent Letter: Identity and Independence in Writing (Resource 3.7)

| Unit Assessment Developing Identity and Independence in Writing | | | PROCESS |
|---|---|---|---|
| Student name: | EMERGING | DEVELOPING | INDEPENDENT |
| Selects an appropriate individual writing goal. | | | |
| Works thoughtfully toward the achievement of this goal. | | | |
| Succeeds in achieving this goal. | | | |
| Works with greater independence during writing time. | | | |
| Asks for writing conferences when necessary. | | | |
| Sets ongoing personal writing goals. | | | |

| Stage of the Unit | Focused Instruction<br>You will | Independent Practice<br>Students will |
|---|---|---|
| **IMMERSION**<br>3 days | • explore the hopes and dreams of the writers in your class.<br><br>• explore writing topics and techniques your writers would like to try.<br><br>• explore ways to improve our writing. | • share their own writing dreams with a partner; list them in their writing notebooks.<br><br>• consider new writing try-its with a partner; list these in writing notebooks.<br><br>• share with a partner things they would like to get better at as a writer; list these in writing notebooks. |
| **IDENTIFICATION**<br>4 days | • explain that writers can set personal goals and work toward these goals, and identify that goals can be within process, genre, strategy, or conventions; list examples of each (show Writing Goals Across the Complete 4, Resource 3.4).<br><br>• model how to choose a final writing goal.<br><br>• identify that some students have similar writing goals, and they may want to work together; share examples of group projects (based on genre, media, author, interests).<br><br>• model planning for a writing goal (gathering materials, setting deadlines, etc.). | • revisit writing dream lists and label as process, genre, strategy, or conventions goals; add to these columns with other possible goals and share with a partner.<br><br>• review lists of goals; select one that can be achieved by the end of this unit and share it with a partner, then write the goal on loose-leaf paper and hand in.<br><br>• conduct short sharing sessions to find other students who may share similar goals; determine whether the goal will be an individual or group goal.<br><br>• meet in groups or individually to plan for achieving the goal and gather necessary materials. |

| | | |
|---|---|---|
| **GUIDED PRACTICE**<br><br>6 days | • ask your class what it means to be an independent writer; list their suggestions (making good topic choices, facing the blank page, etc.).<br><br>• demonstrate strategies to help a student achieve his goal.<br><br>• demonstrate how students can ask for help as writers; introduce the Writing Conference Request (Resource 3.3).<br><br>• ask a student to share the progress of her writing goal.<br><br>• ask students to share what it felt like to work independently.<br><br>• consider possible goals for ongoing writing work and share these with your class; introduce class to writing goal pockets. | • work independently (or in small groups) toward the achievement of their goal.<br><br>• work independently.<br><br>• request conference if needed.<br><br>• work independently and monitor their progress on a calendar.<br><br>• share progress with another writer (or group); work toward completion of their goals.<br><br>• consider future writing goals and list them in writing notebooks; write their current goal on index cards and place in writing goal pockets. |
| **COMMITMENT**<br><br>2 days | • share your observations and pride in individual and group efforts and goals; ask students to reflect on their learning.<br><br>• prepare students to read each other's projects; introduce the Comments for the Author form (Resource 3.6). | • write personal reflections about their learning.<br><br>• read through other students' writing generated during this unit, leaving comments for the authors. |
| **TOTAL: 15 DAYS** | | |

# Getting Started

As you begin your planning for this unit, ask yourself what you notice about your own writing. What do you wish you did? What would you like to learn how to do? Thinking this through in advance will help you model the process for your students throughout this unit.

# Teaching Materials

## Choosing Teaching Texts

Find some inspirational quotes from writers your students know, perhaps using the Meet the Authors and Illustrators series by Deborah Kovacs and James Preller. In Volume 2, you will find Daniel Pinkwater describing where he gets his ideas:

> "Ideas come 60 a minute to everybody, not just me. And like everyone else's ideas, mine are mostly lousy. I take one of those lousy ideas and chew on it, tug at it, and develop it until it starts to be a better sort of idea."

Allow these quotes to spark wonderful conversation and create opportunities for students to share some of the process that published writers experience as they write.

## Differentiation

For one student, learning to face the blank page may be her challenge. For another, it may be finding focus among pages and pages of writing. Some students may want to learn to write fiction, others want to explore new topics—volcanoes, or guinea pigs, or Major League Soccer. Every goal and every student is unique.

# Stages of the Unit

## Immersion

Explore personal writing interests and identities with your students. Let them share where they feel safe and comfortable as writers, and where things get tricky for them. Make their interests and favorite topics public; explore the genres or the ideas they've never tackled. Make lists of things your class of writers would like to try to do or to improve upon. Have students share their writing challenges and interests with partners, as this collaboration is likely to yield even more possible goals for the class. Involve parents in this process by sending home the Parent Letter (Resource 3.7).

## Identification

Talk to your students about their possible goals through the lens of process, genre, strategy, and conventions. Much of what is already on your class lists can and should be categorized in this way.

| Process Goals | Genre Goals | Strategy Goals | Conventions Goals |
|---|---|---|---|
| Face the blank page with success | Write in a new genre | Try a new craft | Write with greater sentence variety |
| Write longer | Get better in a genre that feels hard | Find the focus in my writing | Add more dialogue to my writing |

It is a small step to then begin adding other topics to your writing goal lists. Construct a thoughtful and comprehensive menu of writing goal choices that represents the interests and identities of the writers in your room. Your students will, at the end of this stage, select their own writing goals and discover whether other members of the class have similar objectives. If so, they can gather in groups to help one another work toward achieving their goals.

Writing Goals Across the Complete 4 (RESOURCE 3.4)

## Guided Practice

During this stage, your students will work independently or in their small affinity groups on their writing goals. What a rich and interesting time in your room, as each day, for more than a week, each student will be following his own hopes and dreams as a writer. Every student should be fully engaged, and there should be a great hum and buzz in the room, for each student has chosen his or her own course of study.

Gather mentor texts or other literature resources, use a calendar to plan interim deadlines, and discuss when to ask for help from a teacher. Introduce your fourth graders to the Writing Conference Request form (Resource 3.3).

As this week of inquiry and experimentation comes to an end, your students can say they have completed their independent writing goals. Put these short-term goals in context, and introduce goal-setting as an ongoing expectation in your classroom. Have your students think of new writing goals (direct them to the list of possibilities generated during the Immersion and Identification stages), and then commit to a goal by placing it on the writing goal board.

## Commitment

Recognize and reward your students for their focus, commitment, and independence. Link the work of this unit to the bigger picture of being a learner and a student, and to building the skills necessary to be a lifelong writer of power and responsibility. Find time for the writers in your class to share the outcome of their work. Set each writer's work out on view, along with a Comments for the Author form (Resource 3.6).

# Day-by-Day Lessons

**DAY 1** Immersion

## Focused Instruction

*What are your hopes and dreams as writers? I know that I want to write about the people in my life who are important to me. This is one hope I have for myself as a writer. How about you?*

- List possible ideas.

## Independent Practice

- Students share their own writing dreams with a partner.
- Students list possible dreams in writing notebooks.

## Wrap-Up

*Who would like to share a few things on their list?*

**DAY 2** Immersion

## Focused Instruction

*All of us have things we have never tried before as writers. What is something you'd like to try as a writer? What feels interesting to you?*

- Model identifying your own desired "try-its."
- List possible ideas suggested by students.

## Independent Practice

- Students consider new things they'd like to try as writers and list them in their writing notebooks.

## Wrap-Up

- Two students share something they would like to try as writers.

**DAY 3** Immersion

## Focused Instruction

*Another way to grow as writers is to think of things that we'd like to do better as writers. We know the parts of our writing that feel hard. What is something you could do to improve your writing?*

- List suggestions.

## Independent Practice

- Students share ideas with their partners, then list in writing notebooks.

## Wrap-Up

- Two students share how they would like to get better as writers.

### DAY 4 Identification

### Focused Instruction

*Today we are starting a unit on writing identity and independence. Each of you will set your own writing goal and take on an independent writing project to help you achieve that goal. You can choose a process, genre, strategy, or conventions goal. Let us look together at our writing goals chart to get more ideas.*

- Show Writing Goals Across the Complete 4 (Resource 3.4).

### Independent Practice

- Students review Writing Goals Across the Complete 4 and add possible goals that interest them to their writing notebooks.

### Wrap-Up

*Who added a goal from the chart today? Just give a show of hands.*

### DAY 5 Identification

### Focused Instruction

*What goal will you choose? Remember, you have almost two weeks to achieve your goal, so choose something that you can accomplish in this amount of time.*

- Model your own goal selection.

### Independent Practice

- Students review lists of goals, select one, write it on loose-leaf paper, and hand it in.

### Wrap-Up

*I am going to read aloud a few goals that students have selected. What do you notice?*

Mackenzie                                    10-12-07

My goal is to get all my ideas down
on paper. to do that I should find
a idea I like and stick with it. I
should also jot all my ideas down on
papper before so I'll have many to pick
from.

Mackenzie chooses to focus on a process goal—to help her face the blank page and stay on topic.

Gabriela                                    10-12-07

I think I need to work on
finishing work that needs to get done. I think
I can accoplish that by focusing really
hard and useing my time wisly even though
I have a very slow pace. Or I could just try
not to focus on the people talking around
me. And really think about the details that
I need so I could get a good paragraph.

Gabriela has also chosen a process goal. She wants to learn to complete her work without being distracted by others. Note her personal insight—she knows she writes more slowly than her classmates and this makes writing that much harder for her.

Jason                                    10/12/07

Goal: My goal is to grab the readers attention.
How: I will achieve this goal by telling what it would
feel like if they were there. Tell, my senses and the
setting. I will also tell about my surroundings.

Unlike his classmates above, Jason has chosen a strategy goal. He wants to use sensory detail in his writing.

## DAY 6 Identification

### Focused Instruction

*Most of you probably have your own goal and want to work independently, but a few of you have similar writing goals. Let's look at a list of your goals and see where these connections are. You can then decide whether you want to work together or alone. You have the choice.*

### Independent Practice

- Conduct short sharing sessions to determine groups, if any.
- Students write in search of their goals.

## Wrap-Up

*Who decided to work alone? Who decided to work together? Let's have one student and one group explain their choice.*

### DAY 7 Identification

### Focused Instruction

*Do you need special materials for your writing goals? Do you need mentor texts? I want each of you to use the Project Planner (Resource 3.5) to set your project dates and deadlines. Anything else?*

### Independent Practice

- Students meet in groups or individually to gather materials and plan for their goals.
- Students write in pursuit of their goals.

### Wrap-Up

*I was glad to see so many students setting project dates on their Project Planners. If you didn't do that today, you might do it for homework. It will help keep you on track.*

### DAY 8 Guided Practice

### Focused Instruction

*What does it mean to be an independent writer?*

- List student responses.

*Each of you has set a personal reading and writing goal. Both of these experiences will help teach you to become more independent as a learner and as a person.*

### Independent Practice

- Students work independently or in small groups in pursuit of their goals.
- Confer with students who have struggled to set a personal goal.

### Wrap-Up

*I want to share a quote with you today from Joan Lowery Nixon. She was a great mystery writer (Search for the Shadowman, among others). She told an interviewer that she sits at her desk, staring at the white page "with a bit of fear." She said that when that happens, the best thing to do is just write. "Usually I just push through the fear. By the third or fourth page, I'm at home." This must have been one of her writing goals because she wrote more than twenty books and won four book awards for her mysteries.*

## DAY 9 Guided Practice

### Focused Instruction

*Let's help a classmate today with her goal. Who would like some help from the class?*

- Students make recommendations to the writer.

### Independent Practice

- Students work on their writing in pursuit of their goals.

### Wrap-Up

- Ask one student to share his or her writing.

## DAY 10 Guided Practice

### Focused Instruction

*Other students may need help as they work on their goals, or they may want to share discoveries they have made about themselves as writers. I want to introduce you to a conference form that you will use for the rest of the year to request a private writing conference with me.*

- Introduce Writing Conference Request form (Resource 3.3).
- Model a writing conference with a student. Have the rest of the class observe.

### Independent Practice

- Students write in pursuit of their goals, requesting a conference if necessary.
- Confer with students who need your immediate help.

### Wrap-Up

- Share one student's progress on her goal with the class.

## DAY 11 Guided Practice

### Focused Instruction

*Today I have asked [student name] to share the progress of his writing goal with the class. I'd like for him to tell you about his goal and share with us what he is enjoying about his project.*

### Independent Practice

- Students write in pursuit of their goals.
- Students monitor their own progress using the Project Planner.

### Wrap-Up

- Students share their progress with a partner.

## DAY 12 Guided Practice

### Focused Instruction

*Today is our last day to work on our writing projects. Who would like to share what it felt like to work independently on a writing project?*

- List student comments.

### Independent Practice

- Students finish up writing projects and share writing with a partner.

### Wrap-Up

*Tomorrow we are going to talk about setting new writing goals for the future. Be thinking about this so you have some ideas to share.*

## DAY 13 Guided Practice

### Focused Instruction

*I would like to see you set writing goals throughout the rest of the year. We'll keep them in library pockets here on the bulletin board. I can check on what you are working on as writers by checking your library pockets and seeing what you have written on your index cards. What would you like to do next as writers? What might your next goal be? Let's look back on our Writing Goals Across the Complete 4 chart.*

- Students volunteer possible writing goals.

### Independent Practice

- Students review writing goal possibilities and choose one for themselves.
- Students commit to new goals by writing them down on index cards and putting them in the library pockets.

### Wrap-Up

- Students go around the meeting area sharing their new writing goals.

## DAY 14 Commitment

### Focused Instruction

*I learned a lot about all of you during the last two weeks. I learned what you loved to do as writers, and what is hard, and what challenges you have set for yourselves. I am very proud to be your teacher and to see how well you work independently—staying on schedule and following your own plan. How do you feel about this unit? What did you learn about yourselves as writers?*

## Independent Practice

- Students write personal reflections on their learning.

## Wrap-Up

- Students turn and share their reflections with another student.

### DAY 15 Commitment

## Focused Instruction

*Today we are going to read one another's writing. As you walk around the room, I expect you to read at least five pieces of writing, and leave each of those authors your comments on the Comments for the Author form (Resource 3.6). Remember to sign your name, so each writer knows who gave him or her a compliment.*

## Independent Practice

- Students move through the room, reading the writing outcomes of this work and leaving thoughtful comments.

## Wrap-Up

- Students make some of their comments public. Students take home writing and comments to share with their families.

# The Pressure to Perform

Liz Hollingworth (2007) wrote in a recent issue of *Reading Teacher*, "There is a difference between teaching to the test and teaching what is going to be on the test." Every standardized test follows a format. From one year to the next, this format rarely changes. We see the standardized test as its own genre—complete with a purpose, an audience, and key elements to be considered. If we approach the test as a genre, our students will come to understand what to expect of this genre and how to embrace its oddities, performing well if they see the test as a necessary challenge not to be feared.

Standardized language arts tests often feature several short or extended written responses to literature. Prompt-writing asks students to quickly compose a clear, concise answer to a very specific but not necessarily easy question. The answers are sometimes graded only on content, but often they are graded on the clarity and organization of the response. Let us teach these skills in ways that help our students to see taking tests the way ballplayers see playing in the big game: all the things they have learned will work for them, but there are also a few funny things about playing in the big game they need to know for "game day." If we hope all our children will have the opportunity to continue their education to college and beyond, we do them a good service to make sure they are all fully prepared for the skills of test taking, so they can all play the "game" and succeed.

## Reading the Test                                           GENRE

### Why Teach This?

- To prepare students for the reality of standardized testing, which asks readers to perform in ways very different from regular reading time.
- To remind students to think in different ways as they read different genres.
- To teach students to discriminate between questions that can be answered in the text and questions that require the reader to infer.

### Framing Questions

- How can studying the yearly language arts test as if it were a genre help us uncover its predictable elements?
- How do we know which reading strategies to use to answer the questions on the test?

### Unit Goals

- Students will understand the predictable structure of the test.
- Students will practice key performance strategies associated with multiple-choice questions.
- Students will use their knowledge of multiple genres in order to read in search of specific information.

## Resources

- Sample tests from prior years
- Short reading passages of a variety of genres (found in children's magazines)

| Unit Assessment Reading the Test | | | GENRE |
|---|---|---|---|
| Student name: | EMERGING | DEVELOPING | INDEPENDENT |
| Recognizes the predictable structure and elements of the test. | | | |
| Uses knowledge of genre to read in search of specific information. | | | |
| Understands the type of questions that appear related to genres. | | | |
| Matches key reading strategies to predictable types of questions. | | | |
| Learns to fill in answer bubbles. | | | |

| Stage of the Unit | Focused Instruction<br>You will | Independent Practice<br>Students will |
|---|---|---|
| IMMERSION<br><br>4 days | • browse through last year's test, modeling your observations on its structure and expectations.<br><br>• read aloud and highlight instructions throughout the test, discussing how the wording of the instructions gives the reader clues about the work to be done.<br><br>• point out the varying genre in each passage, and how this knowledge might help you read in search of particular types of information (biography: key dates and turning points; fiction: story elements; poetry: meaning of figurative language).<br><br>• review old tests and notice words or types of questions that regularly turn up. | • explore other "back issues" of old tests, using sticky notes to post what they notice.<br><br>• highlight the instructions in an old test, looking for common language and directions from year to year.<br><br>• read short passages from old tests, noticing the genre and how that awareness changes the way they read the passage.<br><br>• chart typical questions they find in small groups, noting the genre of the passage associated with the questions. |

| IDENTIFICATION<br>3 days | • construct an outline for the test, using back issues; include components and structure.<br>• review strategies for predicting genre in a short passage; list what students might do to confirm their predictions.<br>• list the types of questions frequently found on the test and identify successful strategies to find the correct answer to those questions. | • compare old tests to the working outline to confirm the predictable structure and content of the test.<br>• practice identifying genre using listed characteristics.<br>• work in pairs to build test strategies to match key types of questions. |
|---|---|---|
| GUIDED PRACTICE<br>2 days | • model "taking" an abbreviated test, asking students to notice what you do well and what you do not.<br>• reread the passages in the abbreviated test, looking for evidence that will confirm your answers to key questions. | • practice moving through an abbreviated sample test, noting what feels good and what is hard.<br>• reread the passages and double-check your answers based on evidence found. |
| COMMITMENT<br>1 day | • list five things you want your students to remember to do on test day. | • write their own test pledges, reflecting on what they need to do to be successful on test day. |
| **TOTAL: 10 DAYS** | | |

# Writing to the Literary Prompt

## Why Teach This?

- To teach students to construct written answers that are clear and well organized.
- To help students understand that there are different expectations and assessments for prompt-writing.

## Framing Question

- How do we craft the best possible answers to writing prompts?

## Unit Goals

- Students will learn effective structures with which to craft their responses.
- Students will study the expectations for this type of writing and evaluate their own writing against these expectations.

## Resources

- Sample passages with test prompt questions from prior years' tests
- Classroom-generated chart that lists elements of a prompt response

| Unit Assessment Writing to the Literary Prompt | | | STRATEGY |
| --- | --- | --- | --- |
| Student name: | EMERGING | DEVELOPING | INDEPENDENT |
| Restates question in the answer to writing prompts. | | | |
| Uses details from the text. | | | |
| Stays focused. Does not add extraneous information. | | | |
| Crafts a clear, thoughtful answer to writing prompts. | | | |

| Stage of the Unit | Focused Instruction<br>You will | Independent Practice<br>Students will |
|---|---|---|
| **IMMERSION**<br>2 days | • point out that sometimes the test asks the student to write an answer rather than select an answer from a list of multiple-choice responses.<br><br>• model writing a response to a passage read aloud, noticing your highlighted instructions; as you write, ask students to notice what you include in your answer and how you organize your response. | • walk through back issues of tests, highlighting the questions that require written answers; compare discoveries with a partner.<br><br>• read a short passage and write a response to a supplied prompt; meet in partnerships to compare answers and notice how they organized their answers. |
| **IDENTIFICATION**<br>4 days | • identify the types of written prompts for different genres: How are they the same? How are they different?<br><br>• demonstrate that test prompt questions are open-ended (they are not designed for a yes or no answer or an incomplete response); name the parts of a thoughtful response using your answer from earlier in the unit.<br><br>• model restating question in the first sentence, then writing the answer to the prompt in the second sentence; do this with several prompt questions (do not complete the answers, just practice restating the question).<br><br>• revisit yesterday's prompt-writing; finish the response by adding several facts or details from your reading to substantiate your opinion. | • compare two prompts in different genre passages; work with a partner to imagine how the answers might vary based on the genre.<br><br>• read a short passage and write a response to a supplied prompt, this time looking to include the parts of a thoughtful response.<br><br>• practice restating question prompts.<br><br>• practice using facts or details from the text to bolster individual answers. |

| GUIDED PRACTICE 3 days | • model reading a shared passage and then writing a response to a written prompt, including the elements identified earlier in the unit; reread the response, checking to make sure all elements of a thoughtful answer have been included.<br><br>• model writing a response to yesterday's reading that sends the reader off track with other personal connections; demonstrate that written responses must be focused and single-minded, using the text, not the writer's life, to provide evidence.<br><br>• read aloud a shared passage; show a student response exemplar and ask the class to evaluate the content, structure, and clarity of the response. | • read independently; choose a common prompt question for the genre read and write a response that matches their reading.<br><br>• read independently; choose another common prompt question that matches the genre being read; write a response, making sure you do not add extra non–text-based information.<br><br>• work in partnerships to study other student exemplars and craft written responses that improve upon the examples given. |
|---|---|---|
| COMMITMENT 1 day | • list the elements of any strong written response to a text prompt. | • write a written response to the following prompt: How can we craft the best possible answers to prompt questions? Answers should include all key elements of a thoughtful answer. |
| **TOTAL: 10 DAYS** | | |

# Strengthening Muscles for Reading and Writing

In reading instruction, there is a great deal of focus on comprehension strategies and fluency. However, the building of stamina is often ignored. Especially in fourth grade, as the texts jump up in length and density, our students need our help in building those muscles to read longer and read stronger.

Naturally, some of your students will read very quickly, while others will not. Let's create an environment in which students can take risks as readers and push themselves. If they are worried that they read more slowly than other students, assure them that the slower reader is often the more thoughtful reader, pausing at interesting spots, reflecting and musing on what was read. Simultaneously, discuss techniques to build reading fluency and stamina: skimming, reading words in chunks, getting the gist of a big idea from chapter headings, practicing speedy reading.

So, too, in writing, we see the value of helping our students build stamina. Some children in your class are overflowing with writing ideas while others sit and stare at the blank page. The act of writing can be extremely stressful for some students. They watch while other children are speeding down the page, and they feel slower. Help your students build their confidence, their strategies for facing the blank page, and their stamina for writing longer and stronger. For some of your children, building stamina may mean increasing from one page to two; for some it may mean sustaining an idea they have for more than one class writing session. All of this work is encompassed by the term *stamina*. Let this unit be about creating opportunities and the environment to build and cultivate the muscles for writing longer and stronger.

## Building Stamina: Reading Longer and Stronger

PROCESS

### Why Teach This?

- To help students develop strategies to read for longer periods of time, comfortably.
- To help students develop strategies to read stronger.

### Framing Question

- What are the strategies effective readers use to read longer and stronger?

### Unit Goals

- Students will increase their reading stamina in terms of how many minutes they can read.
- Students will increase their reading stamina in terms of the depth of connection they make with the text.

### Anchor Text

- A short story anthology, such as *Tripping Over the Lunch Lady and Other School Stories*, edited by Nancy E. Mercado, *How Angel Peterson Got His Name* by Gary Paulsen, or *Weird Stories from the Lonesome Café* by Judy Cox

| Unit Assessment Building Stamina: Reading Longer and Stronger | | | PROCESS |
|---|---|---|---|
| Student name: | EMERGING | DEVELOPING | INDEPENDENT |
| Tries several different stamina strategies. | | | |
| Identifies a stamina strategy that is personally effective. | | | |
| Reads for longer periods of time with demonstrable comprehension and enjoyment. | | | |

| Stage of the Unit | Focused Instruction<br>You will | Independent Practice<br>Students will |
|---|---|---|
| **IMMERSION**<br>1 day | • read aloud a short story from your anthology; model optimal reading stamina behavior (active stance, good pace, stop and think, etc.); ask students to notice your reading behavior and how this will help you read long and strong. | • read independently, noticing their own reading behavior. |
| **IDENTIFICATION**<br>1 day | • list several strategies for reading stamina: finding comfortable spots to read, choosing the right text for level and interest, maintaining focus by stopping and thinking or questioning the text; model using one or more of these strategies as you read another short story aloud to the class. | • in their reading notebooks, list one or two strategies they will try in order to build their own personal reading stamina; read to practice these strategies. |
| **GUIDED PRACTICE**<br>2 days | • ask several students to share other strategies that have worked for building personal stamina (such as reading more than one text, reading at or below your level).<br>• share your own favorite strategies for reading stamina. | • try a different stamina strategy as they read independently.<br>• try another stamina strategy as they read independently. |
| **COMMITMENT**<br>1 day | • reflect on what worked for students this week in terms of building stamina | • share an effective stamina strategy with a partner. |
| **TOTAL: 5 DAYS** | | |

## Building Stamina: Writing Longer and Stronger

PROCESS

### Why Teach This?

- To help students develop strategies to write longer.
- To help students develop strategies to write stronger.
- To help students improve their writing pace.

### Framing Question

- What are the strategies effective writers use to write longer, stronger, and faster?

### Unit Goals

- Students will increase their writing stamina in terms of how many minutes they can write.
- Students will increase their writing intensity in terms of the depth of exploration they undertake.

### Anchor Texts

- Autobiographies of writers such as Meet the Author series, published by Richard C. Owen Publishers, Inc.
- Interviews and quotations by a favorite author (such as Jacqueline Woodson found at www.jacquelinewoodson.com)

| Unit Assessment Building Stamina: Writing Longer and Stronger | EMERGING | DEVELOPING | PROCESS INDEPENDENT |
|---|---|---|---|
| Student name: | EMERGING | DEVELOPING | INDEPENDENT |
| Demonstrates one effective strategy for writing longer. | | | |
| Demonstrates one effective strategy for writing more deeply. | | | |
| Identifies the genre of choice for achieving stamina. | | | |
| Identifies the topics of choice for achieving stamina. | | | |

| Stage of the Unit | Focused Instruction<br>You will | Independent Practice<br>Students will |
|---|---|---|
| **IMMERSION**<br>1 day | • read a quote from an anchor author such as Jacqueline Woodson: "I think the thing about being stuck [as a writer] is that you are not writing what you want to be writing." Explore the ways we get stuck as writers; share how you keep going when you get stuck; write to demonstrate. | • write independently in writing notebooks, noticing their own slowing-down or sticking points. |
| **IDENTIFICATION**<br>2 days | • read another quote from Jacqueline Woodson: "The way to learn to write is by reading; read the same books over and over; study them the way you would study a textbook." Name this as one writing stamina strategy—reading or revisiting mentor texts for inspiration; list other effective stamina strategies such as talking with a partner, changing your writing seat, preplanning writing, rereading, and so on.<br><br>• share another quote from Woodson: "When I get stuck, I try something different, like going for a ride, or switching genres." Name this as another stamina strategy; model this strategy by writing in front of your students. | • use one of the stamina strategies to write longer and stronger in writing notebooks.<br><br>• select a topic or genre they feel will allow them to write long and strong; write in notebooks and then evaluate effectiveness of this strategy. |
| **GUIDED PRACTICE**<br>2 days | • read another Woodson quote: "I'm usually working on two or three books at once. When I get bored with one, or get stuck, I go onto the other one." Add this strategy to the stamina list.<br><br>• interview a student on his stamina strategies in front of the class; have him share a snippet of his writing. | • try writing long and strong; switch and write something new in their notebooks when they feel they are losing interest.<br><br>• interview a classmate on her writing stamina strategy; choose a listed strategy not yet tried and write in notebooks. |
| **COMMITMENT**<br>1 day | • ask your students what they have learned from Jacqueline Woodson's writing process that has helped them to write longer and stronger. | • write letters to the author, thanking her for her writing advice and sharing what advice she shared that helped them to build their writing stamina. |
| **TOTAL: 6 DAYS** | | |

## Ask "Why?" and Finding the Answers

Fourth graders are always asking: WHY? They are open and curious about all kinds of things, both outside their own experience and right in their backyards. In fourth grade, our focus in research is on connecting real-world inquiry to research activities.

Asking our students to create their own informational articles is an expression of real-world nonfiction writing. Creating articles that look as if they came right from the pages of a nonfiction children's magazine is a motivating experience for your fourth graders. And you, too, will love their voices as the room fills with of a multitude of whys.

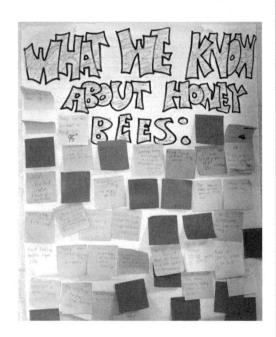

## Planning and Organizing Research

STRATEGY

### Why Teach This?

- To allow students to explore their personal interests in nonfiction reading.
- To connect the research process to real-world inquiry.
- To expand upon prior experiences with research, both in depth and breadth of topic.

### Framing Questions

- What do we wonder about in the world?
- What does it mean to conduct research?

### Unit Goals

- Students will gather material at their reading level that supports their personal inquiry.
- Students will read in search of answers to guiding questions.
- Students will take notes to capture answers to guiding questions.

### Anchor Texts and Resources

- *How Come in the Neighborhood?* by Kathy Wollard
- Nonfiction libraries (classroom, school, town)

| Unit Assessment Planning and Organizing Research | | | STRATEGY |
|---|---|---|---|
| Student name: | EMERGING | DEVELOPING | INDEPENDENT |
| Selects thoughtful guiding research questions. | | | |
| Selects appropriate level of reading material. | | | |
| Reads effectively in search of answers to questions. | | | |
| Takes notes in own words. | | | |
| Is responsible for the care and retention of all research materials. | | | |

| Stage of the Unit | Focused Instruction<br>You will | Independent Practice<br>Students will |
|---|---|---|
| **IMMERSION**<br>3 days | • read aloud from *How Come in the Neighborhood?*; wonder out loud about the world, asking students what they would like to learn more about; create a list of ideas.<br>• explore personal topics of interest for research; choose one topic to focus on.<br>• create a "Think I Know, Want to Know" T-chart for a working topic, establishing guiding questions for research; model creating several key questions for your topic. | • meet in partnerships to share their own wonderings; list wonderings in their reading notebooks.<br>• conduct a school library hunt with supervision; identify several books on different topics and browse through books to help make final topic decisions.<br>• create their own T-charts, establishing several key guiding questions for their own research. |
| **IDENTIFICATION**<br>3 days | • model setting up research materials, listing one of your guiding questions for your topic at the top of each page in your notebooks.<br>• model selecting appropriate Internet content; begin by showing students how to create a keyword list and review rules for visiting appropriate sites.<br>• model selecting and evaluating print research materials (difficulty of text, reading strategies, using features of nonfiction to help find information). | • set up a page for every related research question, listing the question at the top.<br>• create keyword list for an Internet search and find websites using a search engine; bookmark sites, printing key material and placing it in a research folder; read and take notes from these sources.<br>• gather nonfiction books or articles from a school, town, or classroom library; review texts for usefulness and readability. |

| GUIDED PRACTICE<br>6–8 days | • model note-taking by turning over the text and restating information.<br>• model reading in smaller, meaning-based "chunks," asking whether a chunk has answered a guiding question.<br>• model what to do if conflicting facts arise (express facts as a range, choose the more legitimate resource based on publisher or year of publication).<br>• model what to do if important information is found that doesn't match a guiding question.<br>• model what to do if you can't find an answer to your question.<br>• model decision-making: Am I done with my research? | • read selected material in search of answers to guiding research questions; record notes on the appropriate page.<br>• continue to research by "chunking" reading.<br>• continue to research, checking status—what questions have been answered, what questions are remaining; refocus research to find answers to these open questions.<br>• continue to research, adding pages to their research folder or clipboard if new information worthy of recording is found.<br>• evaluate remaining unanswered questions: Can they be answered by a fourth grader? Is the research well-rounded without these questions answered?<br>• complete research process. |
|---|---|---|
| COMMITMENT<br>1 day | • reread guiding questions and collected facts and reflect on the process: What have you learned about your topic? How can you share your learning with the world? | • reread guiding questions and collected facts and share their new expertise with a friend; reflect on learning in writing. |

**TOTAL: 13–15 DAYS**

# Developing Expertise: Informational Articles

## Why Teach This?

- To provide students with real-world avenues to share their newfound knowledge.
- To provide students with a structure and form to use as a model for drafting informational text.
- To share student research with a larger audience through the publication of classroom nonfiction magazines.

## Framing Questions

- How can we share our newfound knowledge with an audience?
- What does powerful informational text include?

## Unit Goals

- Students will create their own multiparagraph informational articles, using the notes gathered in the companion reading unit.
- Students will create powerful expository paragraphs, with student-generated topic sentences and factual details that support each topic sentence.
- Students will use nonfiction text features and graphic aids to clarify and illustrate this information.

## Anchor Texts

- Sample nonfiction articles from children's magazines such as *Kids Discover*, *Time for Kids*, *Scholastic News*, *Ranger Rick*, *Click*, and *Ask*

| Unit Assessment Developing Expertise: Informational Articles | | | GENRE |
|---|---|---|---|
| Student name: | EMERGING | DEVELOPING | INDEPENDENT |
| Selects mentor informational article as a model for an article. | | | |
| Constructs effective expository paragraphs with a student-generated topic sentence and factual details from research as support. | | | |
| Structures multiple paragraphs in a logical order, with effective simple transitions. | | | |
| Uses text features and graphic aids to clarify or explain complicated information. | | | |
| Produces a well-organized, attractive nonfiction informational article. | | | |

| Stage of the Unit | Focused Instruction<br>You will | Independent Practice<br>Students will |
|---|---|---|
| **IMMERSION**<br>5 days | • read aloud a nonfiction informational article; notice topics, favorite parts.<br>• revisit features of nonfiction text by locating and naming them in a shared nonfiction article.<br>• notice how an article begins.<br>• notice how an article ends.<br>• notice what the writer does to make his subject interesting; explore the craft found in nonfiction articles (simile, metaphor, talking to audience, onomatopoeia, repetition, etc.). | • read nonfiction articles independently, noticing topics and favorite parts.<br>• read nonfiction articles, using sticky notes or margin notes to name and locate text features.<br>• read at least one new nonfiction article; compare the beginning of this article with the other two read earlier this week.<br>• read another new nonfiction article; compare the end of this article with the others read this week.<br>• meet in small groups to highlight craft in several key articles. |
| **IDENTIFICATION**<br>5 days | • name the elements of a nonfiction article.<br>• compare and contrast articles to identify required elements.<br>• identify optional craft elements in articles.<br>• select a mentor article to assist you in writing your own article.<br>• create a class checklist for an informational article. | • search for elements of nonfiction articles in magazines.<br>• search and mark required elements in independent articles.<br>• search and mark optional elements in independent articles.<br>• select mentor articles.<br>• use the checklist to plan writing and make choices. |
| **GUIDED PRACTICE**<br>11–13 days | • model reviewing notes (students will use notes gathered in Planning and Organizing Research unit) students in search of main ideas; use the main idea to craft a working topic sentence for each page of research notes.<br>• return to one of your note pages and think aloud about how you would restate and order your research facts to support your topic sentences; draft this first body paragraph in front of your students as a model.<br>• repeat this lesson for several days, as students work through their own body paragraphs. | • review one page of notes and ask what these facts have in common; restate this as a working topic sentence on the bottom of the page; repeat with other notes pages.<br>• return to notes pages and, with topic sentence in place, restate facts gathered as supporting detail sentences that will follow the topic sentence; decide what order of facts works best.<br>• continue to draft body paragraphs for each page of notes. |

| | | |
|---|---|---|
| **GUIDED PRACTICE** *(continued)* | • model revising paragraphs for interest, combining facts with description and comment; repeat this for several days, varying the craft that you model for your students.<br><br>• model writing an introduction using mentor text; write several versions; allow students to choose the winner.<br><br>• model ordering draft paragraphs into a cohesive logical progression, following introductory paragraph.<br><br>• model writing a conclusion; think aloud about the purpose of this paragraph: Why should the reader care about this topic? How can they learn more?<br><br>• plan the final layout of the article in column format; model planning graphic aids BEFORE writing so students can see how they must write around these visuals.<br><br>• write in column format; work around graphic aids to replicate the look of a real magazine article, consulting mentor texts for examples.<br><br>• check draft against the checklist and notice what might be missing; add missing elements.<br><br>• model editing for grammar and spelling. | • revise paragraphs onto clean loose-leaf paper to add description and comment; repeat for several days.<br><br>• revisit mentor text(s) to study introduction; try several approaches and select their favorite introductory paragraph.<br><br>• experiment with the order of the paragraphs following the introductory paragraph.<br><br>• draft a concluding paragraph.<br><br>• use two-column paper or a word-processing program with column formatting to plan the final layout of the article; search for photographs or create graphic aids to explain their concepts.<br><br>• write or type the final draft of the article in column format; work around artwork and graphic aids and add text features such as headings and subheadings, captions, and so on.<br><br>• review final draft against checklist; revise for missing elements.<br><br>• engage in a final edit for grammar and spelling; hand in finished articles. |
| **COMMITMENT**<br>2 days | • reflect on class learning.<br><br>• celebrate class magazine of nonfiction articles. | • reflect in writing on learning.<br><br>• assemble articles into magazines; create covers and tables of contents and share magazines with another class. |
| **TOTAL: 23–25 DAYS** | | |

# From Late Fall to Winter

As winter arrives, you can feel your community has become something special. Your children's voices make it so. They are changing so quickly, it is hard to believe. It almost seems as if they are growing a little bit more every night, and you can see they are a bit taller the next day! You have asked them to become deep thinkers and strong decision-makers. They have built their stamina and become more independent as readers and writers. Now they are ready for some new creative challenges in this next season.

# Chapter 4

WINTER

# The Fourth Grader as Creative Thinker

*"'Never mind the toast,' said Mom. 'Let's have cake for breakfast.' She carried the cake high over her head and set it right in the middle of the table. The golden crust didn't show under the sugar roses and the sugar hearts. 'It's almost too beautiful to eat,' said Mom."*
—from *The High Rise Glorious Skittle Skat Roarious Sky Pie Angel Food Cake* by Nancy Willard

Our fourth graders are wondrously creative. They are dreaming big dreams and small dreams day and night. This season is replete with an attention to their imaginations at work. By studying mysteries and, later, poetry, we feed their hungry minds with the myriad uses and delights of language. Come with us as we explore this next set of units in a busy season of discovery and creativity.

## WINTER UNITS

SPOTLIGHT UNITS

# SPOTLIGHT on Genre

- Reading Mysteries
- Writing Mini-Mysteries

There are a few great writers who have been able to write across several genres. E. B. White comes to mind. He wrote the classic children's books *Charlotte's Web*, *The Trumpet of the Swan*, and *Stuart Little*. He wrote small humorous snippets for *The New Yorker* in the Talk of the Town column. And he cowrote the seminal "how-to" guide to grammar: *The Elements of Style.* White was the rare genius who could accommodate all genres, fitting his observations, his wonderings, his memory, and his imagination into a wide variety of "containers." Great ideas are like water, flowing clear: a stream. Genre is a container we use to hold those ideas. The ideas are the same, but they look different depending on the container that holds them. Loneliness inside a poem, for example, looks different from loneliness inside a science fiction novel. Courage inside a biography looks different from courage inside a letter. A clear idea, held inside the right container, can change someone's mind, even someone's life. See pages 47 through 61 in my book *The Complete 4 for Literacy* for a more detailed description of the elements and categories of genre and the importance of these units to the lives of our students, who are seeking to clarify, extend, and share from their own stream of ideas.

*Pam Allyn*

# Clue Seekers

If you take a close look at your classroom library, you will probably notice that the vast majority of chapter books published for this age are wonderful mysteries—some scary, some funny, some simply clever. Mysteries are compelling reads, the classic "can't-put-'em-downs." What a perfect time of life to grab onto mysteries: fourth graders are building stamina, and not only do they love a good story, they love a fast read. They are nearly jumping out of their skins with the excitement of life itself. The beauty of studying mysteries with this age group is also that the story elements in mystery are so, so strong: characters have powerful characteristics; settings have significance. Everything means something. In writing, our students can play inside this genre. They have the opportunity to create their own mysteries, relishing their own capacity to surprise someone and to use language to be sneaky, funny, intriguing, and clever.

## Reading Mysteries     GENRE

### Why Teach This?

- To engage students in a close study of a fictional genre.
- To encourage students to make inferences about characters, their actions, and their motivations.
- To compare this fictional genre with other fictional genres.

### Framing Questions

- What is a mystery? What are the characteristics of a mystery?
- How does active reading help us solve our mysteries before the book ends?

### Unit Goals

- Students will identify and find examples of mystery characteristics.
- Students will use these characteristics to build theories about suspects.
- Students will identify important details in the text.
- Students will read, gathering evidence to confirm or refute theories.
- Students will use graphic organizers to record important information as they read.

### Anchor Texts

- *Ace Lacewing, Bug Detective* by David Biedrzycki
- *The Case of the Mummified Pigs: And Other Mysteries in Nature* by Susan E. Quinlan
- *Jake Gander, Storyville Detective: The Case of the Greedy Granny* by George McClements
- *The Mystery of Eatum Hall* by John Kelly

## Resource Sheets

- Story Elements in Mystery (Resource 4.1)
- Mystery Case File (Resource 4.2)
- Mystery Mountain (Resource 4.3)
- Project Planner (Resource 3.5)

| **Unit Assessment** Reading Mysteries | | | GENRE |
|---|---|---|---|
| Student name: | EMERGING | DEVELOPING | INDEPENDENT |
| Identifies and finds examples of mystery characteristics in independent reading. | | | |
| Identifies logical suspects. | | | |
| Infers motives for suspects. | | | |
| Predicts the culprit in the mystery, using evidence from the text. | | | |
| Captures important details in the story. | | | |
| Uses questioning to refine or revise theories as reading progresses. | | | |

| Stage of the Unit | Focused Instruction<br>You will | Independent Practice<br>Students will |
|---|---|---|
| **IMMERSION**<br>4 days | • ask students what mysteries they have read previously; build a class list of favorite mystery titles and series.<br><br>• ask students what they expect from a mystery; read aloud *Jake Gander, Storyville Detective*.<br><br>• read aloud *Ace Lacewing, Bug Detective*; notice what tends to be the same in all mysteries and what is different.<br><br>• read aloud *The Mystery of Eatum Hall*; notice what makes reading a mystery different from reading other forms of fiction. | • read and discuss in partnerships a short, shared mystery.<br><br>• read another short, shared mystery and discuss with a partner: Does it deliver on your expectations for a mystery?<br><br>• read another short mystery from the mystery basket and compare different mysteries with partners; create a T-chart of similarities and differences across mysteries.<br><br>• read another short mystery from the mystery basket and create a T-chart of similarities and differences between mystery and other fictional genres. |

| | | |
|---|---|---|
| **IDENTIFICATION**<br>4 days | • revisit *Ace Lacewing, Bug Detective*; compare story elements in mystery to story elements in realistic fiction (e.g., suspect vs. character, crime vs. plot); use Story Elements in Mystery (Resource 4.1).<br>• revisit *Jake Gander, Storyville Detective* in order to name and define specific stages of mystery.<br>• define key language of mystery (alibi, red herring, motive, opportunity, etc.); explain how to keep track of what's happening in a mystery with a Mystery Case File (Resource 4.2).<br>• connect fictional mystery to the scientific process (form hypothesis, gather evidence, test theory); read aloud one short "real" mystery from *The Case of the Mummified Pigs: And Other Mysteries in Nature*. | • read another short mystery; list and name elements of this text on the Story Elements in Mystery form.<br>• search for examples of mystery stages in a short, shared mystery text and mark with sticky notes; add page references to Story Elements form.<br>• use the Mystery Case File (Resource 4.2) to keep track of a mystery read.<br>• read another "real world" mystery; use Mystery Case File to record the steps taken by scientists to solve the mystery. |
| **GUIDED PRACTICE**<br>11 days | • model selecting a level mystery novel for independent reading; discuss reasons for choice with the class.<br>• model setting a reading plan to finish the book by the end of the unit using the Project Planner (Resource 3.5); begin reading the book to the class.<br>• use class read-aloud to study the setup of the mystery; review the last reading in search of important initial information, recording findings on Mystery Case File.<br>• read aloud; discuss progression of mystery; continue to use Mystery Case File to record key developments. | • browse and sample from independent mystery chapter book choices, discuss options with classmates, and then select their preferred text.<br>• set personal reading plans and then begin reading their books.<br>• revisit the first chapter or so of their books to review the setup of the mystery; use the Mystery Case File to record important information.<br>• read their own mysteries.<br>• read their own mysteries, searching for suspects and clues to add to their Mystery Case Files. |

| GUIDED PRACTICE *(continued)* | • model searching for suspects and clues as you read aloud; capture information on your Mystery Case File.<br><br>• explore motive and opportunity by thinking aloud in front of the class; read to confirm or refute these ideas.<br><br>• check in on reading progress by noting pages read and whether you've stuck to the reading plan.<br><br>• continue to read aloud the mystery; investigate where clues hide (scene changes, objects, dialogue, review of case by crime solver).<br><br>• ask the class to help you update your theories, clues, and suspects.<br><br>• use the Mystery Case File to practice summarizing the class mystery. | • read their own mysteries with a focus on motive and opportunity: Who could have committed the crime? Why would he have done so?<br><br>• read in search of opportunity and motive; update suspect list.<br><br>• check their own reading progress, making adjustments in their reading plans, if necessary, to meet the end-of-unit date.<br><br>• read their own mysteries, noticing where clues hide and adding these to Mystery Case Files.<br><br>• read; update Mystery Case Files.<br><br>• practice summarizing what your crime solver thinks about the crime by sharing with a partner; read and gather additional clues. |
|---|---|---|
| COMMITMENT 1 day | • reflect on what you've learned about reading mysteries. | • write in response to the unit's first two framing questions; recommend mystery books to classmates. |
| TOTAL: 20 DAYS | | |

# Getting Started

Mysteries ask your students to practice summarizing, to make thoughtful predictions, and to read for details—all of which are hard to do if you are not an attentive and observant reader. Many students will discover a passion for reading when they first read a mystery. Let this unit be about the absolute pleasures of digging into this genre so you as a community are on the edge of your collective seat.

# Teaching Materials

## Choosing Teaching Texts

We suggest that you consider using short mysteries so that you are able to read quite a few different examples (scary, traditional, funny) in the early stages of this unit. Luckily, these abound! Use mystery picture books. Here is a list to get you started.

### Mystery Picture Books

- *Ace Lacewing, Bug Detective* by David Biedrzycki
- *Bad Bear Detectives* by Daniel Pinkwater
- *Detective Small in the Amazing Banana Caper* by Wong Herbert Yee
- *Grandpa's Teeth* by Rod Clement
- *Jake Gander, Storyville Detective: The Case of Greedy Granny* by George McClements
- *Mystery at the Club Sandwich* by Doug Cushman
- *The Mystery of Eatum Hall* by John Kelly
- *Piggins* by Jane Yolen
- *The Web Files* by Margie Palatini

To allow you to make the connection to mysteries in the real world, you and your students will also enjoy reading from the following.

### Real World Science Mysteries

- *The Case of the Monkeys That Fell From the Trees: And Other Mysteries in Tropical Nature* by Susan E. Quinlan
- *The Case of the Mummified Pigs: And Other Mysteries in Nature* by Susan E. Quinlan

An alternative or addition to picture books is to read aloud very simple early chapter books that are models of mystery such as the Nate the Great series by Marjorie Weinman Sharmat. Most of your students will be familiar with this series, so you can focus on the structure of the mystery—the setup, the crime or disappearance, the search for suspects and clues, and the resolution. Any Nate title can be read in a day or two and can be used to plot the characteristics of the mystery. Or use the Cam Jansen books by David A. Adler.

Finally, for the early stages of the unit, you can read aloud from the short mystery stories found in anthologies and children's magazines. Examples of these are detailed below.

## Choosing Student Texts

During the Immersion and Identification stages of this unit, your students read short, shared mysteries in partnerships. Set up mystery baskets with collections of mystery short stories for each table of students. You can find many of these in *Highlights* magazine, at www.highlightskids.com, or in key anthologies. Place the short mysteries in plastic page protectors, staple these together, and place them in your baskets. Below are some suggested titles.

### Anthologies

- *The Adventures of Sherlock Holmes*, retold from the Sir Arthur Conan Doyle original (Classic Starts series)
- *The Carlton Treasure*, compiled by the editors of *Highlights*
- Encyclopedia Brown books by Donald J. Sobol (each book in the series has several short mysteries included)
- *Smiffy Blue, Ace Crime Detective: The Case of the Missing Ruby and Other Stories* by Walter Dean Myers

### Individual Mystery Stories Found in Children's Magazines

- "The Alien in Apartment 4-B" by Marcie Aboff (available on www.highlightskids.com)
- "The Cottage-Key Caper" by Kitty Clark, *Highlights* (May 2004)
- "The Eerie, Haunting, Terrible Cry" by Sandra Beswetherick (available on www.highlightskids.com)
- "The Last Case of the I.C. Detective Agency" by Carol M. Harris (available on www.highlightskids.com)
- "The Mystery in the Attic" by Jeanne B. Hargett (available on www.highlightskids.com)
- "Mystery in the Old Museum" by Janet Poling (available on www.highlightskids.com)
- "The Squeaky Duck Mystery" by Julie Angeli, *Spider* (November 2006)

By the third week of this unit, each of your students will be reading their own full-length mystery chapter books. These are generally short, fun series books.

### Examples of Mystery Series Books

- American Girl Mysteries by various authors
- Backpack Mysteries books by Mary Carpenter Reid

- The Baker Street Mysteries by Jake and Luke Thoene
- The Boxcar Children books by Gertrude Chandler Warner
- Cam Jansen books by David A. Adler
- Capital Mysteries books by Ron Roy
- Chinatown Mystery books by Laurence Yep
- Clue Jr. books by Della Rowland
- Detective Zack books by Jerry D. Thomas
- Einstein Anderson, Science Detective books by Seymour Simon
- Encyclopedia Brown books by Donald J. Sobol
- Hank the Cowdog books by John R. Erickson
- Herculeah Jones Mystery books by Betsy Byars
- Jigsaw Jones books by James Preller
- Nate the Great books by Marjorie Weinman Sharmat
- Sugar Creek Gang books by Paul Hutchens
- The Three Investigators books by Robert Arthur
- Wishbone Mysteries by various authors

## Differentiation

Some of your students will be reading well above grade level, others perhaps several levels below. Whenever we ask students to study a new genre closely and identify its particular characteristics, we encourage students to read level or downhill books. With this in mind, we suggest the following books to support your vulnerable readers and to extend your strong readers.

### For Vulnerable Readers

- *Aunt Eater Loves a Mystery* by Doug Cushman
- *Aunt Eater's Mystery Vacation* by Doug Cushman
- Bones books by David A. Adler
- *The Case of the Hungry Stranger* by Crosby Bonsall
- *The Case of the Scaredy Cats* by Crosby Bonsall
- *Detective Dinosaur* by James Skofield
- *Detective Dinosaur Lost and Found* by James Skofield
- *The High-Rise Private Eyes* series by Cynthia Rylant
- Houdini Club Magic Mystery books by David A. Adler
- *Rhymin' Simon and the Mystery of the Fat Cat* by Bill Apablasa
- Young Cam Jansen books by David A. Adler

**For Strong Readers**

- American Girl History Mysteries by various authors
- Hardy Boys books by Franklin W. Dixon
- The Lady Grace Mysteries by Jan Burchett and Sara Vogler
- Nancy Drew books by Carolyn Keene
- Red Rock Mysteries by Jerry B. Jenkins and Chris Fabry
- The Roman Mysteries by Caroline Lawrence

## Stages of the Unit

### Immersion

Over four days, read aloud several short mysteries and ask your students to notice the similarities and differences from one mystery to another, and from the mystery genre to other, perhaps more familiar, genres. At the same time, your students will practice these strategies in their independent reading of short mysteries from their mystery baskets. Ideally, they read side by side in partnerships, so they can discuss their observations at the end of each day's practice. By the end of the Immersion stage, your students will have had the opportunity to read or listen to eight short mysteries—a wonderful immersion in this new genre.

Here is an example of a class chart generated during the Immersion stage.

| What we noticed about the mysteries in *The Carlton Treasure* anthology | |
|---|---|
| How Mysteries Begin | Examples From Our Stories |
| Sometimes they begin with descriptions of the setting, including surprising or suspenseful details:<br><br>"Alone on Misery Island" | "The fog hung heavy over Misery Island." |
| Sometimes they start in the middle of the action:<br><br>"The Secret of the Flashing Light" | "Dana didn't know what woke her up." |
| Sometimes they start with the main character introducing himself as a detective:<br><br>"The Case of the Missing Redhead" | "My partner, Murph, and I had worked hard to convert my tree house into a detective agency." |
| Sometimes they start with a warning or a suggestion of a problem:<br><br>"The Zoo Detective" | "Don't look now," said Sammy. "But I think someone's following us." |

## Identification

Make the connection for your students between the elements of story found in all fiction and the specific characteristics and language of mystery fiction. Once we name these characteristics with and for our students, they can find examples of these characteristics in their independent reading of short mysteries.

Here is an example of a chart created by one group of fourth graders.

| The Elements of Story | The Characteristics of Mystery |
|---|---|
| Characters | • Crime-solver, detective, sleuth<br>• Sidekick, assistant, friend<br>• Victim<br>• Witnesses<br>• Suspects<br>• Culprit, criminal |
| Setting | • Sense of foreboding, danger, suspense<br>• Something missing, out of place<br>• Important details, clues<br>• A crime scene |
| Problem | A crime, a riddle, a disappearance, a kidnapping, a problem |
| Plot<br>Rising Action | • Clues are left<br>• Suspense builds<br>• Motives are identified<br>• A theory, prediction, or deduction<br>• Evidence is collected<br>• An alibi<br>• A "red herring" |
| Solution | An arrest, capture, solution |

This form exists as a graphic organizer your students can use to reinforce your teaching and find examples in their short mystery reads. See Story Elements in Mystery (Resource 4.1).

For those who like to make connections with other curricular areas, this is also a wonderful time to link the steps of solving a mystery to the steps in the scientific process (create a hypothesis, gather evidence, test theory). There are many wonderful "real-world" science mysteries that can be woven into science instruction for additional integration.

Mystery Case File

## Guided Practice

With the language and structure of mystery in place, begin reading full-length mysteries. Setting a reading plan helps your students select books that can be read in the time allotted. Include rereading first chapters to capture the important information associated with the mystery and show your students how to find clues, identify suspects, develop theories, and gather evidence in their Mystery Case Files (Resource 4.2).

Students will read their mystery chapter books, gather information for their Mystery Case Files, develop working theories as to "whodunit," and collect evidence to prove or disprove their theories. Model this process for your students with your own read-aloud text and your own Mystery Case File.

Students can read the same book together in partnerships, keep dual case files, and support each other as they try to solve the mystery before the main character does in their books. Some students prefer to read collaboratively; others enjoy being able to read at their own pace and to conduct their own crime-solving.

## Commitment

Your students have read a full-length mystery and several short, shared mysteries. They can now make thoughtful book recommendations to their classmates or other guests. Plan a culminating celebration, such as a Mystery Party. Your students will have the best ideas!

# Day-by-Day Lessons

## DAY 1 Immersion

### Focused Instruction

*Today we begin our unit on the genre of mystery. I have in front of me a bunch of mystery chapter books from our classroom library. What mysteries have you read before?*

- List mysteries and mystery series that students mention.
- Talk up the genre. Read blurbs. Have students share their reading experiences with mystery.

### Independent Practice

*Everyone is going to read the same short mystery story today, so that we can discuss it in partnerships afterward. As you are reading, ask yourself: What makes this story a mystery?*

### Wrap-Up

- Students share why they think this story is a mystery.

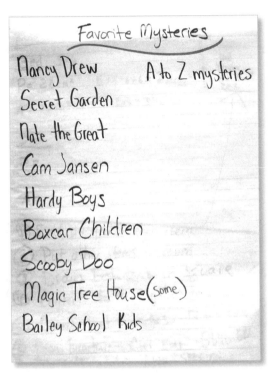

Favorite Mysteries

Nancy Drew          A to Z mysteries
Secret Garden
Nate the Great
Cam Jansen
Hardy Boys
Boxcar Children
Scooby Doo
Magic Tree House (some)
Bailey School Kids

## DAY 2 Immersion

### Focused Instruction

*What do you expect to find inside a mystery?*

- Discuss this question. List comments.
- Read aloud from a mystery picture book or short story.

*Did the story we read today have the elements we talked about?*

### Independent Practice

- Students read another short, shared mystery.
- Students share whether this story has the elements of mystery.

### Wrap-Up

- Add elements to the mystery list.

## DAY 3 Immersion

### Focused Instruction

*Today I want you to begin to notice what is the same in all mysteries and what seems to be different. I am going to read aloud another short mystery. Listen for similarities and differences to the other stories we've read.*

### Independent Practice

- Students read another short mystery out of the mystery baskets at their tables.
- Students compare different mysteries in partnerships.
- Students work at table groupings to build a T-chart of similarities and differences across mystery.

### Wrap-Up

- Students compare content from one chart to another. They look for consistent observations.

## DAY 4 Immersion

### Focused Instruction

- Read aloud another short mystery story or picture book.

*How is the genre of mystery the same as the genre of realistic fiction? How are these genres different?*

### Independent Practice

- Students read another short mystery independently.
- Students meet in table groupings and make a T-chart of similarities and differences between mystery and realistic fiction.

### Wrap-Up

- Hang charts in the meeting area. Compare content from one chart to another. Look for consistent observations.

## DAY 5 Identification

### Focused Instruction

*Mystery is considered fiction, just as realistic fiction is. But mystery has its own characteristics and its own language. All mysteries include the same story elements as every other kind of fiction we read, but they may be called different things. Let's make a list of story elements and what these elements are called in mystery. You may know some of these words already, or you may have heard or read them in your short mysteries.*

- Revisit any of the mystery picture books to reinforce your teaching.

- Create a T-chart with story elements and mystery vocabulary (e.g., characters in mysteries tend to be a victim, sleuth, crime-solver, detective, witness, suspect, or villain). You may want to use Resource 4.1.

### Independent Practice

- Students read another short mystery, listing story elements in their Story Elements in Mystery organizer (Resource 4.1).

### Wrap-Up

- Students turn and compare organizers with one another.

## DAY 6 Identification

### Focused Instruction

*What are the specific stages of a mystery? Let's name what always happens at the beginning, middle, and end of a mystery. I want us to revisit the short mysteries we've read to make sure they follow this pattern all the time. Let's start by looking at one of our read-aloud picture book mysteries.*

### Independent Practice

- Students revisit several mystery stories read previously and put sticky notes on typical stages of the mystery.

### Wrap-Up

- Two students share their discoveries from their reading.

## DAY 7 Identification

### Focused Instruction

*As the plot progresses, the writer of a mystery gives us certain information so we can build theories about who the villain is and what happened. He also gives us information to throw us off track and make solving the mystery more difficult. I want to share the names for these developments in any mystery.*

- List and define: alibi, red herring, motive, opportunity, evidence.
- Revisit short mysteries to illustrate examples of these developments.

### Independent Practice

*As you read another short mystery today, you will use our Mystery Case File (Resource 4.2). Each of you will keep track of the development of your mystery, gathering suspects and clues.*

## Wrap-Up

*Who had a theory as to who the villain was in the mystery? Did you figure it out before the author told you? Were you right?*

- One student shares reading experience.

### DAY 8 Identification

## Focused Instruction

*You may have noticed that a mystery moves forward in the same way that we approach an experiment in science. First we form a hypothesis, an educated guess as to why something happens. Then we gather evidence by testing our theory. We rule out certain explanations, and develop others as we continue to conduct our experiment. Today I am going to read a "real-life" science mystery out loud. I want you to be comparing this nonfiction article to the fictional mysteries you have been reading.*

## Independent Practice

- Students read other examples of real-world mysteries and name the steps taken by the scientists to solve these mysteries.

## Wrap-Up

*How are these real-world mysteries the same as our fictional mysteries? How are they different? Turn and share your thoughts with a classmate.*

### DAY 9 Guided Practice

## Focused Instruction

*Today we take everything we have learned about the genre of a mystery and select a full-length mystery chapter book to read independently. It is important to make the right choice. First, of course, you want to choose a leveled text—a mystery that will neither be too hard nor too easy for you. How do we check to see if a text is the right level for us?*

*You need to read the blurb, or talk to classmates who may have read from that series, to see if it sounds interesting to you. Some people prefer real detective-type books, while others like to read about kids finding missing things. Some prefer more adventure than others. Some even like mystery books that are a little scary. You will be reading this book for the next two weeks, so choose wisely.*

## Independent Practice

- Students browse mystery baskets and interview one another for reading ideas.
- Students select their mystery of choice.

## Wrap-Up

*With a show of hands, who chose a series-book mystery? Hold your books up so we can see who is reading from the same series. You will be good resources for one another.*

### DAY 10 Guided Practice

### Focused Instruction

*One of the frustrating things about reading in a unit of study is when you aren't able to finish your book in the time set aside for the unit. But we can plan our reading so that we make proper book choices and so that we know how much we need to read each day to finish on time. I expect each of you to finish your mystery by the end of the unit. Let me show you how to plan.*

- Students use the Project Planner (Resource 3.5) to plan the number of pages to read each day, based on total page count and reading rate.

### Independent Practice

- Students work with the Project Planner to plan out their reading schedules. If necessary, students select alternative text that they can finish in the time allotted.
- Students begin reading their books.

### Wrap-Up

*Who had to change books today because they realized they chose something too ambitious? Be proud of yourself for making this adjustment. That is a great reading behavior to develop.*

### DAY 11 Guided Practice

### Focused Instruction

*Today, as I read the first chapter of our mystery chapter book, think about the way the author sets up her mystery. How do we find out about the crime or disappearance? What do we notice about the crime scene? Who are presented as suspects? What is missing? Who is the victim? We will keep track of our discoveries on this large version of a Mystery Case File (Resource 4.2).*

- Read aloud to your class.

### Independent Practice

*Today I am going to ask you to reread your first chapter. An author crams a lot of important information into the first chapter or so of any book, but particularly in a mystery. If you miss an important detail, you may not be able to solve the crime or disappearance. So please reread your first chapter and let us know what you noticed the second time around.*

## Wrap-Up

- Students share examples of clues or other information they missed in their "first-draft" reading.

### DAY 12 Guided Practice

#### Focused Instruction

- Read aloud to the class. Discuss the progression of mystery plot.

#### Independent Practice

*Before you continue reading today, fill out your own Mystery Case File. Keep this close to you as you read, adding to it as you make new discoveries.*

- Students read their own mysteries.

#### Wrap-Up

*Did anyone make a new discovery today as they read?*

### DAY 13 Guided Practice

#### Focused Instruction

*We are now several chapters into our mystery read-aloud. I am going to pay particular attention to suspects and clues today as I read. I will stop and think aloud when I come to a part that I think has importance. See whether you agree with me.*

- Read aloud. Model thinking about suspects and clues.

#### Independent Practice

- Students read their own mysteries, searching for suspects and clues.

#### Wrap-Up

*Did anyone rule out a suspect today as you read? How did you discover they could not have committed the crime?*

### DAY 14 Guided Practice

#### Focused Instruction

*The way I identify a suspect is to think about whether they have a motive. A motive is when someone would have a good reason to have committed the crime or taken the object. Maybe they needed it for something else, or they wanted to take it away from the victim. What are the motives for our suspects in the read-aloud mystery?*

#### Independent Practice

- Students read their own mysteries in search of suspects with motives.

## Wrap-Up

*Who would like to share the motive for one of their suspects?*

### DAY 15 Guided Practice

### Focused Instruction

*Another way I identify a suspect is to think about whether any of the characters in the story had the opportunity to commit the crime or take the object. If one of the characters in our books wasn't in the room at the time of the crime, he cannot be a suspect, because he did not have the opportunity. Who are the suspects in our read-aloud who had the opportunity to commit the crime?*

- Revisit prior sections of text to check for opportunity in read-aloud.

### Independent Practice

- Students read their own mysteries, noticing whether any of the suspects had the opportunity to commit the crime. This may require rereading key sections.

### Wrap-Up

*Who ruled out a suspect in their book because their suspect didn't have the opportunity to commit the crime?*

### DAY 16 Guided Practice

### Focused Instruction

*Before I read aloud today, this is a good time to check and see how our reading is going and whether we are still on track with our Project Planners. Let's check on our progress.*

- Read aloud from the mystery.

### Independent Practice

*I want you to check on your own progress in your mystery chapter books. You have had many chances to read your book so far, assuming you read your mystery each night for homework. Are you on track? Will you finish in time?*

- Students continue to read mystery chapter books.

### Wrap-Up

*Is anyone ahead of schedule? What should students who think they might finish early do? Let's give them some suggestions.*

### DAY 17 Guided Practice

#### Focused Instruction

- Read aloud from the class mystery.

*Where do clues hide in the books we read? I've noticed that often there are new clues to be discovered when the scene or chapter changes. I've also noticed that when new objects or new characters are introduced, they usually have some significance. What else signals a clue?*

#### Independent Practice

- Students read their mystery chapter books, looking for where their clues hide.

#### Wrap-Up

*Did anyone find another good way to identify clues in their books?*

### DAY 18 Guided Practice

#### Focused Instruction

- Review the Mystery Case File for the read-aloud.
- Have the class help you update your theories, clues, and suspects.
- Continue to read aloud.

#### Independent Practice

- Students update Mystery Case Files and continue to read.

#### Wrap-Up

- One student takes the class through her Mystery Case File.

### DAY 19 Guided Practice

#### Focused Instruction

*You should be nearly done with your books. Sometimes it is a good idea, toward the end of a mystery, to summarize what has happened and what we've learned. This might be enough to help us solve the mystery if we haven't already. A summary is not a retelling. We don't want to share every single event and detail. We just want to provide a few important pieces of information. We can use our Mystery Case Files to help organize and guide our summaries. Watch me do it with the read-aloud Mystery Case File.*

- Finish the read-aloud mystery.

## Independent Practice

- Students practice summarizing their mysteries with one another.
- Students continue reading their independent mysteries. Mysteries must be finished by class tomorrow.

## Wrap-Up

*What are the most important things to include when you summarize a mystery?*

### DAY 20 Commitment

## Focused Instruction

*What have we learned about reading mysteries? Turn and share your thoughts with the person sitting next to you. How do you think this will help you in reading any kind of fiction?*

## Independent Practice

- Students write in response to the first two unit framing questions: What is a mystery? What are the characteristics of a mystery?

## Wrap-Up

*Many of you may have read a mystery that you liked so much you'd like to recommend it to a friend. Let's use the rest of the time today to make these recommendations to one another. Remember to write the name of your book and the author on the index card, and include your name as the person who is the recommending the book. Then place the index card in that person's mailbox.*

What do we expect from Mysteries?

Clues — problem (crime)
Suspicion — date/time
Climax — solution (solving the case)
Mysterious — detectives
surprise ending — important events
Ask questions — onomatopoeia
evidence — interrogation
many details — fingerprints
suspects — magnifing glass / Crime scene

EARLY FALL    LATE FALL    WINTER    SPRING

# Clue Creators

To write a mystery is to be in full control not only of plot, but of surprise. Let your students surprise you with their creative ideas. Fourth graders love surprises. Let these units embrace the whimsy of the best mysteries by allowing your students to invent their own fictional mini-mysteries.

## Writing Mini-Mysteries

GENRE

### Why Teach This?

- To explore the world of writing fiction.
- To encourage use of vivid language and description to build sense of place.
- To experiment with creating suspense.

### Framing Questions

- How can we become powerful writers of mystery?
- What do writers do to build suspense?

### Unit Goals

- Students will create their own mini-mysteries, including the key elements of the genre.
- Students will use vivid descriptions in their writing.
- Students will explore writing strategies effective for building suspense.

### Anchor Texts

- *A Dark Dark Tale* by Ruth Brown
- *The Mysteries of Harris Burdick* by Chris Van Allsburg

### Resource Sheets

- Mystery Case File (Resource 4.2)
- Mystery Mountain (Resource 4.3)
- Ways to Celebrate Writing (Resource 4.4)

| Unit Assessment Writing Mini-Mysteries | | | GENRE |
|---|---|---|---|
| Student name: | EMERGING | DEVELOPING | INDEPENDENT |
| Includes all the key elements in his or her mini-mystery. | | | |
| Uses vivid, attention-getting language. | | | |
| Uses at least one technique to build suspense for the reader. | | | |

| Stage of the Unit | Focused Instruction<br>You will | Independent Practice<br>Students will |
|---|---|---|
| **IMMERSION**<br>4 days | • reread a shared short mystery the class already knows; tell your students that today they will read this mystery again, but this time read like writers, looking for the way the author structures and resolves the mystery; map out the particulars on a blank Mystery Case File (Resource 4.2).<br>• explain one way writers get their ideas for mysteries (e.g., from the news).<br>• explain that another way writers get their ideas for mysteries is to fictionalize something in their own lives; model doing this as a writer in front of your students, planning a mystery based on something that actually happened to you.<br>• explain a final way that writers get their ideas for mysteries (e.g., from their imaginations); introduce the class to Chris Van Allsburg's book *The Mysteries of Harris Burdick*, reading the opening and several of the "sentence starters" and using one to plan a mystery. | • revisit favorite short mysteries, reading like writers: How did this writer plan out and present his mystery? List ideas for mysteries with a partner; take one idea and try writing about it.<br>• explore possible mystery plots with a partner by skimming copies of the local or national newspaper, current-events magazines, finding puzzling or worrisome news, and developing these into fictional mystery ideas; record possible scenarios in Mystery Case Files and write from one of them.<br>• continue to explore possible mystery plots by rereading writing notebooks and looking for events that could be fictionalized into mysteries; share discoveries with a partner and record possible topics using Mystery Case Files.<br>• continue to explore possible mystery plots. Students may choose to use a sentence starter from the Van Allsburg book; record the possible plots using their Case Files. |
| **IDENTIFICATION**<br>2 days | • explain that each student will be writing his or her own mini-mystery, using what they have learned from the reading unit; review your own Mystery Case Files and choose one to develop into your own mystery.<br>• explain that each mystery must begin with a crime or something that is missing, and that as the mystery progresses, the suspense must build; plot your own mystery on the Mystery Mountain organizer (Resource 4.3). | • select a Mystery Case File to develop into a mini-mystery; share their decision with a partner and make sure their Mystery Case File has all elements listed.<br>• use the Mystery Mountain organizer to plot events in mini-mysteries as a prewriting activity. |

EARLY FALL

LATE FALL

WINTER

SPRING

| GUIDED PRACTICE<br>8 days | • review how different short mysteries begin; return to prior read-alouds and name the different techniques the writer uses to pull the reader into the mystery; choose one and write a beginning for your mystery.<br><br>• read aloud *A Dark Dark Tale*; name one technique a writer uses to build suspense as a mystery begins (describing the location as scary or puzzling or worrisome): How can we portray the place in a way that worries the reader? What is lurking around the corner? Show a mentor example; write to build suspense and mood through developing your setting.<br><br>• revisit *A Dark Dark Tale*; name another suspense technique (e.g., bringing the reader toward the problem, not away from it); show an example and continue to write your own mystery, having the sleuth walk directly into danger.<br><br>• name another suspense technique (e.g., describing your characters). How are they acting? What seems strange or out of place? What is unusual? Continue your mystery, spending some time noticing the appearance and behavior of the "suspects."<br><br>• name another technique that writers use to build suspense as the mystery continues (e.g., having the action take a sudden turn); show a mentor example and write to build suspense in your mystery through unexpected events.<br><br>• model crafting the climax and resolution of your mystery—when your sleuth or detective solves the crime. Who did it? How did your sleuth know? What happens next? | • explore different mystery beginnings with a partner; try several beginnings and choose one to begin their mysteries.<br><br>• continue mystery writing, following their Mystery Mountain organizer; develop and describe the setting to build suspense.<br><br>• continue mystery writing, continuing to build suspense; consider having their character walk toward the danger or problem, rather than away.<br><br>• continue mystery writing, trying to build suspense through vivid description of characters. How are their characters acting? What looks or sounds strange? Think about their word choice and be sure to use modifiers!<br><br>• continue mystery writing and continue to build suspense; consider adding an unexpected event or sudden turn in the plot, building this into their mystery.<br><br>• continue writing; draft the climax and ending of the mystery.<br><br>• revise first drafts.<br><br>• work in partnerships to edit mysteries for conventions. |
|---|---|---|

| GUIDED PRACTICE (continued) | • model the revision of your mystery: What parts are confusing? What is missing? <br> • model editing your mystery for conventions and correct spelling of mystery language. | |
|---|---|---|
| COMMITMENT 1 day | • reflect on what you have learned as a writer of mysteries. | • reflect in writing on their learning; meet in small groups to read their mini-mysteries out loud. |
| TOTAL: 15 DAYS | | |

# Getting Started

We are studying the craft of mystery—how a mystery begins, how the suspense builds, how the writer plans the resolution of the mystery. Revisit your own favorite short mystery. Notice how the writer introduces the crime or disappearance. Notice how she builds suspense. Notice how she walks her main character right into the heart of the problem. Read a short mystery like a writer, and notice what has been done to pull you, the reader, along.

# Teaching Materials

## Choosing Teaching Texts

The main texts that we suggest you use in this unit are short mysteries. These will serve as mentors of topic and plot for your writers. If you have taught the reading unit, your students will already be familiar with these texts.

### Anthologies

- *The Adventures of Sherlock Holmes,* retold from the Sir Arthur Conan Doyle original (Classic Starts series)
- *The Carlton Treasure,* compiled by the editors of *Highlights*
- Encyclopedia Brown books by Donald J. Sobol (each book in the series has several short mysteries included)
- *Smiffy Blue, Ace Crime Detective: The Case of the Missing Ruby and Other Stories* by Walter Dean Myers

### Individual Mystery Stories Found in Children's Magazines

- "The Alien in Apartment 4-B" by Marcie Aboff (available on www.highlightskids.com)
- "The Cottage-Key Caper" by Kitty Clark, *Highlights* (May 2004)
- "The Eerie, Haunting, Terrible Cry" by Sandra Beswetherick (available on www.highlightskids.com)

- "The Last Case of the I.C. Detective Agency" by Carol M. Harris
  (available on www.highlightskids.com)
- "The Mystery in the Attic" by Jeanne B. Hargett
  (available on www.highlightskids.com)
- "Mystery in the Old Museum" by Janet Poling
  (available on www.highlightskids.com)
- "The Squeaky Duck Mystery" by Julie Angeli, *Spider* (November 2006)

In addition, you will appreciate having two picture books as anchor texts. The first is called *A Dark Dark Tale* by Ruth Brown. This story, while not a classic detective tale, is an excellent example of how an author builds suspense with her words. As you ask your students to do this themselves, *A Dark Dark Tale* becomes an important mentor text for your class. It teaches the craft of suspense. Another important picture book is Chris Van Allsburg's *The Mysteries of Harris Burdick*. While not a conventional mystery with rising action, climax, and resolution, this book is beautifully and spookily illustrated, and each page introduces another "mystery moment," in which the writer titles a mystery and provides the first line of text. Some of your writers may struggle with the initial premise of creating a mystery out of their own 9-year-old imaginations. Launch your students' writing ideas using Van Allsburg's picture book.

## Choosing Student Materials

All the preparatory writing (possible mystery ideas, development of these ideas) goes in their writing notebooks, but as they choose a topic to turn into a mini-mystery draft, students then move to a folder. The folder can also be used to store examples of mentor texts.

## Differentiation

Most students will differentiate this work for themselves, choosing an appropriate idea to develop into a mini-mystery. Students with more experience as writers and more experience as readers of mystery will take their writing, and the development of their mysteries, further. You can provide your vulnerable writers with prompt support, using the pages from *The Mysteries of Harris Burdick*, or, for that matter, any first sentence of any mystery novel or short story. Or, you can invite these students to take an existing narrative they have written or can conceptualize and then fictionalize this story into a mystery. What happens when the tickets for their vacation are stolen? Who are the suspects? Why would someone take them? How will they solve the crime?

# Stages of the Unit

## Immersion

During this stage, model where mystery writers get their ideas. Most of Joan Lowery Nixon's ideas for her own mysteries came from reading newspapers. She would read and ask, "What if?" Browse the local news and find a topic that you could develop into a plausible, entertaining mystery. For example, if you read in the paper that your local library has stopped running its mobile library, you could fictionalize this into a scenario where someone has stolen the library bus. Who would want to do that? The local owner of the video store? Why? Because he wants children to stop reading and watch more movies? Use the Mystery Case File (Resource 4.2) to imagine each important element of this mystery scenario. Who are the victims? The suspects? The evidence? Develop the possible mystery.

Mysteries are all about describing something that is difficult or impossible to explain. Taking the news and twisting it is one way to create a concept for a mystery.

Another approach is to model how to fictionalize an event from your own life as a way of sharing where writers of mystery get their ideas and how they develop plots. Your students may know the story of when you drove to Pennsylvania to pick up your puppy, Tucker. What happens if you imagine a story in which you let Tuck out in the yard to play, and when you come to let him in, the dog is gone, but a note has been tacked on the fence? Fill out a Mystery Case File. Who would take him? Why?

The last approach is the most fun, and perhaps the hardest, as it is not bound by reality in any way. This is the imagination. You and your students can invent any possible situation. Favorite stuffed animals disappearing, coded clues left in lunch boxes, doors locked that have never been locked before. The important thing to remember, when you share the vastness of your own imagination, is to remind students that they must ultimately have a plan for their mystery. They must plan the crime, the suspects, the clues, and the evidence for their stories to work.

Here is an example of a class chart showing some of the choices writers have in choosing their mystery inspirations.

| Where Do Mystery Writers Get Their Ideas? | |
|---|---|
| Mystery Inspiration | Writing Ideas |
| Events from the news | • Road closed<br>• Dog missing<br>• Cat stuck in tree<br>• Bank robbery<br>• Opening night of school concert |
| Fictionalizing our own lives | • Trips<br>• New neighbors<br>• Favorite toy is missing<br>• Lunch money is gone<br>• Books disappearing from the library |
| Using our imaginations | • Moving into a haunted house<br>• Meeting a stranger<br>• Suddenly the window opens…<br>• The doorknob turns…<br>• Your house is empty. Where is everyone? |

By the end of the Immersion stage, all students have a chance to use their own lives, the news, and their imaginations to conceptualize various mystery scenarios in possible Mystery Case Files. This is a critical process, as you want them to be able to choose a topic worth developing into a complete mini-mystery. This will be more effective if they have had a chance to explore several possible writing scenarios.

## Identification

Ask your students to select a mystery scenario from their case files. They should choose a topic that feels interesting and deep enough to develop across several days of writing. Once they have selected their topic, they need to plot their mystery on the Mystery Mountain graphic organizer (Resource 4.3). This will give their stories a path and a destination. It is important for fiction writers to plan their stories before they write them. Model this process with your own writing. Take your own mystery topic, imagine how it will progress, what clues you will find, and how you will find the culprit.

## Guided Practice

Over the next eight days, your students will draft mini-mysteries. With a plot planned on your Mystery Mountain, you can focus your instruction on the craft of the mystery. For example, returning to student observations of how mysteries begin will give your student writers ideas for their own opening paragraphs. Return to your read-aloud and shared texts. Revisit the class chart with the different types of beginnings for mysteries.

Use this same approach to help students build rising action. Select key texts to study so you might highlight what the author does to build suspense. *A Dark Dark Tale* by Ruth Brown is a great example of this. Students will discover that she uses repetition, description, and the steady movement of her main character toward the "danger" to build suspense. Here is an example of a teacher's imaginative writing as she models trying to build suspense for the reader:

I told her not to open the door…

The hallway was dark, and cold, and I could hear water dripping. Every sound echoed around me—every creak, every splash, even my foot tapping restlessly on the stone floor. A light glowed from beneath the door. Somehow it wasn't comforting. I wanted desperately to get out of that cold, dark space. The walls felt like they were closing in on me. The hair stood up on the back of my neck and I knew that what was on the other side of that door would not be warm and inviting.

I knew it, and she knew it, but it didn't stop her as she reached out, her hand shaking, and wrapped her cold fingers around the ancient metal knob and turned…

Your ongoing teaching in this stage ultimately brings the writers in your class toward a resolution of their mini-mysteries as they complete and edit their drafts.

## Commitment

Your students all have written mini-mysteries and should be proud. There are many ways to reflect and celebrate this work (see Ways to Celebrate Writing, Resource 4.4). Some can be done within your classroom. Others can have a larger scope. Several children's websites offer young writers the opportunity to "publish" their mysteries online, including Joan Lowry's site at Scholastic.com (teacher.scholastic. com/writewit/mystery/index.htm). Each year the Mystery Writers of America hosts a contest for mystery short stories written by students in second through tenth grades (find out more at www.mysterywriters.org). Ask your students how they would like to celebrate finishing their own stories.

# Day-by-Day Lessons

### DAY 1 Immersion

**Focused Instruction**

- Revisit a short mystery read during the Reading Mysteries unit.
- Notice the way the author plans out and resolves the mystery.
- Map mystery in Mystery Case File.

**Independent Practice**

*Go back into the mystery baskets today. Read like a writer. Look at a mystery you've already read. Notice the way the different mysteries are presented, and how the writer planned out the crime and hid the evidence. With a partner, list your own ideas for a mystery in your writing notebooks. Take one idea and write about it.*

**Wrap-Up**

- One student shares her mystery idea.

### DAY 2 Immersion

**Focused Instruction**

*One way writers get ideas for their mysteries is to look at the news. Sometimes a story strikes you just so, and you think, This would make a great mystery. Taking something that really happened and using it as a place to launch your imagination is one way to get an idea for a mystery.*

**Independent Practice**

- Offer students access to newspapers and current-events magazines so they can brainstorm ideas this way.
- Students gather other mystery topics in new Mystery Case Files.
- Each student chooses a topic and writes to explore this scenario.

**Wrap-Up**

*Did anyone add an idea to his or her list after reading the paper? What was the idea?*

### DAY 3 Immersion

**Focused Instruction**

*Another way writers get ideas for their mysteries is to take something that really happened to them and change it into a mystery. What would happen if you flew to Florida for vacation and you got to Disney World and there was a handwritten sign on the gate that said, "Closed Until Further Notice"? We did take a trip to Florida recently, but the park was open like it always is. I just like the idea of making something unexpected happen. And if the sign was handwritten, it probably wasn't the company that locked the gates and was keeping people out.*

## Independent Practice

*As you work today as a writer, think about things that have actually happened to you. Reread your writing notebook to look for ideas. Can you fictionalize these moments and change the events to turn this real story into a mystery? Try it!*

- Students list additional mystery ideas, using their lives and their imaginations with new Mystery Case Files. Each writer selects a topic of interest and writes about it in their writing notebooks.

## Wrap-Up

*Did anyone change what actually happened to him or her to create a new idea for a mystery?*

### DAY 4 Immersion

## Focused Instruction

*The hardest but sometimes the most entertaining way to get an idea for a mystery is to just start with your imagination. I am going to read a picture book by Chris Van Allsburg called* The Mysteries of Harris Burdick. *In this book, every page suggests another mystery, and each page is just the author letting his imagination and illustration go wild. I'm going to take one of these sentence starters and use it to imagine my own mystery today as I write in front of you.*

## Independent Practice

- Students take another mystery topic and use it to inspire their own writing in their notebooks.
- Offer students access to the pages from *The Mysteries of Harris Burdick.* Encourage children to use these to launch their own mystery ideas.

## Wrap-Up

*Who came up with a new idea after using a sentence starter from our picture book? Tell us your idea.*

## DAY 5 Identification

### Focused Instruction

*Each of you will be writing a mini-mystery during the next two weeks. I am going to write one, too, so watch as I go back through all my possible case files and choose the one I am most interested in turning into a finished piece of writing.*

### Independent Practice

- Students review their case files and their writing notebooks and select a final topic.
- Students share their decisions with a partner.
- Students make sure their Mystery Case File is completely planned for their finished topic, and then they write to explore their topics.

### Wrap-Up

*Let's go around the meeting area and hear what everyone's topic is. Don't say too much, and don't give away the ending. We want to be surprised when you read us the finished piece.*

## DAY 6 Identification

### Focused Instruction

*Every mystery has to start with a crime or something that is missing. Watch me as I plan out my mystery on the Mystery Mountain organizer (Resource 4.3).*

### Independent Practice

- Students plot their own mysteries on the Mystery Mountain organizer.

### Wrap-Up

*How do you think your Mystery Mountain organizer will help when you begin to write your mystery?*

## DAY 7 Guided Practice

### Focused Instruction

*Let's look back on the short mysteries we read during reading time. Let's focus on how mysteries begin. Writers use different techniques for getting us interested in the story. You will each choose one of these and write a beginning for your mystery.*

- Chart different approaches for beginning a mystery.
- Choose one yourself for your modeled mystery. Write off of this beginning.

## Independent Practice

- Students work with partners to explore different mystery beginnings. They write, share, write, trying several beginnings. They choose one and write off of this beginning.

## Wrap-Up

- One or two students share their beginnings with the class.

### DAY 8 Guided Practice

## Focused Instruction

- Read aloud *A Dark Dark Tale* by Ruth Brown.

*Writing with suspense is the most important thing a good mystery writer does. For the next several days we will be looking at ways to build suspense in our writing. One way is to describe the setting as scary or puzzling or worrisome. How can we describe a place in a way that would get the reader's attention?*

- Model your own writing to build suspense by describing the setting in worrisome ways.

## Independent Practice

- Students continue mystery writing, developing and describing their settings to build suspense.

## Wrap-Up

*Who wants to share a piece of writing that demonstrates building suspense?*

### DAY 9 Guided Practice

## Focused Instruction

*Another famous technique in mystery writing is to bring your character closer to the problem or the danger, not away from it. Here is an example from one of our short mysteries.*

- Revisit *A Dark Dark Tale* to demonstrate concept.

*I am going to continue writing my mystery in front of you, but today, I am going to walk my main character right into the heart of the danger. Watch how I do it.*

## Independent Practice

- Students continue writing their mysteries; some may bring their sleuth closer to the danger or problem.

## Wrap-Up

*Did anyone try today's technique? Who would like to share?*

## DAY 10 Guided Practice

### Focused Instruction

*Another thing we can do to build suspense is to describe our suspects and their actions. If they are strange, or acting not quite normal, this builds suspense. Watch me as I continue my mystery. Let's see if I can describe my suspects in a way that makes you suspicious of them.*

- Write using powerful adjectives to build suspense.
- Revisit text written and highlight those modifiers.
- Build a class word bank of spooky and suspenseful adjectives, adverbs, and verbs.

### Independent Practice

- Students continue their mysteries, adding character descriptions to build suspense.
- Students refer to a word bank list to inspire their descriptions.

### Wrap-Up

*Who would like to share their description of a suspect in their mystery?*

## DAY 11 Guided Practice

### Focused Instruction

*The final technique we will try this week will be having the action in our mystery take a sudden turn. All of you should be coming close to finishing your mysteries. Often in a mystery, when you just about think you have it solved, something surprising happens. I will try that today as I write in front of you. I want to choose an event that will surprise and perhaps confuse the reader. Remember, you don't want the reader to figure out "whodunit" right away. That's the fun of writing and reading mysteries.*

### Independent Practice

- Students continue writing. Writers consider adding an unexpected turn or event.

### Wrap-Up

*Who decided to add an unexpected turn? Read it to us.*

## DAY 12 Guided Practice

### Focused Instruction

*Today is the day our sleuths solve their crimes. We need to write our climax scenes and finish drafting our mini-mysteries. This is where your detective or crime solver puts everything together and figures out what happened. Watch as I add the climax scene to my mini-mystery.*

### Independent Practice

- Students draft the climax of their mysteries if they haven't done so already.

### Wrap-Up

*Let's hear how one student had his crime solver solve the crime.*

## DAY 13 Guided Practice

### Focused Instruction

*Today is all about revision. I want you to read your mystery aloud to a partner. As you read aloud, notice the parts that are confusing or seem to have words left out. Fix what doesn't make sense. Add what is missing. One of the most important reasons to revise a mystery is so the crime and the clues and the suspects are clear and not confusing. Revision is IMPORTANT! Take the time to reread your work and check it for clarity. Watch as I do this now.*

### Independent Practice

- Students work with partners to share and revise their final first drafts.

### Wrap-Up

- Students share the kinds of changes they made to their drafts.

## DAY 14 Guided Practice

### Focused Instruction

*What is the last step we always take in the writing process? We need to reread our piece for spelling, capitalization, and punctuation errors. What is likely to be capitalized in our mysteries? What words might we misspell? Can we use the words on our case files to help us double-check our use of mystery language? Remember to make sure that every sentence is a complete sentence, and that each sentence has ending punctuation. We are publishing these stories and sending them home in our very own mystery magazine, so they need to be carefully edited. Watch as I edit my own final draft.*

### Independent Practice

- Students revise for spelling, punctuation, and capitalization.

### Wrap-Up

*Who used mystery language in their story? What words were hard to spell?*

## DAY 15 Commitment

### Focused Instruction

*What have we learned about being writers of mysteries? How do our mini-mysteries show the reader what we understand about the mystery genre?*

### Independent Practice

- Students meet in small groups to read their mysteries aloud.
- Students reflect in writing on their learning, answering one of the framing questions in the unit: What do writers do to build suspense?
- Students brainstorm, vote, and select a name for their mystery magazine.

### Wrap-Up

- Students select two peers to prepare and illustrate the cover and the table of contents for the magazine.

# Hit the "Mark" With Punctuation

By fourth grade, sentences in the books your students read are no longer simple, with obvious subjects and objects. Sentences are now woven from phrases and clauses, with commas and colons weaving those strands together into cohesive structures. Help students' fluency keep pace with their enthusiasm and their other reading skills by explicitly introducing them to the role of "pausing" punctuation, thus improving their comprehension, stamina, and pacing. In writing, help your students seize the joy of language by modeling how to build more complex sentences with the use of pausing punctuation.

## Understanding Pausing Punctuation in Reading

CONVENTIONS

### Why Teach This?

- To help students recognize the purpose of certain punctuation marks and the impact these marks have on comprehension and fluency.
- To teach punctuation in authentic ways.

### Framing Questions

- Why do writers use punctuation inside of sentences?
- What is this punctuation asking us to do as readers?

### Unit Goals

- Students will review and expand upon their understanding of the comma.
- Students will discover and discriminate between the em-dash, the colon, and the semicolon.
- Students will apply this understanding of pausing punctuation to their phrasing and fluency.
- Students will use this growing knowledge to improve comprehension.

### Anchor Texts

- *The House on Mango Street* by Sandra Cisneros
- *My Mama Had a Dancing Heart* by Libba Moore Gray
- *Silent Music* by James Rumford

| Unit Assessment Understanding Pausing Punctuation in Reading | | | CONVENTIONS |
|---|---|---|---|
| Student name: | EMERGING | DEVELOPING | INDEPENDENT |
| Names several important forms of pausing punctuation. | | | |
| Understands the differences between several forms of pausing punctuation. | | | |
| Uses knowledge of pausing punctuation to read aloud in longer, more effective phrases. | | | |
| Uses knowledge of pausing punctuation to read aloud with greater expression. | | | |
| Explains at least two rules for the comma. | | | |

| Stage of the Unit | Focused Instruction<br>You will | Independent Practice<br>Students will |
|---|---|---|
| IMMERSION<br>3 days | • share the history of punctuation with your students, explaining that early punctuation was related more to speaking than reading; emphasize that the marks let the orator know where to give pause or provide emphasis.<br><br>• read aloud from *My Mama Had a Dancing Heart* by Libba Moore Gray; notice the author's use of the comma; ask students what other pausing punctuation they noticed in this shared text and list their observations.<br><br>• read aloud from *Silent Music*; notice that the comma looks like an apostrophe or a single quotation mark, but it differs in that it sits on the baseline of the text and has a different purpose; notice that other pausing punctuation appears in different locations and forms. | • with a partner, read aloud from picture books, practicing phrasing based on punctuation.<br><br>• read from favorite picture books, noting examples of interesting pausing punctuation; copy at least one sentence featuring pausing punctuation onto a sentence strip and practice reading that sentence out loud.<br><br>• compare and contrast different pausing punctuation marks with a partner, using the sentence strips gathered previously; note their appearance, location, and usage, and write working definitions of these marks in reading notebooks. |

| | | |
|---|---|---|
| **IDENTIFICATION**<br>2 days | • revisit anchor text to explain that commas help the reader divide sentences into smaller meaning chunks so that the sentences can be better and more quickly understood; review basic comma rules for series commas, for commas that set off clauses or phrases, for commas used with quotations, and for commas used to form compound sentences.<br><br>• name other punctuation marks that set off segments of text: the em-dash, the colon, and the semicolon; define each mark and its general rule for use; use "My Name" by Sandra Cisneros (from *The House on Mango Street*) as an example of the em-dash. | • highlight different segments of shared text, set off by commas, with different-colored highlighters; practice reading these sentences out loud.<br><br>• find semicolons, colons, and dashes in independent reading; copy one sentence onto a sentence strip. |
| **GUIDED PRACTICE**<br>4 days | • study several of the sentence strips gathered in earlier lessons as mentors for comma usage and explain different forms of comma usage; model reading aloud for fluency and expression.<br><br>• explore various examples of the dash on the sentence strips— including using pairs of this mark to set off a clause with greater emphasis than a comma, and using a single dash to attach clarifying information to the end of a sentence.<br><br>• find examples of colons and semicolons in sentence strips; review rules for usage.<br><br>• ask students to list any other pausing punctuation marks they have encountered, such as parentheses and ellipses; compare these marks to the others: How are they the same? How are they different? | • read independently, finding and naming at least one example of comma usage; mark this spot with a sticky note and share with a partner.<br>• find one use of a dash in independent reading; mark this spot with a sticky note and share with a partner.<br>• find one use of the colon in independent reading; mark this spot with a sticky note and share with a partner.<br>• find an example of ellipses or parentheses in independent reading; mark this spot with a sticky note and share with a partner. |

| COMMITMENT<br>1 day | • think out loud to explain and articulate the differences between each of the marks studied in this unit; reflect on how this learning will help students with their fluency and comprehension. | • meet in small groups to discuss their favorite pausing punctuation and to create their own written explanations of pausing punctuation. |
| --- | --- | --- |
| **TOTAL: 10 DAYS** | | |

# Using Pausing Punctuation in Writing

**CONVENTIONS**

## Why Teach This?

- To allow students to experiment with the use of several forms of pausing punctuation.
- To help our students gain greater command and fluency in crafting compound and complex sentences.

## Framing Questions

- How can we take what we are learning about pausing punctuation in reading and apply it to our own writing?
- How will this understanding help us to become more powerful writers?

## Unit Goals

- Students will use the comma properly in a series.
- Students will apply their growing understanding of commas to set off phrases and clauses.
- Students will apply their growing understanding of using a comma and a coordinating conjunction to join two sentences.
- Students will experiment with using other forms of pausing punctuation in intentional ways.

## Anchor Text

- Newbery acceptance speech from Lois Lowry (available at www.loislowry.com)

| **Unit Assessment** Using Pausing Punctuation in Writing | | | CONVENTIONS |
|---|---|---|---|
| Student name: | EMERGING | DEVELOPING | INDEPENDENT |
| Uses the comma properly in series and lists. | | | |
| Demonstrates understanding of the comma to set off phrases or clauses. | | | |
| Experiments with other forms of pausing punctuation. | | | |
| Connects the use of pausing punctuation to the desired phrasing in written speeches. | | | |
| Presents speech to the class with fluency and expression. | | | |

| Stage of the Unit | Focused Instruction<br>You will | Independent Practice<br>Students will |
|---|---|---|
| **IMMERSION**<br>2 days | • read a short excerpt from Lois Lowry's 1994 acceptance speech; model making pre-writing plans for your own speech about yourself as a writer (where you get your ideas, what writing means to you, etc.).<br><br>• using a preplanning web and a writing prompt (Where do you get your ideas as a writer?), begin to draft your speech in front of your students. | • brainstorm (with a partner) their own ideas for a speech about where they get their writing ideas; list ideas in writing notebooks.<br><br>• create a preplanning web in response to the shared prompt; use the web to begin writing a draft of their speeches. |
| **IDENTIFICATION**<br>1 day | • revisit your speech draft with class as a shared reading and think aloud where you intend to pause when you give your speech; highlight these spots and decide what forms of pausing punctuation would best be used to accomplish this intention; add these marks. | • reread their draft speech, determining where they want to pause as they give their speeches; highlight these spots, deciding what punctuation to use, and reread aloud to a partner to check for planned phrasing. |
| **GUIDED PRACTICE**<br>4 days | • read another excerpt from Lowry's speech; use this to inspire you to add new thoughts to your own speech.<br><br>• revisit new text you've written for your speech; as you phrase out loud for your students, highlight these spots and notice the appropriate punctuation you added yesterday.<br><br>• revisit the mentor speech by Lois Lowry and look at an example of where she has linked her ideas into a complex sentence (see the sixth paragraph of her speech); model revising a sentence or two of your own speech to merge or elaborate on sentences using pausing punctuation. | • continue to draft speeches, returning to individual webs to find new ideas or inspirations.<br><br>• continue to draft speeches, using pausing punctuation to suggest where they plan to pause; read aloud side by side with a partner and have the partner check whether punctuation matches verbal pauses.<br><br>• revisit and revise their speeches, experimenting with combining sentences and adding new punctuation; read out loud side by side with a partner and have the partner check whether punctuation matches verbal pausing.<br><br>• rehearse their speeches. |

| | | |
|---|---|---|
| **GUIDED PRACTICE** *(continued)* | • model practicing your speech—maintaining eye contact, projecting voice, adjusting pace, leaving thinking and pausing spots; list expectations for speech-making with class. | |
| **COMMITMENT** 3 days | • introduce your students as they present their speeches to the class; evaluate their written drafts on the use of pausing punctuation and their actual speeches on fluency and phrasing. (3 days) | • present speeches to classmates.<br>• write a personal reflection on learning. |
| **TOTAL: 10 DAYS** | | |

# The Power of Poetry

The poet Billy Collins was asked, "Why do people turn to poetry in hard times?" He responded, "Poetry tells the history of the human heart." Fourth graders love poetry because they have big hearts. They are old enough to feel the wounds of the world and young enough to still believe magic will cure it. The nuances of poetry suit their own changing moods, at once playful and sunny, and at the next moment, worried and preoccupied. From the silliness of Shel Silverstein to the seriousness of Naomi Shihab Nye, our students can relate to poetry in all its moods.

Fourth graders are still young enough to see things for the first time: their first rainbow, their first cocoon. Images strike them and move them. This unit explores the power and magic of the captured image. Your students have been learning a lot this year about how powerful words are in capturing ideas, emotions, and opinions. Now image, too, can be captured, held forever in the cocoon of a poem.

## Exploring Mood and Imagery in Poetry | STRATEGY

### Why Teach This?

- To uncover the purpose of sensory language in poetry.
- To help readers of poetry learn that images connote feelings, and these feelings are a way of uncovering the meaning of a poem.

### Framing Question

- What is the purpose of mood and imagery in poetry?

### Unit Goals

- Students will identify the mood of a poem and connect this interpretation to evidence in the text.
- Students will explore the significance of imagery in key poems.
- Students will deepen their ability to move beyond the overt meaning of a poem.

### Anchor Texts

Examples of sensory images that imply a deeper meaning:

- "Grandmother's Spit" by Andrew Hudgins
- "I'd Mark With the Sunshine" by Kalli Dakos
- *Soul Looks Back in Wonder*, edited by Tom Feelings
- "Waterfall" by Lilian Moore
- "When Granny Made My Lunch" by Bobbi Katz
- "Where I'm From" by George Ella Lyon
- "Writing Past Midnight" by Alice Schertle

Examples of metaphor in poetry:

- *Angels Ride Bikes and Other Fall Poems/Los Ángeles Andan en Bicicleta y Otros Poemas de Otoño* by Francisco X. Alarcon
- "Dragonfly" by Georgia Heard
- "Every Cat Had a Story" by Naomi Shihab Nye

Examples of extended metaphor in poetry:
- "The Boxing Match" by Lillian Morrison
- "CD a Poem" by Lee Bennett Hopkins
- "How Do I Know When a Poem Is Finished?" by Naomi Shihab Nye
- "Longhouse Song" by Joseph Bruchac

Note: All of the individual poems can be found in *Seeing the Blue Between: Advice and Inspiration for Young Poets*, compiled by Paul B. Janeczko.

| Unit Assessment Exploring Mood and Imagery in Poetry | | | STRATEGY |
|---|---|---|---|
| Student name: | EMERGING | DEVELOPING | INDEPENDENT |
| Defines image and finds an example in a poem. | | | |
| Defines mood and can name the mood of a poem. | | | |
| Monitors his or her emotional response to a poem and uses this to unlock possible deeper meaning(s). | | | |

| Stage of the Unit | Focused Instruction<br>You will | Independent Practice<br>Students will |
|---|---|---|
| IMMERSION<br>3 days | • read "Grandmother's Spit" aloud to your students and explore the imagery the poet presents.<br>• read "When Granny Made My Lunch" and think aloud about the feelings that the poem elicits.<br>• read "Every Cat Had a Story" aloud; discuss how certain images conjure feelings in readers of poetry and how these images may mean different things to different readers. | • explore imagery in their own independent poems, marking favorite descriptions; share these with a partner.<br>• read poetry independently; find one poem that elicits a strong emotional reaction and share with a partner.<br>• read poetry independently and connect imagery to an emotional reaction; consider what the poet intended. |

| IDENTIFICATION 3 days | • define mood and imagery; identify examples of both in mentor poems.<br><br>• read aloud "Dragonfly" and "CD a Poem" and identify the techniques poets use to create images (metaphor, sensory details, other forms of figurative language).<br><br>• read "I'd Mark With the Sunshine" aloud; model how to use our emotional response to poetry to signal a deeper message to the reader. | • find and name examples of mood and imagery in poems they are reading independently.<br><br>• find and name examples of figurative language in independent poems; connect this language with a feeling or mood.<br><br>• find a favorite poem and identify the images and mood of the poem, using these to form an interpretation; keep track of thinking in reading notebook. |
|---|---|---|
| GUIDED PRACTICE 3 days | • explore specific examples of how some poets use descriptive, sensory language to develop images.<br><br>• revisit "Every Cat Had a Story" and explore how some poets use metaphor to paint a picture and mood; highlight the metaphor and name what it is being compared to.<br><br>• read aloud "Longhouse Song" and explore how some poets use extended metaphor to create a single image with a suggested message. | • find favorite examples of descriptive, sensory details in independent poems; connect these details to the poet's larger purpose.<br><br>• find favorite examples of metaphor in independent poems; connect these descriptions to the larger purpose of the poet.<br><br>• read from several shared texts featuring extended metaphor; notice how each poet stretches the metaphor across the breadth of his subject matter. |
| COMMITMENT 1 day | • celebrate your favorite poem by reading it aloud to the class, naming the image and emotion and then sharing your personal interpretation. | • find a favorite poem from reading and copy it into their reading notebook; write a caption to accompany the poem that names the image and emotion that the poem elicits, and then provide a personal interpretation. |
| **TOTAL: 10 DAYS** | | |

# Finding Inspiration in Poetry

## Why Teach This?

- To give students the chance to write poetry with personal significance.
- To give students opportunities to explore figurative language in poetry—not as decoration, but by intention.

## Framing Questions

- What inspires us as poets?
- How can we write poetry that uses mood and imagery to convey a deeper message?

## Unit Goals

- Students will explore their own poetry inspirations.
- Students will build specific images and mood in their own poetry.

## Anchor Texts

Examples of sensory images that imply a deeper meaning:

- "Grandmother's Spit" by Andrew Hudgins
- "Waterfall" by Lilian Moore
- "When Granny Made My Lunch" by Bobbi Katz
- "Where I'm From" by George Ella Lyon
- "Writing Past Midnight" by Alice Schertle

Examples of metaphor in poetry:

- "Dragonfly" by Georgia Heard
- "Every Cat Had a Story" by Naomi Shihab Nye

Examples of extended metaphor in poetry:

- "The Boxing Match" by Lillian Morrison
- "CD a Poem" by Lee Bennett Hopkins
- "How Do I Know When a Poem Is Finished?" by Naomi Shihab Nye
- "Longhouse Song" by Joseph Bruchac

Note: All of these poems can be found in *Seeing the Blue Between: Advice and Inspiration for Young Poets*, compiled by Paul B. Janeczko.

| Unit Assessment Finding Inspiration in Poetry | | | GENRE |
|---|---|---|---|
| Student name: | EMERGING | DEVELOPING | INDEPENDENT |
| Identifies several possible inspirations for poetry. | | | |
| Uses sensory detail to build vivid images in poetry. | | | |
| Uses metaphor in a thoughtful manner to extend levels of meaning. | | | |
| Writes poems that have more than a literal message for the reader. | | | |

| Stage of the Unit | Focused Instruction<br>You will | Independent Practice<br>Students will |
|---|---|---|
| IMMERSION<br>1 day | • share your own poetry inspirations with the class (examples may include memories, observations, wonderings); list these for your students, then use one to inspire you to write a poem in front of your students. | • list some of their own inspirations in their writing notebooks; use one to develop a poem. |
| IDENTIFICATION<br>2 days | • explain to your students that poets often use these inspirations to say something about themselves, about other people, or about the world; list "messages" you have for the world that could themselves become inspirations for poems; write a poem.<br><br>• explain that some poets use sensory language and figurative language to help convey these messages; use a mentor poem from the reading unit to inspire your own attempt at metaphor or imagery in a new poem. | • list "messages" they have for the world in their writing notebooks; use one as an inspiration to develop a poem.<br><br>• study mentor poems to develop the concept of metaphor in poetry and share these concepts with a partner; use discussion to help them craft possible metaphors to include in future poems (example: War is…, Brothers are…, etc.). |

| GUIDED PRACTICE 6 days | • read aloud "The Boxing Match," modeling using an observation to go deeper in your intention: If you write about the wind, how do you want the reader to feel? What are you saying about the world? | • write poems using observations as an inspiration; say something about the world with the poem. |
|---|---|---|
| | • model using a memory to go deeper with your intention: If you write about a special memory, what connection are you making with the reader? How do you want him to feel? | • write poems using a memory as inspiration; say something to the world about life with the poem. |
| | • model using a wondering about the world as an inspiration; make sure to create a strong image and mood in your poem. | • write poems using wonderings as the inspiration; make sure their poems carry a strong sense of image and mood. |
| | • select a poem you have written in your notebook that you will polish and publish and discuss your decision with the class; reread the poem and consider possible revision strategies. | • select a poem from their writing notebook to polish and publish, and read to a partner: What could be clearer? What are you trying to say? |
| | • reread poem for imagery; model strengthening the image with other sensory details. | • revise poems to strengthen sensory images. |
| | • self-assess the poem in front of the class: What have I done well as a poet? What is still hard for me? | • self-assess individual poems, noticing the strengths of their poetry within the topics studied in this unit. |
| COMMITMENT 1 day | • celebrate poems by having students read them in small groups. | • select a favorite poem written in this unit and share it with others in a small group. |
| TOTAL: 10 DAYS | | |

# From Winter to Spring

Spring is coming and your students are blooming. They have worked hard all year, acquiring new skills and understandings as readers and writers. Now we want them to surge toward their own finish lines in this year, using all the strength and stamina they have built and can now enjoy. Their job is challenging, but fun, too. It is time for them to investigate the "why" of words. Why do authors write? Why do they choose the genre they choose? Why do these texts leave us thinking long after we finish them?

Through the lens of allegory and drama, you will ask your students to begin to wonder about these questions as they interpret the world through wide-awake 9-year-old eyes.

# Chapter 5

SPRING

# The Fourth Grader as Interpreter of the World

*"There was once a boy named Nikolai who sometimes felt uncertain about the right way to act. 'I want to be a good person,' he told his friends, 'but I don't always know the best way to do that.' Nikolai's friends understood and they wanted to help him."*

—from *The Three Questions* by Jon J. Muth

Fourth graders are stirring to a new awareness of social justice and what feels right and wrong to them in the world. They are still playful and kind, childlike and cuddly, but they are beginning to take a long look around them. This season is rich with interpretation of all that: through the art of plays, reading and writing them, as well as through a close study of allegory. Join us now for a last season rich with units of deep and joyous study.

EARLY FALL

LATE FALL

WINTER

SPRING

# SPOTLIGHT on Strategy

- Uncovering Theme: Allegory in Picture Books
- Writing in Response to Issues in Our World

Strategy is thinking about what tools (physical or cognitive) we need and have available to understand and solve a problem, create a plan, and put the plan into action to solve the problem. The effective reader and writer and thinker asks: What are the ways of looking at this problem others have successfully employed, and what are the tricks of the trade I can use? We often spend time teaching different strategies separately (making connections or asking questions, for example) when the real challenge is how to help our children understand what type of strategy would be best used to solve a particular problem, and then identifying the particular strategy to solve it. The strategies we use as readers and writers depend on our intuitive understanding of what is happening in that moment as we read and write and how that relates to the goal we are trying to achieve. By properly identifying the problem, we can use the right strategy to fix it.

In *Strategies That Work*, Stephanie Harvey and Anne Goudvis (2000) write:

"The term *strategic reading* refers to thinking about reading in ways that enhance learning and understanding. Researchers who explicitly taught students strategies for determining important ideas (Gallagher, 1986), drawing inferences (Hansen, 1981), and asking questions (Gavelek & Raphael, 1985) found that teaching these thinking/reading strategies improved students' overall comprehension of text. Research by Palincsar and Brown (1984), and Paris, Lipson, and Wixon (1983), however, suggests that it isn't enough for students to simply understand a given strategy. They must know when, why, and how to use it."

In these next units, we will take a close look at how we can help our students become more strategic in thinking about theme, allegory, and symbolism as readers, and we will explore how we feel about these world issues as writers. For more information on strategy units for your fourth grade readers and writers and how we can categorize strategies so as to teach them effectively, see pages 73 through 79 in *The Complete 4 for Literacy*.

# Seeing the Big Picture

Fourth graders are by nature thematic: if they love soccer, their walls at home are full of soccer posters. If they love animals, they dream of them in school and write about them every chance they get. They are natural theme-builders, natural theme-creators. Our fourth graders are ready to look beyond simple plot and into the heart of a story: What is the author trying to say to us?

These days, bookstores and libraries are full of an incredible selection of sophisticated picture books that we can use as tools to help our students uncover and explore the subtleties of theme.

## Uncovering Theme: Allegory in Picture Books

STRATEGY

### Why Teach This?

- To introduce students to theme in an age-appropriate way that allows for reading, rereading, and discussion to build a growing understanding of larger issues embedded in text.
- To uncover the method(s) for revealing theme as we read.

### Framing Questions

- What is theme? How can you recognize theme in literature?
- Why is it important to search for and recognize theme as we read?

### Unit Goals

- Students will be introduced to anthropomorphism and allegory in picture books and folktales.
- Students will infer theme from short allegorical text.
- Students will defend interpretations using details from the text.
- Students will use opinions from classmates to revise personal interpretations of text or consider alternative interpretations.

## Anchor Texts/Resources:

Upper elementary–grade picture books including allegory tales, social commentary, and issues-based literature:

- *Amelia's Road* by Linda Jacobs Altman
- *The Big Box* by Toni Morrison and Slade Morrison
- *Feathers and Fools* by Mem Fox
- *Fox* by Margaret Wild
- *Gleam and Glow* by Eve Bunting
- *The Other Side* by Jacqueline Woodson
- *Peace Crane* by Sheila Hamanaka
- *Riding the Tiger* by Eve Bunting
- *The Stranger* by Chris Van Allsburg
- *Tree of Hope* by Amy Littlesugar

Folktales and fables:

- *Aesop's Fables* by Aesop
- *Fables* by Arnold Lobel
- *The People Could Fly: American Black Folktales* by Virginia Hamilton
- *Spider* magazine

Short stories:

- *Every Living Thing* by Cynthia Rylant

## Resource Sheets

- Picture Book Themes (Resource 5.1)
- Theme Bookmark (Resource 5.2)

| **Unit Assessment** Uncovering Theme: Allegory in Picture Books | | | STRATEGY |
|---|---|---|---|
| Student name: | EMERGING | DEVELOPING | INDEPENDENT |
| Understands the concept of anthropomorphism. | | | |
| Understands the concept of allegory. | | | |
| Is able to state theme, avoiding character names and plot details. | | | |
| Elaborates on his or her personal interpretation of theme, using examples from the text. | | | |
| Explains the steps used in uncovering theme. | | | |
| Makes multiple interpretations of allegorical text. | | | |

| Stage of the Unit | Focused Instruction<br>You will | Independent Practice<br>Students will |
|---|---|---|
| **IMMERSION**<br>4 days | • read aloud from *Feathers and Fools* by Mem Fox and introduce your class to the concept of anthropomorphism—attributing uniquely human qualities to animals.<br><br>• revisit *Feathers and Fools* by Mem Fox and introduce your class to the concept of allegory, in which individuals and actions are equated with a deeper meaning; ask your students to uncover the meaning that lies beyond the narrative itself in this picture book.<br><br>• read aloud *Riding the Tiger* by Eve Bunting, asking your students what this story reminds them of in the world; explore the allegory in this tale.<br><br>• read aloud *The Other Side* by Jacqueline Woodson, asking students what larger issue this story presents; notice that this book carries a message without using animals, but instead uses symbols; explain this is still allegory, as it has a literal and a symbolic meaning. | • read several short fables with a partner, discussing how the animals personify human emotions and traits.<br><br>• read a folktale with a partner and explore what the author is trying to tell the reader: what is the allegorical message?<br><br>• reread the text of *Riding the Tiger* with a partner, exploring how such an unlikely tale could make so much sense to them as readers; find examples in the text to spark discussion.<br><br>• revisit one of Cynthia Rylant's short stories from *Every Living Thing*; read in search of the larger issue presented in one of the stories, and ask whether her stories are allegory. |
| **IDENTIFICATION**<br>4 days | • list issues that children's authors like to write about, referring to familiar picture book text in creating the list.<br><br>• explain that these issues are considered themes in literature, and create a working definition of theme (the theme of a fable is its moral, the theme of an allegory is the social significance of an issue, theme is an author's point of view on an important subject). | • read a selected picture book with a partner and explore the issue presented in this book: Does it use anthropomorphism? Allegory?<br><br>• read another selected picture book with a partner and uncover the theme of the book; explore whether they and their partner agree on the theme.<br><br>• trade reading notebooks and respond in writing to another classmate's interpretation of theme; share their writing with a partner. |

| | | |
|---|---|---|
| **IDENTIFICATION** *(continued)* | • read *Fox* by Margaret Wild and write in response to the reading, asking what your students think the theme of this book is; discuss whether stories can have more than one theme, asking whether different students can have different interpretations.<br><br>• name books or stories that have similar themes. | • work in small groups to read and share text in author sets (Eve Bunting, Cynthia Rylant, Leo Lionni, Dr. Seuss, Maurice Sendak, D. B. Johnson, Allen Say, Ed Young, etc.); work to uncover possible common themes by sharing their thoughts about their stories. |
| **GUIDED PRACTICE**<br><br>6 days | • discuss how a book's theme is not its plot or concept, that when we state theme we avoid using character names or specific details in the story, but rather we state a point; model several theme statements for *Fox* as an example of this process.<br><br>• outline steps to uncover theme; present the Theme Bookmark (Resource 5.2) and use the bookmark to review *Feathers and Fools*.<br><br>• read aloud *The Big Box*; model focusing on character change and character relationships, asking what the characters represent; link this to theme.<br><br>• revisit *Fox*; model noticing the plot—not what happened, but why: why would the author have the fox abandon the bird? Link this to a statement of theme.<br><br>• revisit the picture books *The Big Box*, *Riding the Tiger*, and *The Other Side*; model identifying craft clues—repetitive language, mood, symbols—and link this to theme.<br><br>• model your emotional response to several picture books already read; think aloud about why you connected strongly with the text: what emotion was at work? Link this to theme. | • practice stating theme after reading a picture book with a partner; write working theme statements in reading notebooks.<br><br>• use the Theme Bookmark to practice uncovering theme in a new picture book.<br><br>• read a new picture book, focusing this time on character; consider what the characters represent in determining theme.<br><br>• reread yesterday's picture book with a partner, looking at the plot and asking themselves why the writer moved the plot in this direction—what was she trying to show us? Link this to an interpretation of theme.<br><br>• work in small groups with key picture book texts (*Tree of Hope*, *Peace Crane*, *Amelia's Road*, and *The Stranger*); read in search of symbols that will lead the group to theme.<br><br>• revisit the picture book that elicited the strongest emotional response in this unit: why did you connect with this text? Link this connection to a statement of theme. |

| COMMITMENT 2 day | • ask students what they have learned about allegory and uncovering theme; connect this to future reading.<br>• model creating a theme statement and symbol for a favorite text. | • respond to the framing unit questions in writing, rehearsing their answers with a partner.<br>• select a favorite text with a partner; craft theme statement and a symbol to represent the theme and illustrate. |
|---|---|---|
| **TOTAL: 16 DAYS** | | |

# Getting Started

When Eve Bunting wrote her picture book *Gleam and Glow*, what was she trying to tell us? Does she agree with war? Does she want us to know the consequences are too great? Or does she want us to believe in hope, despite all odds? *Gleam and Glow* is a picture book about goldfish. On the surface it seems like any other picture book. In an author's note, Bunting shares the real events that inspired her fictionalized tale. She tells us of a real village in Bosnia, a real family forced to flee, and a real war. In a podcast (www.justonemorebook.com), Eve Bunting says, "There are things I want to say, things that are really important to me, and I want to say them to the youngest readers who are capable of understanding what I am saying." She explains her childhood in Ireland and the prejudice she learned at an early age. "When I read in my papers things that disturb me terribly, like homelessness or poverty, or unfairness or injustice of any kind, I get this real desire to say to kids, not that I want you to think the way I think, but I just want you to think, I want you to consider this."

Do not underestimate the power of picture books to convey the deepest of themes. They can and will do that for us. The best picture book writers know that their readers, children, are preoccupied with big concerns, but need scaffolding and support to make sense of the world. This unit is about exploring the themes of the world in supported ways.

# Teaching Materials

As you prepare to teach this unit, you have a few choices to make. You may choose a single picture book author and explore the body of his or her work. Toward this end, you may introduce your class to a brand-new author like Eve Bunting or revisit an old one, such as Dr. Seuss. It can be revelatory for your students to revisit books and realize this time around what they really are trying to say.

Another choice is to gather books around common themes such as war or intolerance, written by different authors. Finally, and most important, you can always select books or authors based on your personal passions and interests. The choices are up to you.

**Picture Book Themes**

| Book Title | Author | Theme |
|---|---|---|
| Henry Climbs a Mountain | D. B. Johnson | Human rights, civil disobedience |
| Henry Builds a Cabin | D. B. Johnson | Simple living, respect for nature |
| Where the Wild Things Are | Maurice Sendak | Mastering anger and fear |
| Seven Blind Mice | Ed Young | Working together, seeing the big picture |
| The Three Questions | Jon J. Muth, Leo Tolstoy | Compassion, living in the moment |
| Stranger in the Mirror | Allen Say | Age discrimination, accepting differences |
| The Sign Painter | Allen Say | Following dreams |
| Dreamland | Roni Schotter | Importance of imagination, following dreams |
| The Dot | Peter H. Reynolds | Encouragement, compassion, belief in oneself |
| The Other Side | Jacqueline Woodson | Racism, segregation |
| White Socks Only | Evelyn Coleman | Racism |
| Prayer for the Twenty-First Century | John Marsden | Fear, hope, learning from mistakes |
| Harold and the Purple Crayon | Crockett Johnson | Power of imagination |
| The Carrot Seed | Ruth Krauss | Conviction, faith, perseverance |
| Riding the Tiger | Eve Bunting | Peer pressure, gangs, bullying |
| Terrible Things | Eve Bunting | Racism, intolerance |
| Fox | Margaret Wild | Greed, envy, friendship |
| Feathers and Fools | Mem Fox | Consequences of war, appreciating others' differences, tolerance |
| The Big Box | Toni Morrison and Slade Morrison | Conformity, individuality, creativity |
| Gleam and Glow | Eve Bunting | Hope, overcoming adversity |
| The Lorax | Dr. Seuss | Humans' impact on the environment |
| Swimmy | Leo Lionni | Cooperation |
| The Seed | Isabel Pin | Antiwar message |
| Peace Crane | Sheila Hamanaka | Urban violence, war |
| Amelia's Road | Linda Jacobs Altman | Displacement, setting down roots |
| Tree of Hope | Amy Littlesugar | Hope |
| The Stranger | Chris Van Allsburg | Renewal, change |

RESOURCE 5.1

## Choosing Teaching Texts

In Resource 5.1, we offer you a starter list of picture books, each of which tackles tough and interesting subjects.

## Choosing Student Texts

Picture books can be challenging for fourth graders to interpret independently. Read aloud from the picture books and model your interpretation for students while they practice similar thinking in equally short but simpler text, such as fables and folktales. You may also have students revisit the text from your picture books as a shared reading activity after you have read the book aloud to search for their own interpretation. As your students gain some practice in reading for larger issues, you might shift into short stories, by revisiting the realistic fiction in Cynthia Rylant's collection *Every Living Thing*. Finally, allow them to move into other picture book texts with partners to help uncover theme.

## Differentiation

Steer your vulnerable readers toward simple fables with clear messages and simple plots. The choice of text will be the scaffold they need. Encourage your strong readers to look for multiple interpretations of a text and support each possible theme with examples from the story. Or ask them to work in more realistic forms of fiction, as this will be harder. In *The Other Side* by Jacqueline Woodson, they will hear a story of a girl who wants to make friends, but isn't allowed to cross over her fence because it isn't "safe." Students will be able to connect with the subtle hints of segregation presented by the author, and conclude that the fence is a metaphor, and "sitting on the fence" is a gentle way for the author to explore the idea of breaking down the barriers of racism.

# Stages of the Unit

## Immersion

Read aloud allegory-based picture books. Introduce your class to the idea of *anthropomorphism*, where an author gives animals uniquely human characteristics, and *allegory*, where a text has been written to deliver a second distinct meaning, partially hidden inside the literal events. Explore why an author would choose to do this. Hint at, but don't give away, your own interpretation of the texts. Ask your students to think about deeper meanings in the texts. Then give your students short fables, folktales, or copies of the picture books to explore the possible messages embedded in these stories. Finally, apply these strategies to a realistic-fiction picture book, like *The Other Side* by Jacqueline Woodson. Point out how the author conveys a similarly important message to us as readers without using symbols that are harder to interpret. As you explore the symbol of the fence in *The Other Side*, your students can hunt for symbols in Cynthia Rylant's short stories. All of her animals are symbols of saving people from their own loneliness, from other people, or from themselves.

## Identification

Take the big ideas uncovered in the first three read-aloud texts and list them as "issues" in the world. Add to this list with other issues that writers like to write about, like those listed in Resource 5.1. Read quotes from authors or play radio interviews and podcasts for your students. Let students hear the voices of their authors talking about why they write issue-based fiction for children. Begin to chart book titles, authors, and themes. Look for connections across authors, but within themes. Below is an example of one class chart completed during this unit by a group of fourth graders studying a common theme.

| Book Title | Author | Theme |
| --- | --- | --- |
| The Wall | Eve Bunting | Heroism, consequences of war |
| Gleam and Glow | Eve Bunting | Hope in the face of war |
| Feathers and Fools | Mem Fox | Consequences of intolerance, war |
| Prayer for the Twenty-First Century | John Marsden | Fear, hope, learning from our mistakes |
| The Seed | Isabel Pin | Borders, war, territory, bridging peace |
| Peace Crane | Sheila Hamanaka | Urban violence, war |

The key to this stage is to work with your students to create a definition of theme. It is theme they are searching for, as they explore alternative meanings for the stories they are reading. But theme is, by nature, elusive. We must search for it and then name it.

## Guided Practice

Students uncover and articulate theme during Guided Practice. Most young readers will want to use details from the stories as they try to give voice to their interpretation. We counter this tendency during this stage, encouraging them instead to make a statement that is connected to the world. To help students in this process of uncovering and stating theme, we ask them to use our Theme Bookmark (Resource 5.2).

If students are grasping theme well in the allegory texts, add a layer of difficulty to your instruction—either for individual students, small ability-based groups, or for the whole class. Pull or revisit picture books that deliver their thematic messages through symbolism. For example, study the tiger as a symbol of peer pressure and gangs in *Riding the Tiger* by Eve Bunting.

## Commitment

In the closing days of this unit, ask students what they have learned about reading that will help them as they grow. Offer your students the opportunity to select a favorite picture book, craft a theme statement, and illustrate a symbol of their own design to represent theme. These can be assembled into a paper quilt of understanding at the end of the unit.

# Day-by-Day Lessons

### DAY 1 Immersion

## Focused Instruction

- Read aloud from *Feathers and Fools* by Mem Fox.

*Some authors use animals to tell us a story. But their intention from the beginning is not to tell us a cute animal tale. It is to tell us something about being human. When a writer does this, when she gives animals like swans and peacocks human personalities, this is called "anthropomorphism." What human traits do the birds have in the story? How do they act like humans, rather than birds?*

## Independent Practice

*Folktales and fables are another place where you can find anthropomorphism. Today you are going to read several short fables with a partner. Think about the human characteristics or traits that the authors of these fables give to the animals.*

## Wrap-Up

*Let's list the traits that different authors have given to the animals in their stories. What do we notice about this list?*

### DAY 2 Immersion

## Focused Instruction

*Today we are going to look back on yesterday's story,* Feathers and Fools *by Mem Fox. What do you think Mem Fox was trying to tell us about being a person in our world?*

- Take a picture walk back through the picture book. Point out key scenes.
- List student responses to your question.

*When authors use animals to teach us lessons about being human, they are writing allegory. This is a form of literature that has two meanings: the story of the birds, and then the underlying, more important message that the author has for us to uncover.*

## Independent Practice

*You are each going to read the same folktale with a partner, so we can talk about it together. When you are done reading, meet with your partner and see if you can figure out what the author is trying to tell the reader. What is the allegorical message?*

## Wrap-Up

- Students share possible interpretations.

### DAY 3 Immersion

#### Focused Instruction

- Read aloud *Riding the Tiger* by Eve Bunting.

*This is another allegorical tale. Tigers do not give rides to boys in the middle of cities. They don't talk or brag or tease people. So what does this story remind you of in the world?*

- List connections and possible interpretations.

#### Independent Practice

*I have given each partnership a typed excerpt from* Riding the Tiger. *Revisit this text with your partner and find examples that help support your own opinion as to what this story is really about. Leave sticky notes on these text details so you can refer to them later.*

#### Wrap-Up

- Encourage a powerful conversation about the issue(s) raised in the text.

### DAY 4 Immersion

#### Focused Instruction

*Today I am going to read a different kind of picture book. There are no talking animals, just kids like you. There are no unbelievable events, only kids playing and talking. But I believe this book still presents some important issues. I believe this book is also an example of allegory. As you listen, see if you can figure out the symbolic as well as the literal meaning of the story.*

- Read aloud *The Other Side* by Jacqueline Woodson. Stop two or three times as you read to get feedback and theories from your students.

#### Independent Practice

*Select one Cynthia Rylant's short stories to read today, and just as we did with* The Other Side, *search for the symbolic meaning of the story. Since there is no anthropomorphism, your job is harder. But see what you can figure out. Ask yourself what the author is trying to tell you about life.*

#### Wrap-Up

- List possible interpretations of the Rylant stories.
- Look for connections in message across her texts. What do pets represent in each story?

## DAY 5 Identification

### Focused Instruction

*So far we have read three picture books together, and each of you has read several fables or folktales and one short story. What do the writers of these stories like to write about? What issues in the world do they like to explore?*

- Students turn and talk to discuss.

*Today we are going to begin to make a list of the books and stories we read and what the issues are that we think the author wants us to think about. We will keep adding to this list as we move through the unit.*

### Independent Practice

- Partners choose picture books from baskets of preselected books.
- Partners read in search of the issue presented in the book.

### Wrap-Up

*So was your picture book an example of allegory? Does it use anthropomorphism? Let's hear a few partnerships share their interpretations of their picture books.*

## DAY 6 Identification

### Focused Instruction

*When authors tell two stories with one book—the events on the page, and then the message they have for us as readers—we refer to the message as the theme of the book. The theme of a fable is its lesson or moral. The theme of an allegory is the author's point of view on a subject. So we could say one theme in* Feathers and Fools *is that we must be tolerant of one anothers' differences. And we could say that one theme in* Riding the Tiger *is that peer pressure is hard to avoid, and another theme in this book is respect is not the same thing as fear.*

  *Let's create our own definition of theme.*

### Independent Practice

*Today you and your partner get to choose the picture book you are going to read together. When you are done reading, discuss your interpretation. What is the theme of your book? Do you agree on the theme? Or do you have different interpretations?*

### Wrap-Up

- Add book titles and student interpretations to the growing list of books and themes begun on Day 5.

## DAY 7 Identification

### Focused Instruction

- Read aloud *Fox* by Margaret Wild (if you taught the Using Modifiers writing unit in Chapter 2, your students will already be familiar with this text).

*Instead of talking about what you think the theme of* Fox *is, sit with your reading notebooks and write your thoughts down first. Then we will share them. As you write, try to move yourself toward a statement of theme. This is another allegory, and it features anthropomorphism. The author isn't trying to teach us something about dogs and birds and foxes. What is her message to us as humans?*

- Students share snippets from their reading notebooks.

*This book is great for helping us see that our interpretations of theme are very personal. They are the result of who we are and what we are thinking about at the time. Books can have more than one interpretation. Some of you can think this is a book about the consequences of temptation, others can say it is about friendship, and some will say it is about jealousy. You would all be correct, as I can return to the text and find examples that support each of these ideas. The interpretation is harder to prove when you can't find any text evidence.*

### Independent Practice

- Students trade reading notebooks. Each student returns to the text of *Fox* to see if they agree with the notebook writer's interpretation and responds to this interpretation by writing the owner of the reading notebook a response.

### Wrap-Up

*Who found that their partner had a believable interpretation of theme? Would you like to share what you wrote back to her?*

- Students meet in partnerships and share their responses to one another.

## DAY 8 Identification

### Focused Instruction

*If we look at our growing book and theme list, we can see that writers often choose to write about similar themes.*

- Note recurrent themes.

*Today I am going to put you in author groups. Read from the picture books in these collections, and then meet and discuss some possible common themes across text. If you think your books or some of your books share a theme, go back into the books and find evidence to prove your interpretation. Then we can add these books to our list.*

## Independent Practice

- Students read from author baskets.
- Groups meet to share possible common themes.

## Wrap-Up

*As I walked around and listened to your group conversations, I noticed that several different authors liked to write about war and violence. The Eve Bunting group read two stories that had this theme,* The Wall *and* Gleam and Glow. *But we could add Mem Fox's book to this, too, couldn't we? Why do you suppose such different writers, from such different lives and countries, would write about similar themes?*

### DAY 9 Guided Practice

## Focused Instruction

*Finding theme is one of the hardest things to do. The author hides her message for us in gentler stories that allow us to think about and consider difficult issues. Today we are going to practice stating theme. Just as it is hard to find it, it is equally hard to say it. Let's look back at* Fox *by Margaret Wild. Together we will write several theme statements for this book. Notice how I don't use character names or plot details. Notice how I make a clear statement or point. Notice how I try to say the theme in a sentence and not a single word. If a book is about friendship, I want to push myself further and ask: What does the author want me to know about friendship?*

- Create multiple theme statements with the class that exemplify the elements you desire.

## Independent Practice

- Students read a new picture book with a partner.
- Students discuss themes and write working theme statements in reading notebooks.

## Wrap-Up

- Create a list of theme statements to hang in the classroom.

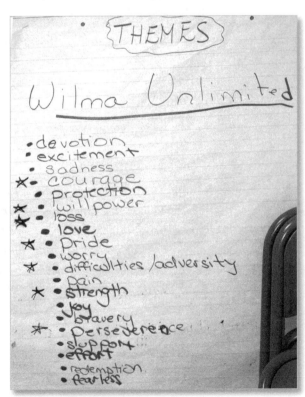

### DAY 10 Guided Practice

#### Focused Instruction

- Introduce the Theme Bookmark (Resource 5.2).
- Use to review *Feathers and Fools* by Mem Fox.

#### Independent Practice

- Students use the Theme Bookmark to practice uncovering theme in a new picture book.

#### Wrap-Up

*Does it help to have the bookmark? What does it remind you to do as a reader when searching for theme?*

### DAY 11 Guided Practice

#### Focused Instruction

- Read aloud *The Big Box* by Toni Morrison and Slade Morrison.

*This book has a message for us, and it's clearly allegory because children don't get sent to boxes where they are locked inside. But the authors have something they are trying to say. One good place to practice looking for theme is to study character. Let's look at the three children in this book. What does each of them represent?*

#### Independent Practice

- Students read new picture books, focusing on character to uncover theme.

#### Wrap-Up

*Who wants to share who or what their character represents?*

### DAY 12 Guided Practice

#### Focused Instruction

*Another way to uncover theme is to study plot—not what happened, but why. Let's go back and look at a few of our picture books from this unit. In* Fox, *Dog and Magpie had a great relationship; they helped each other through a very difficult time and were supporting each other. Then the author has a fox come along. Why? What was she trying to say? And why was the new character a fox instead of a rabbit or a deer?*

## Independent Practice

- Review several key picture books in partnerships, studying plot developments as hints to theme.

- Students link this to an interpretation of theme.

## Wrap-Up

*Every decision an author makes is an intentional one. If something surprising or unusual happens, that is your clue to dig around for the significance of this event. That is one secret to finding theme.*

## DAY 13 Guided Practice

### Focused Instruction

*So far we've noticed that studying characters or studying plot can help us uncover theme. There is another technique that can work, too. We need to look at the author's craft— how she has written her story. Sometimes writers will leave clues by using repetitive language or symbols or a particular mood in their stories. Let's look at* The Big Box. *Did you notice when I read this book to you the first time that the authors repeat the phrase "and the doors only open one way" over and over again? And also, the word* freedom *appears 16 times! Repeating words or phrases are a big hint in this book.*

*In* The Other Side, *there is the symbol of the fence. It is both a real fence and a metaphorical one, keeping whites and blacks apart.*

*In* Riding the Tiger, *first Eve Bunting describes the tiger in glorious, exciting, admirable terms, but as the story progresses, her descriptions become more threatening and ominous. You know something bad is going to happen, and that the tiger is no longer such a great friend to the boy. The mood is a dead giveaway that the boy has made the wrong choice to "ride the tiger."*

### Independent Practice

*I have placed copies of several picture books at your tables. Work in small groups to read these books. Each one of them has strong symbols, and these symbols will help you uncover theme. Read independently, and then talk to one another about what you think is going on. What do these symbols represent?*

> ## Symbolism in Because of Winn Dixie
>
> ## By: Seth
>
> In the realistic fiction book <u>Because of Winn Dixie</u> by Kate DiCamillo there are many examples of symbolism. Symbolism is something that stands for something, you can touch, a feeling, a sense, or a problem.
>
> For example Gloria Dump's bottles of alcohol that are hanging on her tree are symbols of mistakes. Gloria hangs up one bottle every time she makes a mistake. The mistakes Gloria calls the ghosts of her past. She pays attention to them so she does not do it again.
>
> Winn Dixie is a symbol for happiness because everywhere he goes with Opal he makes friends for Opal and himself. When Opal moved to Naomi, Florida she had no friends. She has friends now because of Winn Dixie.
>
> Kate DiCamillo put many examples of symbolism into <u>Because of Winn Dixie</u> The next time I write a story I'll try to put a lot of symbolism in my story too.

Here, fourth grader Seth has written a statement of symbolism based on his class read-aloud, *Because of Winn-Dixie.*

**Wrap-Up**

*I listened carefully to the group conversations. The students who read* Amelia's Road *got the symbol right away—it was the tree that she liked to visit. The character had no home, and she traveled with her family everywhere, and all she really wanted to do was "set down roots." What does that expression mean?*

### DAY 14 Guided Practice

### Focused Instruction

*Today we are going to explore the last method for uncovering theme. I am going to go back through some of my favorite picture books from this study, and all I am going to do is remember the feelings I had as I read them. When I read* Fox, *I was angry. I was angry at Fox, but even more angry at Magpie for going with him. When I read* The Big Box, *I was angry, too, but this time at the parents who didn't seem to understand that children need to be children. When I read* The Other Side, *I felt sorry for both girls, who clearly wanted to be friends. And at the end of the book I felt proud of them for finding a solution. If you think about your emotional reaction to a text and ask yourself why the author wants you to feel that way, this is another clue for theme. In* The Big Box, *my anger was due to the unfair treatment and unrealistic expectations for children. Kids are kids, not adults. So my anger led me right to the theme of this book.*

### Independent Practice

*Go back and find the picture book you read in this unit that you had the strongest emotional reaction to. Think about why you connected so strongly to the text. See if this can help you write a theme statement for this book.*

### Wrap-Up

*Let's share the range of emotions we had in connection to our books in this unit.*

## DAY 15 Commitment

### Focused Instruction

*What have you learned about allegory and uncovering theme? How do you think this will help you as a reader going forward?*

### Independent Practice

- After rehearsing their answers with their partners, students write to respond to the framing unit questions: What is theme? How can you recognize theme? Why is it important to search for theme as we read?

### Wrap-Up

- Select students share written responses.

## DAY 16 Commitment

### Focused Instruction

*This is the last day of our unit on theme and allegory. Let us celebrate our experiences by choosing our favorite picture books, creating a theme statement and a visual symbol that represents this theme. Here is the symbol I created for* Fox. *It is a drawing of three friends holding hands. Notice how I didn't use any of the pictures from the book in my illustration, because I wanted to come up with my own picture to represent the theme. I wanted all three friends to hold hands, because this is what I think Fox wanted but didn't know how to ask for. Instead, he broke the chain of friendship by running away with Bird.*

### Independent Practice

- Students choose partners based on favorite picture books.

- Students conceive and illustrate a symbolic image and write a theme statement to match their books.

### Wrap-Up

*Let's all hold up our pictures so everyone can see them. I am going to take all of these squares, and I am going to put them together into a quilt of our thinking. I'll hang this quilt outside for all the other classes to admire. I am so proud of the work you have done in this unit!*

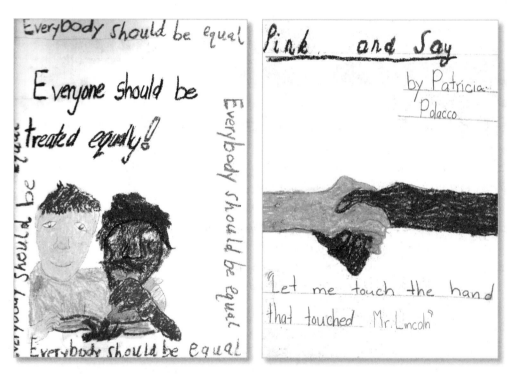

Two students, Aaron and Olivia, pair up to create a theme statement and a visual symbol for *Pink and Say* by Patricia Polacco. In addition to their symbol and their theme statement, they decide to include a key quote from the text.

# Changing the World With Words

Nine-year-olds have strong and passionate opinions about so many things. Your classroom will feel richer for knowing what they are. As Heather Lattimer (2003) says in her book *Thinking Through Genre*, "I want [my students] to be able to take their frustrations, joys, and sorrows, recognize the large issues surrounding their experiences, and craft [writing] that has the power to create change in their communities."

## Writing in Response to Issues in Our World

**STRATEGY**

### Why Teach This?

- To allow students to express their opinions and a point of view about the world.
- To provide opportunities to practice persuasive writing.
- To demonstrate growing insight about the world.

### Framing Questions

- How do the themes in literature inspire me as a writer?
- What do I feel strongly about in the world? What do I want to say to the world?

### Unit Goals

- Students will make connections between their reading and writing lives.
- Students will learn that our thoughts and feelings can inspire our writing ideas.
- Students will practice crafting opinion-based writing in their writing notebooks.
- Students will learn that opinions require examples or facts to back up the argument.

### Anchor Texts

- Student-opinion writing found in children's magazines such as *Creative Kids*, picture books such as *A Little Peace* by Barbara Kerley, *Prayer for the Twenty-First Century* by John Marsden, and *Somewhere Today: A Book of Peace* by Shelly Moore Thomas

### Resource Sheet

- Parent Letter: Writing in Response to Issues in Our World (Resource 5.3)

| Unit Assessment Writing in Response to Issues in Our World | | | STRATEGY |
|---|---|---|---|
| Student name: | EMERGING | DEVELOPING | INDEPENDENT |
| Makes a connection between a shared text and an issue in the world. | | | |
| Develops a personal point of view on this issue. | | | |
| Supports this point of view with examples from his own life. | | | |
| Makes a genre choice based on intention as a writer: Will this be a poem? A picture book? A nonfiction piece? | | | |

| Stage of the Unit | Focused Instruction You will | Independent Practice Students will |
|---|---|---|
| IMMERSION 3 days | • ask students to list issues in the world that concern them as human beings.<br>• ask students to list things they love, dream, or hope for in the world.<br>• read aloud *Prayer for the Twenty-First Century*; discuss the writer's dreams for the world; ask students to add any new issues to their lists. | • write in response to one of the issues that concern them about the world.<br>• write in response to one of the things they love about the world.<br>• write in response to issues raised in the shared texts or taken from their personal lists. |
| IDENTIFICATION 3 days | • read aloud an editorial from *Creative Kids* magazine; identify the purpose of writing about issues in the world.<br>• read aloud *A Little Peace*; choose a topic to develop.<br>• read aloud *Somewhere Today: A Book of Peace*; name the genre choices writers make when they choose to write about issues: poetry, essay, picture books, etc. | • consider how they might convince others of their point of view: What could be said? Select a topic and explore ways to persuade others of their point of view.<br>• choose a topic to develop.<br>• explore genre possibilities for writing topics and choose one. |

| GUIDED PRACTICE 6 days | • model writing to explore your topic, making sure to include your thoughts, feelings, and personal experiences.<br><br>• list other forms of proof to help persuade an audience; model adding this to writing.<br><br>• notice how great issue-based writing begins; model trying out these techniques in your notebook.<br><br>• think about who you are trying to convince: What do they believe? How can you acknowledge their point of view?<br><br>• read your latest writing to the class: is it convincing? Ask the students what you should add.<br><br>• model rereading and revising your draft. | • write to explore their topic, making sure to include thoughts, feelings, and personal experiences.<br><br>• gather other proof; add to their written argument.<br><br>• try out two great beginnings for issue-based writing; choose one.<br><br>• try acknowledging the counterpoint to an argument.<br><br>• read their draft to a partner; ask what should be added to make it more persuasive.<br><br>• reread and revise their draft to strengthen the power of their argument. |
|---|---|---|
| COMMITMENT 1 day | • ask your students to consider what they have learned about writing in response to themes in the world. | • celebrate their writing by reading it out loud to a small group; write a personal reflection on their learning. |
| **TOTAL: 13 DAYS** | | |

# Getting Started

Mahatma Gandhi wrote: "Be the change you wish to see in the world." Fourth graders are feeling their new awareness of the world around them. They see themselves as the big kids now. They feel the power of their new young voices. This unit is an opportunity for them to feel that power and exercise it on the page.

# Teaching Materials

## Choosing Teaching Texts

Locate back issues of the children's magazine *Creative Kids*. In every issue, students submit their own opinion writing under the feature heading "Write On." In this magazine, students slightly older than your class write about school uniforms and bicycle safety and the effects of watching too much television. They also write about issues farther way from home, like illiteracy or world hunger. There are great read-alouds and mentor texts.

Another suggestion is to gather picture books or poems that are written as wishes or dreams or prayers for the people of our world. Examples of these include

*A Little Peace* by Barbara Kerley, *Prayer for the Twenty-First Century* by John Marsden, or the gentler *Somewhere Today: A Book of Peace* by Shelley Moore Thomas. Each of these recommendations present opinion writing in picture book form.

Also, keep an eye out for student-friendly op-ed pieces in your local papers and in *The New York Times* and use them as read-alouds during this unit. It is wonderful for your students to hear your voice reading persuasive nonfiction aloud.

## Differentiation

You will ask your students to explore a range of topics about which they feel strongly. They will have much to choose from as they approach a topic choice, but all of the choices will come from their own writing lives. A vulnerable writer might take on something closer to home and simpler to construct—such as how annoying siblings can be, or how they wish their parents didn't work such long hours. A stronger writer might be interested in the same topics, but will be able to develop them more fully. Or this same writer might take on more worldly and less personal issues that she is exposed to every day through the news and the conversation that centers around the adults in her life. This may mean she wants to write about something happening in world news, or urgent causes such as hunger and poverty. Choosing an appropriate genre for their topic will also help them match their abilities and interests.

# Stages of the Unit

## Immersion

Have fun experimenting with possible topics in this stage. Ask students to think about things that bother them in their families or homes, like brothers or bedtimes. Then ask them to think about things that bother them or they disagree with at school, like indoor recess or gym class. Then ask them to think about things that bother them in their local community, like the skate park that is always closed, or the busy street that is impossible to cross. Finally, ask them to think about things that bother them in the world, like war, or global warming, or racism. You can repeat this same activity the next day, only asking students to list things they love about home, school, town, and country. Each day, following these lessons, students return to their writing spots and take one item on their list and write off of it.

Let parents know what you are working on by sending home a letter with students (see Resource 5.3). They can help to positively reinforce your efforts by sharing their own opinions with their children.

**Parent Letter: Writing in Response to Issues in Our World**

Dear Parents,

It is hard to believe the year has gone by so quickly. Your child has grown so much this year and is stepping up to the challenge of fourth grade! Toward this end, we have been looking at big issues in the world—or at least issues that feel big and important to your child.

We first explored these issues in literature and practiced looking for theme in some very powerful picture books and short stories.

Now we are exploring some of these issues as writers. Your child will be working in his or her writing notebook over the next several days, discovering what it feels like to write about one's opinions.

You can support this work at home by sharing with your child the places you turn to for written opinions—perhaps the editorial page of the newspaper or magazine you read, or a blog you visit on the Internet, or the book reviews you check each week before you head to the library.

Children need to learn that adults are influenced by writing each and every day. Please share your own thoughts and experiences with your child. It will help him or her see the value of this kind of writing in the world.

Warmly,

RESOURCE 5.3

## Identification

Your students select a topic from those they have explored already in their notebooks and develop this topic more fully. Will their piece become a poem? A picture book? A letter to the principal or a parent? Students will identify the qualities of opinion writing.

## Guided Practice

Your students write to explore their topics. Model each step you ask your students to take, including making a genre choice, selecting a mentor text, looking at great beginnings, and drafting and revising their writing.

## Commitment

At the end of this unit, ask your students what they have learned. Do they feel more connected to the world by putting their words out into the open? Do they think they have the power to change someone's mind? Do they have an official audience for their piece? Will they send it out into the world?

# Day-by-Day Lessons

### DAY 1 Immersion

### Focused Instruction

*Today we are going to undertake a quick listing activity in our writing notebooks. I am going to ask you a series of questions, and each time I ask, I want you to list a few answers to my question. These answers will be things that bother you in the world. Ready?*

- Ask students to list things that bother them at home, at school, in town, and as a human being in the world.
- Share some of the responses. Ask students to asterisk their favorite topic—the one they feel most strongly about.

### Independent Practice

*For writing time today I want you to take the topic that you starred in your notebook, write it at the top of a new page, and then write in response to this topic. You can write anything you want, but be sure to explore your honest feelings about this topic. Tell us why something bothers you and what you wish you could change about this situation.*

### Wrap-Up

- Writing partners share their writing with each other.

### DAY 2 Immersion

#### Focused Instruction

*Today we are going to do the same listing activity, except this time you are going to list things you love or dream about or hope for in the world. It will be the opposite of yesterday's lists. For example, I hope for peace in every country, but I also hope for more time in my life to read books. These can be big dreams or small ones.*

- Ask students to list things they love or hope for or dream about in their family, in their home, in their school, town, country, world.
- Share some of these responses. Have students asterisk the one that is the most interesting.

#### Independent Practice

*For writing time today, I want you to take the topic that you starred in your notebook, write it at the top of a new page, and then write in response to this topic. You can write anything you want, but just make sure to honestly explore your feelings about this topic. Tell us why you love something so much or what you hope and dream about.*

#### Wrap-Up

- Writing partners share their writing with each other.

### DAY 3 Immersion

#### Focused Instruction

*Today I am going to read aloud from a favorite picture book of mine. It was written by John Marsden and it is called* Prayer for the Twenty-First Century. *What do you think it will be about?*

- Read aloud the picture book.
- Discuss the writer's dreams for the world. Imagine why he wrote this as a picture book instead of as a poem or a speech or an article in the newspaper.

#### Independent Practice

*As you write today, you may choose from one of the items on your lists, or you can choose an issue or theme we have been exploring in our picture books during reading time. Put the topic at the top of a clean page in your notebook and write. You may write anything—just make sure to express your opinion.*

#### Wrap-Up

- Several students share their opinions with the class.

## Focused Instruction

- Read aloud an editorial from "Write On" in *Creative Kids* magazine.
- Discuss the issues raised in this editorial.

*Why do people write books like John Marsden's or editorials like this one? What is the purpose of this kind of writing? The purpose is to try to influence other people, to get them to change their minds or their beliefs or their behaviors.*

## Independent Practice

*As you write today, think about how your writing might change someone's mind. Take a new topic from your lists. Write off that topic, but this time try to include information or ideas or examples that might help convince others of your point of view.*

## Wrap-Up

*What kind of information did you include to try and convince people in your writing today?*

> Athletes are getting more money than you can imagine, and your parents work equally as hard, if not harder, than these athletes. That's not fair, because these athletes love the game they play!
>
> I'm sure there are many many people with almost no money, who'd do anything to get a job. I'm sure lots of these people are just as good people as these athletes.
>
> My dad goes to work every

> day, struggling, almost ten hours, to finish. What's more important, being a good athlete, or a good person?
>
> I go to school over six hours a day, and get paid nothing and athletes play sports, and get paid millions of dollars. Talk about crazy—Alex Rodriguez is getting paid 250 million dollars! One guy playing baseball isn't worth that much!

Here, Aaron chooses to explore the problem with salaries for professional baseball players. As his piece progresses, he defends his position by comparing the hard work that both he and his father do each day, for which neither receives millions of dollars a year!

## DAY 5 Identification

### Focused Instruction

- Read aloud *A Little Peace*.

*You have now been writing about issues for the last week in school and for homework. Today we are all going to choose a topic from those we have explored already. This writer chose to focus on peace. I'm going to share my decision-making with you. I have chosen to write about wishing I had more time to spend with my father because I think I still have a lot to say, and I feel very strongly about it. I could spend the next several days working on it and not feel like I would run out of things to say.*

### Independent Practice

- Students meet in partnerships to read each other's notebooks and provide suggestions on topic choice.
- Individual writers make final topic choices.

### Wrap-Up

- Share final topic choices.

## DAY 6 Identification

### Focused Instruction

*I have thought about my topic, and have decided I am going to turn my writing idea into a letter. I am going to send this letter to my father, because I am writing about how I wish we had more time to spend together. A letter seems like the right choice, because the only audience for my writing is my dad. He is the only person I am trying to convince. Some of you may make other choices because there are different kinds and numbers of people you are trying to convince with your words. Whom will you try to convince? Where can you find this audience?*

- List genre options (letter, speech, editorial, picture book, script).

### Independent Practice

- Students identify their audience and make genre choices.

### Wrap-Up

- Several students share their decision-making process.

## DAY 7 Guided Practice

### Focused Instruction

*Now that I have selected my topic and the form in which my writing will appear, it is time for me to develop my point of view. I am going to put my topic at the top of the page and write to develop my thoughts, my feelings, and to share my personal experiences and memories with my father. I am going to stop several times to reread my writing, to see what else I might include that would help convince my dad to spend more time with me.*

- Model writing to explore your topic in front of your students.

## Independent Practice

*Today you are going to take your topic, and you are going to think about your audience, and you are going to write to try to convince your audience of your point of view. Remember to add your thoughts and feelings and anything else you think might be convincing.*

- Students write to develop their opinion in writing and defend it with examples.

## Wrap-Up

- Several students share their writing pieces.
- Class makes constructive suggestions to strengthen arguments.

### DAY 8 Guided Practice

## Focused Instruction

*Sharing my opinions with my dad may not be enough to convince him. Reminding him of our trips together might make him want to spend more time with me, but how do I make sure I can convince him? Could I include other support that would be convincing? What else could I include?*

- List other forms of proof—facts, statistics, primary research, quotes from experts, and so forth.
- Choose another form of proof and add to your written piece.

## Independent Practice

*Today you need to reread your written argument. What else could you include that would persuade the reader? Use today to gather other proof. You may do some Internet research or interview your classmates. When you have more proof, add this to your written argument to make it more convincing.*

## Wrap-Up

*Who would like to share how they made their writing more convincing today?*

### DAY 9 Guided Practice

## Focused Instruction

*Today we are going to explore different ways to begin our writing. We'll list several on the chart, and then when you go to write I want you to try at least two different ways to begin your piece. Then choose the one you like the best. One way to begin is to start right away with your opinion. Just say what you believe.*

- Model writing a beginning in this fashion for your students.

*Another way is to save your opinion for the end, and start with a story instead. Start with a very visual description of the situation or issue. Since I am writing about time with my father, I think I will start with a memory of hiking with him in the White Mountains. That should get his attention and make him remember the good times we spent together.*

- Model writing this beginning.

## Independent Practice

*Open your notebook to two clean pages, side by side. Try one beginning on one side and another beginning on the other side. When you are done, meet with a partner and choose the beginning you like best.*

## Wrap-Up

*Using a show of hands, who chose a beginning that starts with your opinion? Who started with a description or story? Why did you make the choice you did?*

### DAY 10 Guided Practice

## Focused Instruction

*Who is the audience for your writing? Whom are you trying to convince? Remember, we aren't trying to convince people who already agree with us. It is always a good idea to think about your audience and why they believe what they believe or do what they do. Then you can appeal to them by thinking about your issue from their point of view. I want to tell my father how I feel, so maybe we can spend more time together—just the two of us. He is really busy and so am I, but we need to make more time for each other.*

- Model adding to your writing to reflect the point of view of the audience. Recognize their side of the issue, but still encourage them to consider yours.

## Independent Practice

*As you write today, try to acknowledge how your audience feels about your topic. If you aren't sure, ask a partner what he or she thinks. Then write off your favorite beginning and try to convince them of your point of view.*

## Wrap-Up

- Two students share how they acknowledged the audience's differing point of view in their writing.

## DAY 11 Guided Practice

### Focused Instruction

*Is my writing convincing? Do you think I will convince my dad to find more time to spend with me? What should I add? Is there anything that I should take out? Anything that makes it harder for my dad to agree with me?*

### Independent Practice

- Students read their drafts to a partner. Partners discuss what should be added or removed to make the writing more persuasive and effective.

### Wrap-Up

- Read aloud one student's draft. Discuss.

## DAY 12 Guided Practice

### Focused Instruction

*Today is the last day for my writing. So I need to reread it carefully and make any final changes. What should I check for? How will I know when my writing is ready to publish?*

- Model revising for clarity and persuasiveness.
- Model editing for conventions.

### Independent Practice

- Students finish, revise, and edit their drafts.

### Wrap-Up

- Students share what they fixed when they edited their writing.

## DAY 13 Commitment

### Focused Instruction

*What have you learned about being a writer in this unit? What should we do with our finished writing?*

### Independent Practice

- Students make decisions regarding "publishing." This may include sending letters (have stamps available), submitting for publication, or simply reading their finished writing aloud.
- Students write to answer two of the framing questions of the unit: What do I feel strongly about in the world? What do I want to say to the world?

### Wrap-Up

- Teacher reads aloud one or two written reflections.

## "All the World's a Stage"

Your students play every day. They make up games, change the rules, and play again. They meet, imagine scenes together ("Let's be horse trainers," or, "I'm the teacher, you're the student"), assign roles, and act out their stories. Their imaginations drive the drama in their lives.

One of the best ways to bring drama alive for our students is to allow them to write and stage their own plays. We aren't talking about months of rehearsal and heavy-duty memorization. Instead, fourth graders can use their imaginations to craft their own simple plays, and then act out their plays in a manner that will allow them to feel the power of their words and all of the joy without the pressure of performance. Toward this end, this unit asks students to work in playwriting clubs to create their own three- or four-person simple plays. This should be light and fun, and a great way to get your students up and out of their seats, actively engaged in the pleasures of oral language inside a great literary tradition.

## Reading Plays: An Introduction to Drama

GENRE

### Why Teach This?

- To introduce students to the genre of drama.
- To focus on characters and their interactions, intentions, and motivations.
- To practice fluency through reading dialogue aloud.

### Framing Questions

- How does drama compare to other forms of literature?
- How can we be powerful readers of plays?

### Unit Goals

- Students will learn the key elements, format, and conventions of the play.
- Students will compare and contrast the play with the chapter book.
- Students will practice reading/performing short skits with phrasing and expression.

### Anchor Texts

- A play to read aloud and then perform as a class, such as *How to Eat Like a Child* by Delia Ephron, John Forster, and Judith Kahan (available at www.samuelfrench.com)
- Plays for independent reading during Immersion and Identification, such as *12 Fabulously Funny Folktale Plays* by Justin McCory Martin, *12 Fabulously Funny Fairy Tale* Plays by Justin McCory Martin, *Cinderella Outgrows the Glass Slipper and Other Zany Fractured Fairy Tale Plays* by Joan M. Wolf, and, for the vulnerable readers, *25 Just-Right Plays for Emergent Readers* by Carol Pugliano-Martin
- For stronger readers, plays adapted from the works of Roald Dahl, such as *Charlie and the Chocolate Factory*, adapted by Richard George; *James and the Giant Peach*, adapted by Richard George; *The BFG: A Set of Plays*, adapted by David Wood; *The Twits: A Set of Plays*, adapted by David Wood; *The Witches: A Set of Plays*, adapted by David Wood.

| Unit Assessment Reading Plays: An Introduction to Drama | | | GENRE |
|---|---|---|---|
| Student name: | EMERGING | DEVELOPING | INDEPENDENT |
| Identifies the key differences between reading fiction and drama. | | | |
| Understands the structure and characteristics of a play. | | | |
| Follows the progression of a play without support of narration. | | | |
| Explains the relationships between characters and how this moves the plot forward. | | | |
| Reads dialogue with fluency and expression. | | | |

| Stage of the Unit | Focused Instruction<br>You will | Independent Practice<br>Students will |
|---|---|---|
| IMMERSION<br>3 days | • read aloud an excerpt from a short play like *How to Eat Like a Child*; ask students: "What is a play?" (a story told through dialogue) and "How is reading drama different from reading a chapter book?"<br><br>• continue to read aloud from your play; list the growing observations of a play vs. a chapter book (absence of narration, description).<br><br>• continue to read aloud from your short play; think aloud when you reach a part in the play that is hard(er) to understand. | • read side by side in partnerships from play collections, noting similarities and differences to fiction.<br><br>• read side by side in partnerships from play collections, adding observations about the genre to their reading notebooks.<br><br>• notice when reading a play feels harder than reading a novel or short story. |

| **IDENTIFICATION**<br>4 days | • continue to read aloud your play; use shared reading of an excerpt already read to identify the specific formatting of drama—cast of characters, stage directions using parentheses, dialogue with speaker tags and colons, and so on.<br>• continue to read aloud your play; use shared reading of an excerpt already read to identify the conventions of a play: acts versus chapters, scenes versus paragraphs, stage directions versus narration, dialogue versus exposition.<br>• finish reading the play aloud to your class; review and identify the story elements in the play as the same as those in fiction.<br>• use a passage from a class play to explain that drama focuses on the character, and that the reader's job is to infer as much as possible about a character through his actions and his conversation. | • read and name examples of the cast of characters, stage directions, and speaker tags in their own plays.<br>• read from a collection of short plays, gathering examples of the conventions of a play.<br>• revisit a play read with a partner; use the story elements to retell the play to one another.<br>• revisit a play read with a partner; explore the path of the character(s) in the play: What did they learn about the character? |
|---|---|---|
| **GUIDED PRACTICE**<br>6 days | • explain that the class is going to act out the class play, and that each "group" of actors will select a skit in which to perform.<br>• assign skits to groups, preferably giving groups their first or second choice; model how to choose roles, prepare a list of props, costumes, and so on.<br>• model rehearsing—ways to memorize their lines.<br>• model rehearsing—ways to portray their characters (facial gestures, body movements, movement across the stage). | • meet in teacher-assigned groups and review the read-aloud play to identify favorite skits.<br>• meet in groups, choose roles, prepare a list of props, and highlight speaking roles on a copy of their skit.<br>• rehearse lines individually, then come together and do a "table reading" of their skits.<br>• rehearse lines in pairs and then come together and do a standing reading with each other.<br>• rehearse lines in pairs and then do another standing rehearsal. |

| GUIDED PRACTICE (continued) | • model rehearsing—have a few students share ways to memorize their lines.<br>• model rehearsing—have one group "perform" while you direct how they might move across the stage. | • conduct a dress rehearsal with props. |
|---|---|---|
| COMMITMENT<br>2 days | • introduce the acting groups and their skits to an audience of parents or peers.<br>• ask students to respond in writing to their learning. | • perform skits for classmates.<br>• reflect on their learning experience in drama. |
| TOTAL: 15 DAYS | | |

## Making Plays

GENRE

### Why Teach This?

- To allow students to demonstrate their growing understanding of drama as a genre by writing and acting out their own plays.
- To provide opportunities for students to write collaboratively.

### Framing Questions

- Why might a writer choose to write a play, rather than another genre?
- How can we use what we have learned about reading plays to help us write our own?

### Unit Goals

- Students will work in small groups to create simple plays.
- Students will develop relationships between characters through active use of dialogue.
- Students will use the formatting and structure of a play in designing their scripts.

### Anchor Texts

- Mentor plays from companion reading unit
- Playbills from actual productions

| Unit Assessment Making Plays | | | GENRE |
|---|---|---|---|
| Student name: | EMERGING | DEVELOPING | INDEPENDENT |
| Successfully completes the writing of a simple play. | | | |
| Works collaboratively and productively with peers. | | | |
| Uses specific formatting and structure for a play. | | | |
| Moves the story forward using dialogue. | | | |
| Brings the play to a resolution. | | | |

| Stage of the Unit | Focused Instruction<br>You will | Independent Practice<br>Students will |
|---|---|---|
| **IMMERSION**<br>2 days | • explain that students will become playwrights in this unit, working together in playwriting clubs; use model plays from the reading unit to explore what should be included in students' own plays.<br>• explore possible topics for class plays (revisit themes from allegory and poetry units); select a topic that will be the concept you develop into a play with help from the class; model for students what they will do in their own playwriting clubs. | • meet in teacher-selected playwriting clubs; review mentor plays and list elements required for every play.<br>• share topic ideas for their plays within their clubs, deciding upon a theme or message that their one-act play will explore. |
| **IDENTIFICATION**<br>3 days | • determine and develop your characters and relationships between characters with help from students, with the class acting as the other members of your writing club.<br>• determine and develop setting and stage requirements for your play with help from students.<br>• determine plot for your play with help from students. | • meet in their clubs and develop their characters and how the relationship between these characters will move their plays forward.<br>• meet in their clubs and develop the setting and stage requirements for their plays.<br>• meet in their clubs and determine rising action and a turning point in the plot for their plays. |
| **GUIDED PRACTICE**<br>9 days | • model drafting your own simple play with help from students; focus on possible beginnings.<br>• model drafting with help from students; focus on rising action.<br>• model drafting with help from students; focus on climax.<br>• model drafting with help from students; focus on resolution.<br>• reread your play and focus on a revision strategy—tightening the dialogue in the climax; have students help you revise the play. | • meet in clubs and discuss possible beginnings; collectively draft a preferred beginning.<br>• meet in clubs and draft the body of the play, moving the characters through the rising action that has been agreed upon.<br>• meet in clubs and draft the key scene—the climax and the turning point for the character.<br>• meet in clubs and draft the falling action and resolution in their plays. |

EARLY FALL    LATE FALL    WINTER    SPRING

| GUIDED PRACTICE (continued) | • ask several students to help you do a table reading of the play; "cast" students informally to read roles in the center of the meeting area; ask the rest of the class to comment on the play with constructive questions.<br><br>• model gentle rehearsing techniques to keep the playacting lively and fun; minimize the pressure to memorize scripts.<br><br>• conduct one additional rehearsal for your play; focus on how characters can move and act to reinforce their roles.<br><br>• model creating a simple program for your play; use examples from real stage productions as models. | • meet in clubs and reread their plays, revising for tighter, more meaningful dialogue in the climax scene.<br><br>• meet in clubs and do table readings; revise again if necessary and submit final scripts for copying.<br><br>• meet in clubs to begin rehearsals, using copies of the play.<br><br>• meet in clubs for one final "dress" rehearsal, imagining how characters will move on "stage."<br><br>• create a simple program for the play. |
|---|---|---|
| COMMITMENT 2–3 days | • celebrate across two or three days by having playwriting groups act out their plays for the class; invite parents or other classes to join you in the audience; throw a cast party at the end of the unit. | • hand out programs for their plays; act out plays; write to reflect on the learning in this unit. |
| **TOTAL: 16–17 DAYS** | | |

# Stepping Into Summer

We come to the end of the school year. The windows are open, attentions are scattered. We are all eager for summer vacation. We need to measure our growth, like the height marks on the side of a door frame. It is time for our students to admire who they have become and where they are going next.

## Looking Back, Looking Forward: Making Summer Reading Plans

PROCESS

### Why Teach This?

- To develop a habit of self-reflection and goal setting.
- To be proud of one's accomplishments this year as a reader.
- To plan forward as a reader, setting personal goals and expectations.

### Framing Questions

- What have I learned about myself as a reader this year?
- What have I learned about reading across multiple texts as a reader?

### Unit Goals

- Students will revisit all books read and notice how they have grown or changed as a reader.
- Students will make summer reading plans and share these with their families.

### Resources

- Book review websites (such as www.spaghettibookclub.com and www.bookhive.org)
- Printed book reviews from children's magazines such as *Storyworks*, *Scholastic News*, and *Stone Soup*
- Students' reading history (logs or other record-keeping tools that allow students to look back over their reading life), reading notebooks, and summer reading book lists

| **Unit Assessment** Looking Back, Looking Forward: Making Summer Reading Plans | | | PROCESS |
|---|---|---|---|
| Student name: | EMERGING | DEVELOPING | INDEPENDENT |
| Names what has been learned this year as a reader. | | | |
| Draws broader conclusions about reading across text and/or genres. | | | |
| Identifies specific successes and interests. | | | |
| Identifies particular challenges. | | | |
| Writes a thoughtful reflection statement, including plans for summer reading. | | | |

| Stage of the Unit | Focused Instruction<br>You will | Independent Practice<br>Students will |
|---|---|---|
| **IMMERSION**<br>1 day | • model how you feel your reading has changed this year. | • look back on texts they have read independently this year and share findings with a partner; talk through observations. |
| **IDENTIFICATION**<br>3 days | • name your reading accomplishments and your reading challenges.<br>• model choosing a favorite text and naming what you learned reading this text.<br>• model making connections to other texts—how you have learned some important big ideas about reading across multiple texts. | • name their reading accomplishments and reading challenges; share these with a partner.<br>• revisit a favorite text, describing what they learned reading this text.<br>• meet in small groups and discuss some of the larger things they have learned about being a reader from many different texts. |
| **GUIDED PRACTICE**<br>4 days | • make reading plans for the summer; share favorite books with the class.<br>• visit websites and/or read reviews for summer reading; add to a list.<br>• explore book recommendations on websites such as Amazon ("Customers who bought this item also bought…")<br>• meet with a fifth-grade class and teacher; ask the teacher to model her recommendations for summer reading. | • make reading plans for the summer; meet with different partners and share their favorite books from the year.<br>• visit websites and/or read reviews for summer reading; add to their list.<br>• write "If you like this…" suggestions for their favorite books; share them with friends.<br>• meet with fifth graders in small groups; exchange book recommendations. |
| **COMMITMENT**<br>1 day | • model writing a year-end reflection, using examples from your reading life to make your points. | • write a year-end reflection, using examples from their own reading lives to make their points. |
| **TOTAL: 9 DAYS** | | |

# Looking Back, Looking Forward: Making Summer Writing Plans

## Why Teach This?

- To develop a habit of self-reflection and goal-setting.
- To be proud of one's accomplishments this year as a writer.
- To plan forward as a writer, setting personal goals and expectations.

## Framing Questions

- What have I learned about myself as a writer this year?
- What inspires me?
- What have I learned by reading multiple texts and genres that I now can do myself as a writer?

## Unit Goals

- Students will reflect on their writing this year, noting growth, inspirations, successes, and challenges.
- Students will share their reflections with an audience (family, next year's teacher, etc.).
- Students will think across the body of their work, looking for common techniques and influences.
- Students will appreciate the importance of writing during the summer.

## Resources

- Writing notebooks
- Writing portfolios
- Reflection writing gathered across the year

| Unit Assessment Looking Back, Looking Forward: Making Summer Writing Plans | | | PROCESS |
|---|---|---|---|
| Student name: | EMERGING | DEVELOPING | INDEPENDENT |
| Names what has been learned this year as a writer. | | | |
| Identifies specific successes and interests. | | | |
| Identifies particular challenges. | | | |
| Writes a thoughtful reflection statement, including plans for this summer and next year. | | | |

| Stage of the Unit | Focused Instruction
You will | Independent Practice
Students will |
|---|---|---|
| **IMMERSION**
1 day | • model how you feel your writing has changed this year and how students can talk to each other to about their reflections. | • look through writing portfolios with a partner, noticing what they are most proud of, and how they have grown. |
| **IDENTIFICATION**
1 day | • model choosing a favorite piece of writing and naming its qualities. | • meet with others and share favorite writing pieces. |
| **GUIDED PRACTICE**
2 days | • name one technique that worked for you regardless of author or genre this year.
• make writing plans for the summer. | • revisit their portfolio in search of craft techniques or inspirations that they used in multiple writing samples.
• make writing plans for the summer. |
| **COMMITMENT**
1 day | • model writing a year-end reflection, using examples from your own writing to make your points. | • write a year-end reflection, using examples from their own writing portfolios to make their points. |
| **TOTAL: 5 DAYS** | | |

# Circular Seasons: Endings and Beginnings

You will miss these children. And they will miss you. For the rest of their lives, they will remember your name. There should be more of a ritual for you to let go of these children and to prepare to embrace the new ones.

In Japan every fall there is a traditional chrysanthemum festival to celebrate the last blooming before the winter comes. The people journey to view the beautiful flowers and to celebrate the changing seasons. There are special horticulturists who work for a full 11 months of the year to prepare for this festival, creating spectacular chrysanthemum arrangements, which they feature in *uwaya*, serene shelters for the beautiful plantings. In this way, the people can contemplate and reflect upon the changing seasons.

We wish we had such a thing for the work we do. The seasons go around, and then come around again, and there is a beauty in that: we know they will always come again. But these precious children will never come again quite like this, and that is the pang we feel. As we enter our summer and curl up on the couch with our mug of tea once again, let the last moments of this book be an *uwaya* for us, a serene shelter for reflection. The work you do with your students is, well, once in a lifetime. Remember this as the seasons of your teaching life begin once again.

# Chapter 6

## TRACKING STUDENT PROGRESS ACROSS THE YEAR

# The C4 Assessment

Assessment is the beginning, the middle, and the end of our teaching. It is the heart of our instruction, the age-old dilemma, the most gratifying, frustrating, and rewarding aspect of our work, because it reveals in stark relief: How are we all doing? Done well, it is not offensive, harmful, hurtful, or unpleasant for children. Done well, it is engaging, reflective, fascinating, and insightful for teachers. Done poorly, it is demeaning, demoralizing, and useless to everyone. Done poorly, it is unhelpful, uninteresting, and slightly boring. We have created rubrics as formative assessments and a yearlong assessment tool we call the C4 Assessment that we believe will lead you to the "done well" column. Done well, assessment is meaningful, as J. Richard Gentry (2008) points out: "...you can loop together assessment and instruction and use both simultaneously to support your students in targeted and powerful ways."

## Unit Rubrics as Formative Assessments

Within each unit we have written for this book, we have given you a model assessment rubric such as the following:

| Unit Assessment The ARCH: Thinking Across Books | | | PROCESS |
|---|---|---|---|
| Student name: | EMERGING | DEVELOPING | INDEPENDENT |
| Understands and follows the routines and structures of reading time. | | | |
| Has an accurate sense of oneself as a reader, including challenges faced. | | | |
| Sets personal reading goals. | | | |
| Uses classmates for book/genre/author suggestions. | | | |
| Demonstrates a developing ability to talk across text. | | | |

These rubrics can and should be used as formative assessments. By this we mean that you can construct rubrics such as these with your students during the Identification stage of any unit. As you name the expectations for process behaviors, or the elements of a genre, or the type of strategy or convention you would like to see your students use, you can add this list of performance indicators to your rubric. Then you can give the rubric to your students to use during their Guided Practice. If we give students our upfront expectations in writing, and they have helped to form and understand these expectations, we can be sure that they will know what we want them to do as readers and writers. They can use these rubrics as placeholders for our teaching—reminding them on a daily basis what we want them to practice, even when we are not sitting next to them.

By keeping the rubric alongside your conferring conversations with individual readers and writers, you will be able to focus your observations and record your comments on how each student is performing throughout the length of the unit. Using the rubric to supplement your conferring plans will also allow you to refer back on these conversations to plan for future instruction—either for the entire class when you see something that nearly everyone is having difficulty with, or for individual or small-group work.

# Unit Rubrics as Summative Assessments

Of course these rubrics can also be summative. You may use them to measure your students' performance at the end of each unit, and you may gather these collective unit assessments to plan and draft your report cards. We believe these rubrics will be extremely helpful on several levels. They will help you focus your instruction toward the expectations listed on the rubric. They will help guide and focus your students practice within any unit of study, and they will allow for self-reflection— for our students and for ourselves. By the end of any unit, we should be able to see what students accomplished and what we still need to work on.

# The C4 Assessment

Rubrics are not the only form of assessment that we would like you to consider. As our entire year has been built around the premise of balanced instruction across process, genre, strategy, and conventions, we would like to suggest that you consider your students' growing skills and abilities within these four categories. To help you accomplish this task, we have created the C4 Assessment (C4A) forms seen at the end of this chapter. These forms merge many of the teaching points across the year into collective assessments of students' understanding of process, genre, strategy, and conventions. The C4A is clear and simple to use, yet provides a great deal of information for teachers so that we may differentiate our instruction for all students; for parents so we may share students' growth or challenges; and for schools.

# Tracking Our Students Across the Grades

We have designed specific C4 Assessments for each grade level. While their format and organization are the same, the content varies, as we have given a great deal of thought to the articulation of instruction across the grades. We recommend that these assessment forms be filled out each year and passed on to the next year's teacher. This will give teachers a clearer sense of their students as readers and writers at the beginning of the year than traditional packaged reading or writing assessments.

# Using These Forms

There are many different ways to incorporate these forms into your year. You may choose to:

- use them to conduct more formal reviews of student performance at the beginning, middle, and end of the year.
- keep these forms with your other conferring materials and use them to note when students demonstrate progress within a particular unit.
- keep these forms with you as you read through your students' published writing, so you can use their written work as evidence of learning.

No matter which method you use, we ask you to consider how your children are developing as readers and writers inside the Complete 4 components. What have they learned to do as readers and writers? What have they come to understand about genre? What have they learned about reading and writing strategies? What do they now understand about the world of conventions? Our job is to create lifelong readers and writers in our classrooms. Instruction-linked assessment through the Complete 4 is the key to achieving this objective.

| **Complete 4 Component: Process** Fourth Grade | | | KEY: **E**=emerging **D**=developing **I**=independent |

Student: _____  School Year: _____

| CAPACITIES | BEGINNING OF THE YEAR | MIDDLE OF THE YEAR | END OF THE YEAR |
|---|---|---|---|
| Reads familiar text smoothly (fluency). | | | |
| Reads independently for 35 to 45 minutes (stamina). | | | |
| Reads at home independently for 20 minutes. | | | |
| Sustains book talk independently for 15 minutes (stamina). | | | |
| Selects books according to level and interest (independence). | | | |
| Explains personal criteria for choosing reading material. | | | |
| Reads and understands written directions. | | | |
| Writes independently for 25 to 30 minutes (stamina). | | | |
| Writes at home independently for 15 minutes. | | | |
| Sustains a selected writing piece over five or more days (stamina). | | | |
| Rereads own writing to add on, revise, or fix grammar and spelling (independence). | | | |

| ROLES | BEGINNING OF THE YEAR | MIDDLE OF THE YEAR | END OF THE YEAR |
|---|---|---|---|
| Follows the rules and routines of reading time. | | | |
| Asks for reading conferences when necessary. | | | |
| Is prepared to share thoughts in a reading conference with a teacher. | | | |
| Understands the responsibilities of the ideal reading partner. | | | |
| Listens to reading partner and connects to partner's ideas. | | | |
| Participates thoughtfully in group discussions. | | | |
| Follows the rules and routines of writing time. | | | |
| Asks for writing conferences when necessary. | | | |
| Is prepared for teacher conferences with writing and writing tools. | | | |
| Presents and discusses own writing in conferences with the teacher. | | | |
| Presents and discusses own writing in conferences with a peer. | | | |
| Discusses peer's writing in a conference with a peer. | | | |

## Complete 4 Component: Process Fourth Grade (continued)  KEY: E=emerging D=developing I=independent

Student:                                                                     School Year:

| IDENTITIES | BEGINNING OF THE YEAR | MIDDLE OF THE YEAR | END OF THE YEAR |
|---|---|---|---|
| Is able to express specific growth as a reader. | | | |
| Sets appropriate reading goals. | | | |
| Achieves personal reading goals. | | | |
| Is able to express specific growth as a writer. | | | |
| Sets appropriate writing goals. | | | |
| Achieves personal writing goals. | | | |
| Communicates with others using writing. | | | |

| COLLABORATION | BEGINNING OF THE YEAR | MIDDLE OF THE YEAR | END OF THE YEAR |
|---|---|---|---|
| Uses classmates for book/genre/author suggestions. | | | |
| Offers own suggestions to others for reading. | | | |
| Demonstrates the rules of conversation and collaboration. | | | |
| Uses partnerships or groups to explore and develop reading ideas. | | | |
| Listens effectively to others in reading collaborations. | | | |
| Considers other points of view in discussions about reading. | | | |
| Offers own suggestions to others for writing ideas. | | | |
| Uses partnerships or groups to explore and develop writing ideas. | | | |
| Provides constructive support to other writers. | | | |

## Complete 4 Component: Genre Fourth Grade

KEY: **E**=emerging **D**=developing **I**=independent

Student:          School Year:

| GENERAL | BEGINNING OF THE YEAR | MIDDLE OF THE YEAR | END OF THE YEAR |
|---|---|---|---|
| Recognizes and articulates differences in genres of narrative, nonfiction, and poetry. | | | |
| Reads in a variety of genres. | | | |
| Writes in a variety of genres. | | | |

| NARRATIVE | BEGINNING OF THE YEAR | MIDDLE OF THE YEAR | END OF THE YEAR |
|---|---|---|---|
| Captures important details in the story. | | | |
| Understands the concepts of anthropomorphism and allegory. | | | |
| States theme, avoiding character names and plot details. | | | |
| Elaborates on his or her personal interpretation of theme, using examples from the text. | | | |
| Understands the structure and characteristics of a play. | | | |
| Is able to follow the progression of a play without support of narration. | | | |
| Writes narrative texts that include all of the elements of a story. | | | |
| Writes using vivid, attention-getting language. | | | |
| Successfully completes the writing of a simple play. | | | |

## Complete 4 Component: Genre Fourth Grade (continued)    KEY: **E**=emerging **D**=developing **I**=independent

Student:                                                    School Year:

| NONFICTION | BEGINNING OF THE YEAR | MIDDLE OF THE YEAR | END OF THE YEAR |
|---|---|---|---|
| Reads in search of answers to questions. | | | |
| Develops a personal point of view on an issue. | | | |
| Supports opinions with examples or facts as evidence. | | | |
| Identifies main ideas and supporting details in informational texts. | | | |
| Compares and contrasts information on one topic from two different sources. | | | |
| Identifies and interprets facts taken from visuals in a nonfiction text. | | | |
| Uses graphic organizers to record significant details from informational texts. | | | |
| Collects data, facts, and ideas from nonfiction texts. | | | |
| Uses multiple sources of information in writing a nonfiction text. | | | |
| Writes expository paragraphs with topic sentence and factual details. | | | |
| Names and uses a variety of text features to make meaning from a text. | | | |
| Writes in response to the reading of informational texts. | | | |

| POETRY | BEGINNING OF THE YEAR | MIDDLE OF THE YEAR | END OF THE YEAR |
|---|---|---|---|
| Is able to define image and mood and is able to find examples in a poem. | | | |
| Monitors his or her emotional response to a poem and uses this to unlock possible deeper meaning(s). | | | |
| Identifies several possible inspirations for poetry. | | | |
| Uses sensory detail to build a vivid image in poetry. | | | |
| Uses metaphor in a thoughtful manner to extend levels of meaning. | | | |
| Writes poems that have more than a literal message for the reader. | | | |

## Complete 4 Component: Strategy Fourth Grade

KEY: **E**=emerging **D**=developing **I**=independent

Student: _____  School Year: _____

| INPUT (The strategies writers use to comprehend text) | BEGINNING OF THE YEAR | MIDDLE OF THE YEAR | END OF THE YEAR |
|---|---|---|---|
| Is able to identify point of view independently. | | | |
| Demonstrates ability to build understanding of main character (appearance, thoughts, feelings, actions, motivations). | | | |
| Finds text examples of evidence of character change. | | | |
| Effectively explores the author's purpose in changing the main character. | | | |
| Infers underlying theme or message from written text. | | | |
| Distinguishes between fact and opinion. | | | |
| Makes connections across authors and genres. | | | |
| Recognizes when reading comprehension has been disrupted and initiates self-correction strategies. | | | |
| Makes inferences and draws conclusions about a text. | | | |
| Skims text in search of information. | | | |

| OUTPUT (The strategies writers use to create text) | BEGINNING OF THE YEAR | MIDDLE OF THE YEAR | END OF THE YEAR |
|---|---|---|---|
| Demonstrates ability to add thoughts and feelings to narrative scenes. | | | |
| Can explain what an inner monologue is, and has written one. | | | |
| Has added meaningful, appropriate dialogue to narrative scenes. | | | |
| Has attempted to include gesture as a further indication of character feelings. | | | |
| Takes notes in own words. | | | |
| Constructs effective expository paragraphs with a student-generated topic sentence and factual details from research as support. | | | |
| Structures multiple paragraphs in a logical order, with simple, effective transitions. | | | |
| Uses text features and graphic aids to clarify or explain complicated information. | | | |

## Complete 4 Component: Conventions Fourth Grade

KEY: **E**=emerging **D**=developing **I**=independent

Student: _____ School Year: _____

| SYNTAX | BEGINNING OF THE YEAR | MIDDLE OF THE YEAR | END OF THE YEAR |
|---|---|---|---|
| Uses varied sentence structure in writing. | | | |
| Writes sentences in logical order. | | | |
| Uses paragraphs to organize topics. | | | |
| Effectively uses grade-level vocabulary in writing. | | | |

| PUNCTUATION | BEGINNING OF THE YEAR | MIDDLE OF THE YEAR | END OF THE YEAR |
|---|---|---|---|
| Reviews work independently for spelling, capitalization, and punctuation. | | | |
| Identifies and understands the difference between pausing punctuation. | | | |
| Uses a variety of punctuation in writing. | | | |
| Uses common nouns, pronouns, and proper nouns properly in writing. | | | |
| Uses action, state-of-being, and helping verbs in writing. | | | |
| Uses adjectives and adverbs in writing. | | | |
| Presents speech to the class with fluency and expression. | | | |

| SPELLING/DECODING | BEGINNING OF THE YEAR | MIDDLE OF THE YEAR | END OF THE YEAR |
|---|---|---|---|
| Uses knowledge of letter-sound correspondence to blend sounds when reading unfamiliar grade-level words. | | | |
| Decodes by analogy using knowledge of syllable patterns. | | | |
| Decodes grade-level words using knowledge of word structure. | | | |
| Sight-reads high-frequency grade-level words. | | | |
| Analyzes word structure to learn word meaning. | | | |
| Connects words and ideas in books to spoken language and background knowledge. | | | |

# Chapter 7

# Essential Reading for the Complete 4 Educator

## *The Complete 4 for Literacy*
## by Pam Allyn

Pam's book *The Complete 4 for Literacy* introduces us to the idea of the four major components for literacy instruction: Process, Genre, Strategy, and Conventions. She illuminates the components and how they interact throughout the year. In your school communities, we encourage you to form study groups around these components. Begin with Pam's book and study it together to orient yourself. Then, each year or each season, select one of the components to focus on. We can use each component to discuss not just whole-class instruction but also how best to confer with individual students, how to work with struggling readers and writers, and how to assess our students. We have prepared a special selection of professional texts to foster your investigation of each of the components.

## *Writing Above Standard*
## by Debbie Lera

Debbie Lera will help you to frame a year of teaching writing that really helps your students soar using your state standards as a guide. With the Complete 4 as the backbone of her thinking, Debbie takes us on a journey through state standards and how to make them work for us. In the spirit of the Complete 4 and the Complete Year which is all about building flexible frameworks, this book furthers your thinking by helping you to benefit from the structure provided by the standards while attending to the individual needs of your students.

# Professional Books on Process

There are wonderful classics in the field of the teaching of reading and writing that help remind us why process work is so, so critical. Learning routines, talking about books, choosing topics—all form the bedrock of a lifetime of success as readers and writers. Remind yourself that process is the key to a happy life: how you live your life is as important as what you do with it. The process work is the how.

Our favorites include:

- *Guiding Readers and Writers: Teaching Comprehension, Genre, and Content Literacy* by Irene C. Fountas and Gay Su Pinnell
- *Notebook Know-How: Strategies for the Writer's Notebook* by Aimee Buckner
- *Reading Essentials: The Specifics You Need to Teach Reading Well* by Regie Routman
- *Reconsidering Read-Aloud* by Mary Lee Hahn
- *What Really Matters for Struggling Readers: Designing Research-Based Programs* by Richard L. Allington

# Professional Books on Genre

Genre units allow our fourth graders to try on many hats and to be deeply involved in the world of reading and writing. Genre is also power. If you know which genre matches your purpose, you can communicate most effectively.

Helpful books for your learning include:

- *Awakening the Heart: Exploring Poetry in Elementary and Middle School* by Georgia Heard
- *The No-Nonsense Guide to Teaching Writing: Strategies, Structures, and Solutions* by Judy Davis and Sharon Hill
- *Reality Checks: Teaching Reading Comprehension With Nonfiction K–5* by Tony Stead
- *Thinking Through Genre: Units of Study in Reading and Writing Workshops, 4–12* by Heather Lattimer

# Professional Books on Strategy

In this book, you can see how strongly we believe in the strategic mind of the fourth grader!

Your fourth grader can plan a sleepover party weeks in advance. Your fourth grader is plotting out his summer vacation in the dead of winter. Your fourth grader creates fantastic games and ideas with groups of friends in the playground. In literacy, his mind is awakening in the same kinds of ways: capable of planning, of making connections.

The following books contain some helpful information on strategy work:

- *Better Answers: Written Performance That Looks Good and Sounds Smart* by Ardith Davis Cole

- *Cracking Open the Author's Craft: Teaching the Art of Writing* by Lester L. Laminack

- *Critical Literacy: Enhancing Students' Comprehension of Text* by Maureen McLaughlin and Glenn DeVoogd

- *Investigate Nonfiction* by Donald H. Graves

- *Strategies That Work: Teaching Comprehension to Enhance Understanding* by Stephanie Harvey and Anne Goudvis

# Professional Books on Conventions

We are lucky that these last few years have given us a new explosion of books offering interesting perspectives on conventions: grammar, punctuation, and syntax. This is the hardest hurdle for us to overcome. Most of us grew up remembering either no grammar instruction or terrible grammar instruction. Spelling and grammar and punctuation can all be fun, truly! Conventions instruction is empowering—students want to learn how to spell, and they want to be in on the secrets of language. The following books are invaluable:

- *A Fresh Approach to Teaching Punctuation: Helping Young Writers Use Conventions With Precision and Purpose* by Janet Angelillo

- *Getting It Right: Fresh Approaches to Teaching Grammar, Usage, and Correctness* by Michael W. Smith and Jeffrey D. Wilhelm

- *Teaching for Comprehending and Fluency: Thinking, Talking, and Writing About Reading, K–8* by Irene C. Fountas and Gay Su Pinnell

# Resource Sheets

# Reading Goals Planner

Student Name _____ Goal Period: From _____ to _____

| Genre Goals | Number of Books | Completed? Y/N |
|---|---|---|
| Fiction | | |
| • Realistic Fiction | | |
| • Mystery | | |
| • Fantasy/Science Fiction | | |
| • Sports Fiction | | |
| • Adventure Fiction | | |
| • Historical Fiction | | |
| Nonfiction | | |
| Poetry | | |

| Process | Specific Goal | Completed? Y/N |
|---|---|---|
| Stamina | | |
| Pacing | | |
| Collaboration | | |
| Routines | | |

| Other Goals* | Specifics: | Completed? Y/N |
|---|---|---|
| | | |
| | | |

* Such as author studies, reading across topic, selecting more challenging text, and so on.

Name _____ Date _____

# Idea Generator

My Topic Is:

# Reading Goals Across the Complete 4

Examples include:

| Process | Genre | Strategy | Conventions |
|---------|-------|----------|-------------|
| Noticing and adjusting pacing | Realistic fiction | Reading across author | Oral fluency |
| Building stamina | Fantasy | Reading across interest category or subject (e.g., for baseball— read biography, read fiction, read essays, etc.) | Author's use of punctuation |
| Generating thoughtful reading responses | Science fiction | Reading magazines | Reading with expression |
| Talking well about books with others | Historical fiction | Reading newspapers | Learning to read dialogue more powerfully |
| Reading in the content area | Adventure fiction | Interpretation | Exploring word origins |
| | Series | Visualizing | |
| | Informational nonfiction | Determining importance | |
| | Biography | Inferring character motivations | |
| | Autobiography | Note-taking | |
| | How-to books | | |
| | Question-and-answer books | | |
| | Folktales | | |
| | Mythology | | |
| | Plays | | |
| | Short stories | | |
| | Memoir | | |
| | Poetry | | |
| | Picture books | | |

**RESOURCE 3.1**

# Reading Conference Request

_____ would like a reading conference.  Date: _____
(Student Name)

I am reading: _____

_____

I want to share with you:

☐ a problem I'm having      ☐ something I've figured out about my book

☐ something I'm proud of    ☐ something I am wondering about

Details: _____

_____

_____

# Reading Conference Request

_____ would like a reading conference.  Date: _____
(Student Name)

I am reading: _____

_____

I want to share with you:

☐ a problem I'm having      ☐ something I've figured out about my book

☐ something I'm proud of    ☐ something I am wondering about

Details: _____

_____

_____

# Writing Conference Request

_____ would like a writing conference.  Date: _____
(Student Name)

I am working on: _____

_____

I want to share with you:

☐ a problem I'm having     ☐ something I've figured out about my writing

☐ something I'm proud of    ☐ something I am wondering about

Details: _____

_____

_____

# Writing Conference Request

_____ would like a writing conference.  Date: _____
(Student Name)

I am working on: _____

_____

I want to share with you:

☐ a problem I'm having     ☐ something I've figured out about my writing

☐ something I'm proud of    ☐ something I am wondering about

Details: _____

_____

_____

# Writing Goals Across the Complete 4

Examples include:

| Process | Genre | Strategy | Convention |
|---|---|---|---|
| Noticing and adjusting pacing | Realistic fiction | Using mentor texts or authors | Sentence variety |
| Building stamina | Fantasy | Writing across interest category or subject (e.g., for baseball—read biography, read fiction, read essays, etc.) | Writing with more dialogue |
| Finding writing ideas | Science fiction | Writing with more description | Paragraphing |
| Writing under timed conditions | Historical fiction | Studying craft strategies | Exploring new forms of punctuation |
| Prewriting | Adventure fiction | Close study of an anchor text | Linking thoughts through compound and complex sentences |
| | Series | Read like a writer | |
| | Informational nonfiction | Focus | |
| | Biography | Elaboration | |
| | Autobiography | Writing in certain structures | |
| | How-to books | | |
| | Question-and-answer books | | |
| | Folktales | | |
| | Mythology | | |
| | Plays | | |
| | Short stories | | |
| | Memoir | | |
| | Poetry | | |
| | Picture books | | |

© 2008 LitLife, Inc. *The Complete Year in Reading and Writing: Grade 4* page 222

# Project Planner

Members: _____

Project Description: _____

Start Date: _____  Finish Date: _____

Meeting Days (circle 2 or 3):   Monday   Tuesday   Wednesday   Thursday   Friday

| Monday | Tuesday | Wednesday | Thursday | Friday | Sat. | Sun. |
|---|---|---|---|---|---|---|
| Date:<br><br>Plans:<br><br><br><br>Homework: | Date:<br><br>Plans:<br><br><br><br>Homework: | Date:<br><br>Plans:<br><br><br><br>Homework: | Date:<br><br>Plans:<br><br><br><br>Homework: | Date:<br><br>Plans:<br><br><br><br>Homework: | | |
| Date:<br><br>Plans:<br><br><br><br>Homework: | Date:<br><br>Plans:<br><br><br><br>Homework: | Date:<br><br>Plans:<br><br><br><br>Homework: | Date:<br><br>Plans:<br><br><br><br>Homework: | Date:<br><br>Plans:<br><br><br><br>Homework: | | |
| Date:<br><br>Plans:<br><br><br><br>Homework: | Date:<br><br>Plans:<br><br><br><br>Homework: | Date:<br><br>Plans:<br><br><br><br>Homework: | Date:<br><br>Plans:<br><br><br><br>Homework: | Date:<br><br>Plans:<br><br><br><br>Homework: | | |
| Date:<br><br>Plans:<br><br><br><br>Homework: | Date:<br><br>Plans:<br><br><br><br>Homework: | Date:<br><br>Plans:<br><br><br><br>Homework: | Date:<br><br>Plans:<br><br><br><br>Homework: | Date:<br><br>Plans:<br><br><br><br>Homework: | | |

**RESOURCE 3.5**

# Comments for the Author

**Share a compliment with:**

|  |  |
|---|---|
|  |  |
|  |  |
|  |  |

# Parent Letter: Identity and Independence in Writing

Dear Parents,

In class we are beginning a unit on Identity and Independence in Writing. This is a wonderful opportunity for students to take on writing projects that are of personal interest to them and to learn to work independently to achieve these goals. This kind of experience is good practice for your child, as the movement toward middle school brings with it many independent projects.

It is also a chance for your child to choose exactly what he or she wants to work on as a writer. Some children choose to write in new genres, others choose to practice writing with craft. Some will work on facing the blank page, or writing more than a page in their notebooks. Whatever each child chooses, it should be something that interests them and that will be fun and challenging.

You can support this work at home by showing interest in your child's project, and by encouraging their hopes and dreams for themselves as writers in the world. Our focus in this unit is to learn independence and to reflect on who we are as writers, so ask your child to explain his or her project to you, and then step back and watch him or her fly!

Warmly,

# Story Elements in Mystery

Mystery: _____

| Story Elements in Fiction | Mystery Language | Examples in the Text |
|---|---|---|
| Characters | Detective<br>Sleuth<br>Crime solver | |
| | Victim | |
| | Witness(es) | |
| | Suspect(s) | |
| | Criminal/villain | |
| Setting | Crime scene | |
| Problem | Disappearance, kidnapping, crime | |
| Plot | Crime | |
| | Gather clues | |
| | Interview witnesses | |
| | Develop theories | |
| | Thrown off the scent/red herring | |
| Solution | Solve crime | |

# Mystery Case File

Mystery Case File # _____

Detective/Sleuth: _____

Crime/Disappearance/Mystery: _____

_____

Witnesses:

_____   _____

What they saw/What happened:

_____

_____

Suspects:                                    Motives:

☐ _____      _____

☐ _____      _____

Clues/Evidence:

_____

_____

_____

_____

Case Solved:

_____

_____

# Mystery Mountain

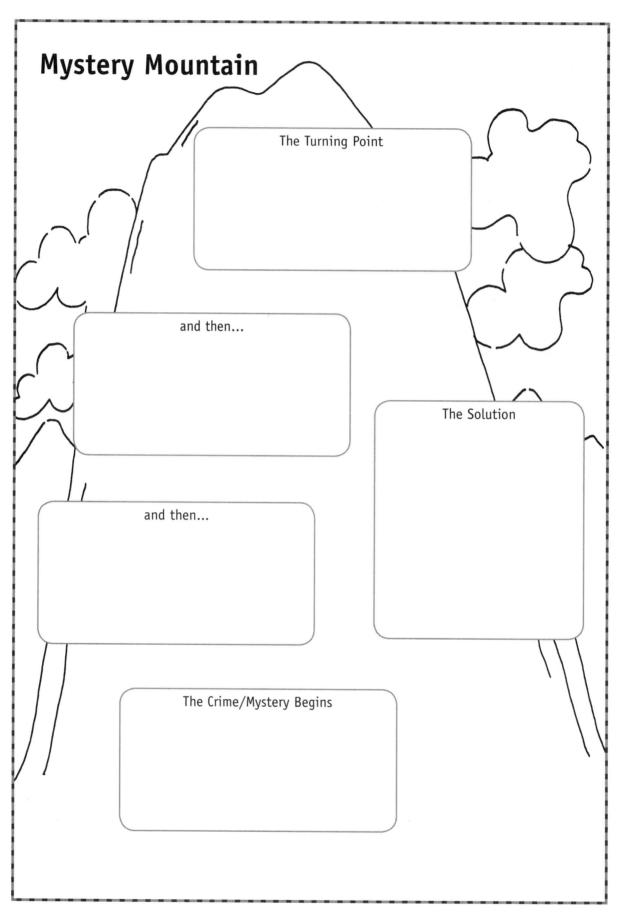

The Turning Point

and then...

The Solution

and then...

The Crime/Mystery Begins

# Ways to Celebrate Writing

✿  Author's chair: read your writing to the class

✿  Reading snippets and collecting comments—
    move around the room

✿  Looped class readings—bring in guest classes

✿  Frame our writing

✿  Author of the week

✿  Write a letter to someone (and get a response)

✿  Writing "museums" with several pieces and related
    artifacts (photos, mementos)

✿  Open mike—lunch activity

✿  Writing buddies

✿  Parent breakfast

## Celebrate Your Writing at Home:

✿  Read it to your whole family in the living room.

✿  Read it on the phone to someone far away.

✿  Share it with your family before dinner.

✿  Share your story over some cheese and crackers.

✿  Read your story to a friend on the bus.

✿  Read your story while you are taking a long car ride.

# Picture Book Themes

| Book Title | Author | Theme |
|---|---|---|
| *Henry Climbs a Mountain* | D. B. Johnson | Human rights, civil disobedience |
| *Henry Builds a Cabin* | D. B. Johnson | Simple living, respect for nature |
| *Where the Wild Things Are* | Maurice Sendak | Mastering anger and fear |
| *Seven Blind Mice* | Ed Young | Working together, seeing the big picture |
| *The Three Questions* | Jon J. Muth, Leo Tolstoy | Compassion, living in the moment |
| *Stranger in the Mirror* | Allen Say | Age discrimination, accepting differences |
| *The Sign Painter* | Allen Say | Following dreams |
| *Dreamland* | Roni Schotter | Importance of imagination, following dreams |
| *The Dot* | Peter H. Reynolds | Encouragement, compassion, belief in oneself |
| *The Other Side* | Jacqueline Woodson | Racism, segregation |
| *White Socks Only* | Evelyn Coleman | Racism |
| *Prayer for the Twenty-First Century* | John Marsden | Fear, hope, learning from mistakes |
| *Harold and the Purple Crayon* | Crockett Johnson | Power of imagination |
| *The Carrot Seed* | Ruth Krauss | Conviction, faith, perseverance |
| *Riding the Tiger* | Eve Bunting | Peer pressure, gangs, bullying |
| *Terrible Things* | Eve Bunting | Racism, intolerance |
| *Fox* | Margaret Wild | Greed, envy, friendship |
| *Feathers and Fools* | Mem Fox | Consequences of war, appreciating others' differences, tolerance |
| *The Big Box* | Toni Morrison and Slade Morrison | Conformity, individuality, creativity |
| *Gleam and Glow* | Eve Bunting | Hope, overcoming adversity |
| *The Lorax* | Dr. Seuss | Humans' impact on the environment |
| *Swimmy* | Leo Lionni | Cooperation |
| *The Seed* | Isabel Pin | Antiwar message |
| *Peace Crane* | Sheila Hamanaka | Urban violence, war |
| *Amelia's Road* | Linda Jacobs Altman | Displacement, setting down roots |
| *Tree of Hope* | Amy Littlesugar | Hope |
| *The Stranger* | Chris Van Allsburg | Renewal, change |

# Theme Bookmark

**1.** Read your story.

**2.** Understand the basic narrative.

**3.** Revisit the text.

**4.** Ask the important questions:

- Think above the plot—not what happened, but why it happened.

- Think above the character—not what it means for her, but what the writer is trying to tell us about the world.

**5.** Use what you know about the world to restate the message as a literary theme.

Examples of themes:

- Social justice (poverty, equality, illiteracy, homelessness, famine, racism)

- Friendship, bullying

- Importance of family, heritage, culture, respect

- War, conflict resolution, freedom

- Love, loss, loneliness

- Tolerance, working together

- Courage, bravery, struggling through adversity

**6.** Make a statement. Avoid character names and plot details. Explain the message to the reader.

_____

_____

_____

_____

# Theme Bookmark

**1.** Read your story.

**2.** Understand the basic narrative.

**3.** Revisit the text.

**4.** Ask the important questions:

- Think above the plot—not what happened, but why it happened.

- Think above the character—not what it means for her, but what the writer is trying to tell us about the world.

**5.** Use what you know about the world to restate the message as a literary theme.

Examples of themes:

- Social justice (poverty, equality, illiteracy, homelessness, famine, racism)

- Friendship, bullying

- Importance of family, heritage, culture, respect

- War, conflict resolution, freedom

- Love, loss, loneliness

- Tolerance, working together

- Courage, bravery, struggling through adversity

**6.** Make a statement. Avoid character names and plot details. Explain the message to the reader.

_____

_____

_____

_____

# Parent Letter: Writing in Response to Issues in Our World

Dear Parents,

It is hard to believe the year has gone by so quickly. Your child has grown so much this year and is stepping up to the challenge of fourth grade! Toward this end, we have been looking at big issues in the world—or at least issues that feel big and important to your child.

We first explored these issues in literature and practiced looking for theme in some very powerful picture books and short stories.

Now we are exploring some of these issues as writers. Your child will be working in his or her writing notebook over the next several days, discovering what it feels like to write about one's opinions.

You can support this work at home by sharing with your child the places you turn to for written opinions—perhaps the editorial page of the newspaper or magazine you read, or a blog you visit on the Internet, or the book reviews you check each week before you head to the library.

Children need to learn that adults are influenced by writing each and every day. Please share your own thoughts and experiences with your child. It will help him or her see the value of this kind of writing in the world.

Warmly,

# Glossary of Terms for the Complete Year Series

We try to avoid jargon as much as possible, but it is inevitable that a community creates or uses specific terminology to identify important aspects of its work. We want you to feel comfortable with all the language inside this book. What follows are some of the key words we have used throughout this book and throughout the Complete Year series.

**Anchor texts** These are the books that moor us to the places of our learning. An anchor holds a ship in place, in water that may be moving fast. Texts are like that for us in our teaching. We are in moving water all the time, but great literature anchors us down to our teaching, to our learning, to our goals and outcomes. Anchor texts connect us to the teaching inside our units of study. They keep our teaching on course, steady, focused, anchoring our big ideas, our commitments and indeed, the essence of each unit. Anchor texts may also be used throughout the year in both the teaching of reading and the teaching of writing. For example, one text may be used in a reading unit for retelling, or sensory image, or prediction. The same text may also be used as a demonstration text for writing with detail, strong leads and endings, and the use of dialogue. There are some special texts that can travel with you throughout the year. They are great, lasting titles that transcend any one teaching point. These are considered anchor texts for the year.

**Book clubs** Working in book clubs allows students to build their collaboration skills and their ability to talk about texts. Book clubs may form from two sets of successful partnerships, or for a variety of teaching purposes. You may group a club according to skill sets or according to interests. Students in a club do not all have to be reading the same book. For example, in a nonfiction unit, the students may meet to discuss editorials or historical writing, using different texts at their own reading levels. You should give clear guidelines for the purposes of a club, its duration, expected outcomes, and how it will be assessed.

**Commitment** The fourth stage of a unit of study, the Commitment stage, is the bridge from the end of one unit to the beginning of the next one. Look for and make public examples of student work and behaviors that are becoming more integrated into the ongoing work of the individual and the community. This stage asks the question: How is what we have learned in this unit going to inform our learning as we begin the next one? It also requires a response to the question: What have you learned?

**Conferences/conferring** This is a process for informally assessing your students' progress, and for differentiating your instruction for individual readers and writers. Ideally, you will meet with each student at least once a week in a brief, focused conference session. Stages of a conference are:

- **Preread/Research** (be very familiar with your student's work and processes in advance of the conference)
- **Ask** (pertinent questions relating to your lesson, the ongoing work, and the plans going forward)
- **Listen** (take notes, with attention to next steps)
- **Teach** (one target point)
- **Plan** (what the student will do when you leave the conference: today, tomorrow, throughout the unit and the year)

**Conventions** The fourth component of the Complete 4, Conventions refers to grammar, punctuation, and syntax. Understanding the conventions of the English language has a direct impact on reading comprehension and writing mechanics and fluency.

**Downhill texts** These are texts we can rest and relax into—to practice building our stamina or our fluency or to revisit favorite characters, authors, or series. They are books that do not require a great deal of decoding to be done by the reader, as the text is generally below the reader's independent reading level.

**Focused Instruction** The first part of every day's reading and writing time, Focused Instruction is the short, focused lesson at the beginning of each workshop session in the teaching of reading or writing. Each lesson should build on the ones before it. No lesson is taught in isolation.

**Four Prompts** In order to help our students learn how to find ideas for writing, we have developed a set of prompts to guide them. They are I wonder, I remember, I observe, and I imagine. You can use these to support your students' writing in any genre.

**Genre** The second component of the Complete 4, Genre typically refers to a type of text such as poetry, nonfiction, or narrative. Within each of these genres are subgenres, which may include a specific focus on persuasive nonfiction writing, or informational nonfiction writing in nonfiction studies. In a narrative study, the focus might be on the short story, the memoir, or story elements. We want students to focus on how they engage with a particular genre. How do we read a newspaper, for example, and how do we read a poem? How are they different, and how are they the same? We will talk about uses for a genre, the reasons we read inside one genre for a length of time, and how our thinking grows and changes as a result of that immersion.

**Guided Practice** In the third stage of any unit of study, Guided Practice, we use mentor texts, transcripts, teacher or student writing, think-alouds, role plays, and read-alouds to model exemplary attributes, behaviors, and qualities related to the unit. Over the course of this stage, students are given increasing responsibility for this work. It is generally the longest stage of a unit, as all students need time for practice.

**Identification** The second stage of any unit of study, Identification, is the time when we begin to develop the common language we will use throughout the study. We identify attributes of a genre, behaviors in a process, qualities of a craft element, rules for a convention or mark. Our thinking is recorded in public charts, student writing notebooks, and our notebook.

**Immersion** The first stage of any unit of study, Immersion is the initial period of inquiry during which we surround our students with the sounds, textures, and qualities of a Genre, Process, Strategy, or Conventions focus. We marinate our students in the literature, the actions and reflections, and the attention to detail and conventions that are part of the study. During this stage, students construct a working understanding of the topic under discussion.

**Independent Practice** Following each day's Focused Instruction, Independent Practice provides time for students to read or write independently and authentically. Students independently read a variety of texts matched to their reading levels. Students also write a variety of texts independently, depending on the unit and their ability levels. They practice the skills and strategies taught in the whole-group sessions. We provide daily lessons to support their work, and confer regularly with the students to assess their individual needs.

**Mentor text** Somewhat interchangeable with an anchor text, we are more inclined to use mentor text to describe books that have particular appeal to individual students. Mentor texts inspire students' reading and writing, whereas anchor texts are specific texts chosen in advance by the teacher to prepare a unit. So in a poetry unit, one mentor text might be a Langston Hughes poem, "The Dream Keeper," because the student loves it and wants to write like that, whereas another student might choose a Valerie Worth poem because she likes the brevity of her language.

**Partnerships** At times you may choose to pair children for different reasons and different lengths of time. Partnerships can be very fluid, lasting for just one session, a week, or an entire unit. Partnerships may be based on reading levels, similar interests in particular books or subjects, or because you would like to work with the partners on a regular basis on small instructional reading or writing work.

**Process** The first of the Complete 4 components, Process asks readers and writers to become aware of their habits and behaviors, and to move forward in developing them. Process units can investigate roles, routines, capacity, or collaboration.

**Read-aloud** During read-aloud, you read from carefully chosen texts that reflect the reading and writing work the community is doing together. Listening to fluent and expressive read-alouds helps students identify the many aspects of text and develop their own deeper understandings of Process, Genre, Strategy, or Conventions. You may read from a book or short text that illustrates the topic of the Focused Instruction for the day, and encourage students to pursue that thinking in their independent reading and writing. During and at the end of the read-aloud, the whole class may have a conversation relating to the ideas in the story.

**Reading notebook** *See* Writing Notebook.

**Shared reading/shared writing** During this activity, you and your students read together from a shared text (on an overhead, chart, or a SMART Board, or using copies of the text). While teachers of younger children use shared reading and writing to help build decoding skills, teachers of older children may use shared reading to teach word analysis, new vocabulary, or punctuation skills. It's also a good way to work with older students on big-picture thinking such as developing an idea about a text, asking questions, or making inferences. Teachers of older students may use shared writing to guide their students toward new writing strategies in a public writing context, or model use of details and elaboration to improve their writing.

**Small instructional groups** This structure is used to differentiate and direct instruction to the specific needs of a small group of learners. You pull small groups of readers or writers with similar needs to explicitly teach targeted reading and writing skills. You select and introduce the texts for reading and make specific teaching points. You may prompt students in small writing groups to do a short, focused writing exercise based on their needs. These groups are flexible and will change as the year unfolds.

**Stages of the lesson** Each day, we should work with our students in a whole-small-whole routine. First we bring everyone together for the lesson (see Focused Instruction), then we send students off to practice something we have taught (see Independent Practice), and finally we call them back to join us for a recap and reiteration of our teaching (see Wrap-Up).

**Stages of the unit** Each unit of study follows a progression of instruction, from Immersion to Identification to Guided Practice to Commitment. These stages provide students with the necessary opportunities to notice, name, practice, and share their learning—all of which contribute to a deeper understanding and application of our teaching (see Immersion, Identification, Guided Practice, and Commitment).

**Steady reader or writer** This student is making steady progress and meeting appropriate grade-level expectations.

**Strategy** The third component in the Complete 4, Strategy consists of two types: reading and writing. In reading, Strategy refers to individual or grouped strategies for reading comprehension that impact reading development. These include visualizing, synthesizing, questioning, and inferring. A unit focused on strategy can be embedded in another study or illuminated on its own. Strategy units also include the study of theme, interpretation, building an argument, and story elements. In writing, Strategy refers to craft. This may include the external or internal structures of writing. Units in writing strategy may include structures of nonfiction or narrative texts, a focus on a particular author, or, internally, units focused on the use of repetition, varied sentence length, or the artful use of punctuation.

**Strong reader or writer** This student is performing above grade-level expectations.

**Turn and talk** This common technique helps students warm up for their reading or writing work. By asking students to "turn and talk" to someone in the meeting area to rehearse their thoughts, we give all students a chance to have their voices heard. It is an effective management technique for making sure students are prepared for the work ahead.

**Unit of study** A one- to six-week period of intensive study on one aspect of reading or writing. The Complete 4 curriculum planning system helps teachers and administrators plan an entire school year in the teaching of reading and writing.

**Uphill texts** This descriptor refers to a text that is above a student's independent reading level. Sometimes we want our readers to challenge themselves with a harder text. Sometimes readers have very good reasons for why they would like to keep an uphill book close by. Other times, though, we ask them to recognize that the book is too uphill for the task, and that they need to find a level text with which they can feel successful.

**Vulnerable reader or writer** This describes the reader or writer who struggles to keep up with the demands of the grade level. These are students who need extra support and scaffolding through appropriate texts or individualized or small-group instruction. Our vulnerable readers and writers need special care to feel successful and to flourish in our classrooms.

**Wrap-Up** The final step in each day's reading or writing time, the Wrap-Up is when we ask our students to return to a whole-group setting for reflection and reinforcement. For example, you may share one or two examples of student work or student behaviors ("Today I noticed..."), or one or two students might briefly share their thinking processes or the work itself.

**Writing clubs** These are recommended for all ages. Children may create clubs based on common interests, from the block area and writing in kindergarten to mystery writing in fourth grade. Give clear guidelines for the purposes of the clubs, the length of time they will last, the expectations, the outcomes, and how you will assess the progress of each club.

**Writing notebook/reading notebook/ writing folder/reading folder** These are containers for thinking and tools for collecting ideas, wonderings, observations, questions, research, lists, snippets of texts, and responses to literature. The form of the container is not the important thing; what is important is having containers for student work that make sense to your students and work well for you in terms of collecting and preserving a history of student reading and writing.

# Grade 4 Anchor Texts

## Early Fall

### The ARCH: Thinking Across Books

- "Anti-Bullying Buddies" by Elizabeth Carney, *Scholastic News* (10/9/06)
- "The Bully" by Donald Graves, taken from *Baseball, Snakes and Summer Squash*
- *Riding the Tiger* by Eve Bunting
- *Whoever You Are* by Mem Fox
- *Zen Ties* by Jon Muth

### The ARCH: Becoming Inspired by Writers

- Lois Lowry's 1994 Newbery acceptance speech (www.loislowry.com)
- *Owen and Mzee: The True Story of a Remarkable Friendship* by Isabella Hatkoff, Craig Hatkoff, and Dr. Paula Kahumbu
- "Poem" by Langston Hughes, taken from *The Dream Keeper and Other Poems*
- *Stone Soup* magazine (www.stonesoup.com)
- "Where I'm From" by George Ella Lyon (from *Seeing the Blue Between: Advice and Inspiration for Young Poets*, edited by Paul B. Janeckzo)
- *Wings* by Christopher Myers

### Getting to Know the Job of Words: Parts of Speech

- *From the Mixed-up Files of Mrs. Basil E. Frankweiler* by E. L. Konigsburg

### Adding Description to Writing: Using Modifiers

- *Fox* by Margaret Wild

### Deepening Collaboration: Reading Partners

- *Bone Detective: The Story of Forensic Anthropologist Diane France* by Lorraine Jean Hopping

- *A Lucky Thing* by Alice Shertle
- *The Van Gogh Cafe* by Cynthia Rylant

### Deepening Collaboration: Writing Partners

- *A Chair For My Mother* by Vera B. Williams
- *Family Pictures/Cuadros de Familia* by Carmen Lomas Garza

### Exploring Changes in Characters

Choose one to read aloud:
- *The Birchbark House* by Louise Erdrich
- *Bud, Not Buddy* by Christopher Paul Curtis
- *In the Shade of the Nispero Tree* by Carmen T. Bernier-Grand
- *Junebug* by Alice Mead
- *Just Juice* by Karen Hesse
- *Milkweed* by Jerry Spinelli
- *My Name Is Maria Isabel* by Alma Flor Ada
- *The Paint Brush Kid* by Clyde Robert Bulla
- *A Single Shard* by Linda Sue Park
- *The Storyteller's Beads* by Jane Kurtz
- *When Zachary Beaver Came to Town* by Kimberly Willis Holt

### Adding Thoughts and Feelings to Writing

- Use monologue excerpts from read aloud in Exploring Changes to Characters unit, OR
- *Every Living Thing* by Cynthia Rylant
- *Just Juice* by Karen Hesse
- *Milkweed* by Jerry Spinelli
- *A Single Shard* by Linda Sue Park

## Late Fall

### Developing Identity and Independence in Writing

- Meet the Authors and Illustrators series by Deborah Kovacs and James Preller

### Reading the Test

- Sample tests from prior years
- Short reading passages from children's magazines, anthologies, and test-prep materials

### Writing to the Literary Prompt

- Test prompt questions from prior years' tests

### Building Stamina: Reading Longer and Stronger

Short story anthologies such as:
- *How Angel Peterson Got His Name* by Gary Paulsen
- *Tripping Over the Lunch Lady and Other School Stories*, edited by Nancy E. Mercado
- *Weird Stories from the Lonesome Café* by Judy Cox

### Building Stamina: Writing Longer and Stronger

Autobiographies of authors, as found in:
- Meet the Author series, published by Richard C. Owen Publishers

Interviews and quotes of a favorite author, such as:
- Jacqueline Woodson (www.jacquelinewoodson.com)

### Planning and Organizing Research

- *How Come in the Neighborhood?* by Kathy Wollard

### Developing Expertise: Informational Articles

Sample nonfiction articles from children's magazines, such as:
- *Ask*
- *Click*
- *Kids Discover*
- *Ranger Rick*
- *Scholastic News*
- *Time for Kids*

## Winter

### Reading Mysteries
- *Ace Lacewing, Bug Detective* by David Biedrzycki
- *The Case of the Mummified Pigs: And Other Mysteries in Nature* by Susan E. Quinlan
- *Jake Gander, Storyville Detective: The Case of the Greedy Granny* by George McClements
- *The Mystery of Eatum Hall* by John Kelly

### Writing Mini-Mysteries
- *A Dark Dark Tale* by Ruth Brown
- *The Mysteries of Harris Burdick* by Chris Van Allsburg

### Understanding Pausing Punctuation in Reading
- *The House on Mango Street* by Sandra Cisneros
- *My Mama Had a Dancing Heart* by Libba Moore Gray
- *Silent Music* by James Rumford

### Using Pausing Punctuation in Writing
- Lois Lowry's Newbery Award acceptance speech (www.loislowry.com)

### Exploring Mood and Imagery in Poetry

Select poems found in:
- *Angels Ride Bikes and Other Fall Poems* by Francisco X. Alarcon
- *Seeing the Blue Between,* compiled by Paul B. Janeczko
- *Soul Looks Back in Wonder,* edited by Tom Feelings

### Finding Inspiration in Poetry

Select poems found in:
- *Seeing the Blue Between,* compiled by Paul B. Janeczko

## Spring

### Uncovering Theme: Allegory in Picture Books
- *Amelia's Road* by Linda Jacobs Altman
- *The Big Box* by Tony Morrison and Slade Morrison
- *Feathers and Fools* by Mem Fox
- *Fox* by Margaret Wild
- *Gleam and Glow* by Eve Bunting
- *The Other Side* by Jacqueline Woodson
- *Peace Crane* by Sheila Hamanaka
- *Riding the Tiger* by Eve Bunting
- *The Stranger* by Chris Van Allsburg
- *Tree of Hope* by Amy Littlesugar

Folktales and fables:
- *Aesop's Fables* by Aesop
- *Fables* by Arnold Lobel
- *The People Could Fly: American Black Folktales* by Virginia Hamilton
- *Spider* magazine

Short stories:
- *Every Living Thing* by Cynthia Rylant

### Writing in Response to Issues in Our World
- *A Little Peace* by Barbara Kerley
- Student editorials written in *Creative Kids* magazine
- *Prayer for the Twenty-First Century* by John Marsden
- *Somewhere Today: A Book of Peace* by Shelley Moore Thomas

### Reading Plays: An Introduction to Drama
- *Cinderella Outgrows the Glass Slipper and Other Zany Fractured Fairy Tale Plays* by Joan M. Wolf
- *How to Eat Like a Child* by Delia Ephron, John Forster and Judith Kahan (available for purchase at www. samuelfrench.com)
- *12 Fabulously Funny Fairy Tale Plays* by Justin McCory Martin
- *12 Fabulously Funny Folktale Plays* by Justin McCory Martin

### Looking Back, Looking Forward: Making Summer Reading Plans

Book review websites such as:
- www.spaghettibookclub.com
- www.bookhive.org

Printed book reviews from children's magazines such as:
- *Scholastic News*
- *Stone Soup*
- *Storyworks*

# Professional References

Akhavan, N. (2008). *The content-rich reading and writing workshop: A time-saving approach for making the most of your literacy block.* New York: Scholastic.

Allington, R. L. (2005). *What really matters for struggling readers: Designing research-based programs.* Boston: Allyn & Bacon.

Allyn, P. (2007). *The complete 4 for literacy.* New York: Scholastic.

Alston, L. (2008). *Why we teach: Learning, laughter, love, and the power to transform lives.* New York: Scholastic.

Anderson, C. (2005). *Assessing writers.* Portsmouth, NH: Heinemann.

Anderson, C. (2000). *How's it going? A practical guide to conferring with student writers.* Portsmouth, NH: Heinemann.

Anderson, J. (2005). *Mechanically inclined: Building grammar, usage, and style into writer's workshop.* Portland, ME: Stenhouse.

Angelillo, J. (2002). *A fresh approach to teaching punctuation: Helping young writers use conventions with precision and purpose.* New York: Scholastic.

Angelillo, J. (2008). *Grammar study: Helping students get what grammar is and how it works.* New York: Scholastic.

Bomer, R. (1995). *Time for meaning: Crafting literate lives in middle and high school.* Portsmouth, NH: Heinemann.

Buckner, A. (2005). *Notebook know-how: Strategies for the writer's notebook.* Portland, ME: Stenhouse.

Calkins, L. (1994). *The art of teaching writing.* Portsmouth, NH: Heinemann.

Cole, A. D. (2002). *Better answers: Written performance that looks good and sounds smart.* Portland, ME: Stenhouse.

Cruz, M. C. (2004). *Independent writing: One teacher, thirty-two needs, topics, and plans.* Portsmouth, NH: Heinemann.

Davis, J., & Hill, S. (2003). *The no-nonsense guide to teaching writing: Strategies, structures, and solutions.* Portsmouth, NH: Heinemann.

Edinger, M., & Fins, S. (1998). *Far away and long ago: Young historians in the classroom.* Portland, ME: Stenhouse.

Fletcher, R. (1993). *What a writer needs.* Portsmouth, NH: Heinemann.

Fletcher, R., & Portalupi, J. (2007). *Craft lessons: Teaching writing K–8.* Portland, ME: Stenhouse.

Fletcher, R., & Portalupi, J. (2001). *Nonfiction craft lessons: Teaching information writing K–8.* Portland, ME: Stenhouse.

Fountas, I. C., & Pinnell, G. S. (2001). *Guiding readers and writers: Teaching comprehension, genre, and content literacy.* Portsmouth, NH: Heinemann.

Fountas, I. C., & Pinnell, G. S. (2006). *Teaching for comprehending and fluency: Thinking, talking, and writing about reading, K–8.* Portsmouth, NH: Heinemann.

Gentry, J. R. (2008). *The easy assessment guide: A breakthrough for beginning reading and writing.* New York: Scholastic.

Goodlad, J. (2004). *A place called school.* New York: McGraw-Hill.

Graham, P. (Ed.). (1999). *Speaking of journals: Children's book writers talk about their diaries, notebooks, and sketchbooks.* Honesdale, PA: Boyds Mills Press.

Graves, D. H. (1989). *Investigate nonfiction.* Portsmouth, NH: Heinemann.

Hahn, M. L. (2002). *Reconsidering read-aloud.* Portland, ME: Stenhouse.

Harvey, S., & Goudvis, A. (2008). *Strategies that work: Teaching comprehension to enhance understanding* (2nd ed.). Portland, ME: Stenhouse.

Harwayne, S. (1992). *Lasting impressions: Weaving literature into the writing workshop.* Portsmouth, NH: Heinemann.

Heard, G. (1999). *Awakening the heart: Exploring poetry in elementary and middle school.* Portsmouth, NH: Heinemann.

Heard, G. (2002). *The revision toolbox: Teaching techniques that work.* Portsmouth, NH: Heinemann.

Hindley, J. (1996). *In the company of children.* Portland, ME: Stenhouse.

Hollingworth, L. (2007). Five ways to prepare for standardized testing without sacrificing best practice. *Reading Teacher.*

Hoyt, L. (2008). *Mastering the mechanics, grades 4–5: Ready-to-use lessons for modeled, guided, and independent editing.* New York: Scholastic.

Hoyt, L. (2004). *Spotlight on comprehension: Building a literacy of thoughtfulness.* Portsmouth, NH: Heinemann.

Jorgensen, K. (2001). *The whole story: Crafting fiction in the upper grades.* Portsmouth, NH: Heinemann.

Kaufman, D. (2000). *Conferences and conversations: Listening to the literate classroom.* Portsmouth, NH: Heinemann.

Keene, E., & Zimmerman, S. (2007). *Mosaic of thought: Teaching comprehension in a reader's workshop* (2nd ed.). Portsmouth, NH: Heinemann.

Krashen, S. (2004). *The power of reading: Insights from the research, second edition.* Portsmouth, NH: Heinemann.

Laminack, L. L. (2007). *Cracking open the author's craft: Teaching the art of writing.* New York: Scholastic.

Lattimer, H. (2003). *Thinking through genre: Units of study in reading and writing workshops, 4–12.* Portland, ME: Stenhouse.

Le Guin, U. (1998). *Steering the craft: Exercises and discussions on story writing for the lone navigator or the mutinous crew.* Portland, OR: The Eighth Mountain Press.

Lera, D. (2009). *Writing above standard: Engaging lessons that take standards to new heights and help kids become skilled, inspired writers.* New York: Scholastic.

Lipson, M. (2007). *Teaching reading beyond the primary grades: A blueprint for helping intermediate students develop the skills they need to comprehend the texts they read.* New York, Scholastic.

McAfee, D. (1981). *Effect of sentence combining on fifth grade reading and writing achievement.* Paper presented at the Annual Meeting of the National Reading Conference. Dallas, TX.

McLaughlin, M., & DeVoogd, G. L. (2004). *Critical literacy: Enhancing students' comprehension of text.* New York: Scholastic.

Miller, D. (2002). *Reading for meaning: Teaching comprehension in the primary grades.* Portland, ME: Stenhouse.

O'Connor, P. T. (2004). *Woe is I: The grammarphobe's guide to better English in plain English, expanded edition.* New York: Penguin.

Pearson, D., & Gallagher. M. (1983). The instruction of reading comprehension. *Contemporary Educational Psychology, 8*(3), 317–345.

Ray, K. W. (2002). *What you know by heart: How to develop curriculum for your writing workshop.* Portsmouth, NH: Heinemann.

Ray, K. W. (1999). *Wondrous words: Writers and writing in the elementary classroom.* Urbana, IL: National Council of Teachers of English.

Ray, K. W., & Laminack, L. (2001). *The writing workshop: Working though the hard parts (and they're all hard parts).* Urbana, IL: National Council of Teachers of English.

Rich, M. (2007, November 19). Study links drop in test scores to a decline in time spent reading. *New York Times*, pp. E1, E7.

Routman, R. (2002). *Reading essentials: The specifics you need to teach reading well.* Portsmouth, NH: Heinemann.

Samway, K. D., & Taylor, D. (2007). *Teaching English language learners: Strategies that work.* New York: Scholastic.

Servis, J. (1999). *Celebrating the fourth: Ideas and inspiration for teachers of grade four.* Portsmouth, NH: Heinemann.

Shertzer, M. (1986). *The elements of grammar.* New York: Collier Books.

Smith, M., & Wilhelm, J. (2007). *Getting it right: Fresh approaches to teaching grammar, usage, and correctness.* New York: Scholastic.

Stead, T. (2006). *Reality checks: Teaching reading comprehension with nonfiction K–5.* Portland, ME: Stenhouse.

Strunk, W., & White, E. B. (1999). *The elements of style* (4th ed.). New York: Longman.

Szymusiak, K., & Sibberson, F. (2001). *Beyond leveled books: Supporting transitional readers in grades 2–5.* Portland, ME: Stenhouse.

Szymusiak, K., & Sibberson, F. (2008). *Day-to-day assessment in the reading workshop.* New York: Scholastic.

Weaver, C. (2006). *The grammar plan book: A guide to smart teaching.* Portsmouth, NH: Heinemann.

Welty, E. (1984). *One writer's beginnings.* Cambridge. MA: Harvard University Press.